Heresy

A History of Defending the Truth

Alister McGrath

HarperOne
An Imprint of HarperCollins*Publishers*

HarperOne

HarperCollins books may be purchased for educational, business, or sales promotional use. For information please write: Special Markets Department, HarperCollins Publishers, 10 East 53rd Street, New York, NY 10022.

HarperCollins Web site: http://www.harpercollins.com
HarperCollins®, ▲®, and HarperOne™ are
trademarks of HarperCollins Publishers

FIRST EDITION
Designed by Level C

Library of Congress Cataloging-in-Publication Data
McGrath, Alister E.
Heresy : a history of defending the truth / Alister McGrath. — 1st ed.
p. cm.
Includes index.
ISBN 978–0–06–082214–9
1. Heresies, Christian. 2. Apologetics. I. Title.
BT1315.3.M35 2009
273—dc22
2009004883

09 10 11 12 13 RRD(H) 10 9 8 7 6 5 4 3 2 1

Contents

foreword by Dr. Rick Warren   v

introduction Our Love Affair with Heresy   1

part one
What Is Heresy?

one Faith, Creeds, and the Christian Gospel   17

two The Origins of the Idea of Heresy   33

part two
The Roots of Heresy

three Diversity: The Background of Early Heresy   43

four The Early Development of Heresy   61

five Is There an "Essence" of Heresy?   81

part three
The Classic Heresies of Christianity

six Early Classic Heresies:
Ebionitism, Docetism, Valentinism   101

seven Later Classic Heresies:
Arianism, Donatism, Pelagianism   135

part four
The Enduring Impact of Heresy

eight Cultural and Intellectual Motivations
for Heresy   175

nine Orthodoxy, Heresy, and Power   197

ten Heresy and the Islamic View of Christianity 223

conclusion The Future of Heresy   231

Notes   235

Index   271

Foreword

In the eighteenth century, Irish philosopher, author, and statesman Edmund Burke famously stated, "Those who ignore history are destined to repeat it." That's why this book is so invaluable. Written by another great Irish philosopher, author, and theologian—my friend Alister McGrath—this volume brilliantly shows us why we cannot afford to ignore the lessons of church history.

One hundred and fifty years after Burke, George Santayana restated Burke's aphorism in his book *Reason in Common Sense*: "Those who cannot remember the past are condemned to repeat it." Nowhere else is this principle more obvious than in the historic heresies of the Christian faith. Because most believers have little or no knowledge of church history, they fail to recognize old errors that reappear on the scene after being refuted and rejected by previous generations of orthodox Christians.

We know that truth is unchanging and eternal. If it's true, it's not new. But many lies are not new either. In Ecclesiastes 1:9, Solomon noted, "History merely repeats itself. It has all been done before. Nothing under the sun is truly new" (New Living Translation).

What goes around in one generation eventually comes back around again in another generation. The name or label of the heresy may change, but the error is likely one that has been proven wrong repeatedly over the past two thousand years.

For instance, there's nothing at all new about New Age philosophy. The New Age is just Old Lies repackaged. The belief that you are God (or can be) is as old as Eden. It was the first temptation.

This is an extremely important book for our day, especially since the media do not consider orthodoxy worthy of coverage. We must equip our people with the historical knowledge they need to discern that fad theologies and current challenges to our faith are merely regurgitated heresies from the past.

I thank God for Alister McGrath. You will too when you've finished this book. His insights and his writing are clear, compelling, and comprehensive.

Don't just read this book. Strengthen the church by giving copies to others.

Dr. Rick Warren
Saddleback Church
Lake Forest, California

Our Love Affair with Heresy

Never has there been such interest in the idea of heresy. Ancient heresies, seen by earlier generations as obscure and dangerous ideas, have now been sprinkled with stardust. The lure of the religious forbidden never seems to have been so strong. As Geoffrey Chaucer shrewdly observed back in the fourteenth century: "Forbid us something, and that thing we desire."[1] For many religiously alienated individuals, heresies are now to be seen as bold and brave statements of spiritual freedom, to be valued rather than avoided.[2] Heresies are the plucky losers in past battles for orthodoxy, defeated by the brute power of the religious establishment. And since history is written by the winners, heresies have unfairly lost out, their spiritual and intellectual virtues stifled by their enemies. The rehabilitation of heretical ideas is now seen as a necessary correction of past injustices, allowing the rebirth of suppressed versions of Christianity more attuned to contemporary culture than traditional orthodoxy. Heresy has become fashionable.

It is clear there has been a shift in the cultural mood, leading to a new way of seeing and valuing heresy. The Yale cultural historian Peter Gay has recently written of the "lure of heresy," an intriguing catchphrase that points to an overwhelming and enticing longing to subvert—or at the very least to challenge—conventional cultural expectations.[3] Modern art, he argues, is thus characterized by a desire to offend tradition. The badges of honor of the movement were thus the persecution, prosecution, and outrage that it evoked. All revolutions require an enemy. In this case, the enemy is an orthodoxy that is both dull and dulling, suppressing the vital sparks of human originality and creativity.

Attitudes like these have become deeply embedded in contemporary Western culture. Heresy is radical and innovative, whereas orthodoxy is pedestrian and reactionary. As the Jewish writer Will Herberg (1901–77) astutely noted at the height of the American revolt against God in the 1960s, whereas religious orthodoxy seemed to be dry and desiccated, heresy seemed to exude intellectual energy and cultural creativity: "Today, people eagerly vaunt themselves as heretics, hoping that they will thereby prove interesting; for what does a heretic mean today but an original mind, a man who thinks for himself and spurns creeds and dogmas?"[4]

The force of Herberg's point cannot be overlooked. Where religious orthodoxy is seen to be moribund or oppressive, the appeal of religious alternatives—including the wholesale rejection of religion—grows in intensity. The surge of interest in atheism in Western culture, especially during the nineteenth century, is a further measure of cultural disillusionment and disenchantment with religious orthodoxy. The recent surge in interest in the "new atheism" suggests that this reading of things remains important in the West in the early twenty-first century.[5]

Yet the appeal of heresy in contemporary Western culture goes far beyond any popular perception, however unreliable, of the irretrievable dreariness or moral inadequacies of religious orthodoxies. The deep-seated postmodern suspicion of the corrupting influence of power permeates, often subliminally, contemporary discussions of heresy. Everyone knows that history is written by the winners. "Orthodoxy" is nothing more than a heresy that happened to win out—and promptly tried to suppress its rivals and silence their voices. This was the thesis developed by the German scholar Walter

Bauer (1877–1960), who argued that the earliest and most authentic form of Christian belief was probably heretical rather than orthodox. Orthodoxy was a later development, he suggested, which tried to suppress types of Christianity that had earlier been accepted as authentic.[6] Bauer's work was originally published in German in 1934 and attracted relatively little attention. It was finally translated into English in 1971, by which time the cultural mood had shifted decisively away from the modernism of the 1930s and toward the postmodernism of the late 1960s. Bauer's ideas now resonated with the suspicions and values of an increasingly antiauthoritarian culture. The book rapidly became a talisman for postmodern critics of orthodoxy.

Bauer's thesis suggests that heresy is essentially an orthodoxy that was suppressed by those with power and influence in the Christian world—above all, the dominant church of Rome. We must therefore recognize the existence of a group of "lost or suppressed Christianities," which were repressed and silenced by those who wished their own ideas to be acclaimed as orthodoxy.[7] In this view, the distinction between heresy and orthodoxy is arbitrary, a matter of historical accident. *Orthodoxy* designates the ideas that won, *heresy* those that lost. The cultural authority of this viewpoint is such that it needs detailed examination, especially in relation to the connections between orthodoxy, heresy, and power. We shall explore these issues thoroughly in the course of this work.

Others, however, went still further. For them, orthodoxy was not just about one set of ideas gaining the ascendancy through dubious means. It was about those ideas' deliberate invention, to secure the religious power base of the Christian church in the Roman Empire. This is one of the controlling themes of Dan Brown's blockbuster *The Da Vinci Code,* published in 2003, which topped bestseller lists throughout the West for a year.[8] Its plotline was influenced by a highly speculative theory advanced in 1982 by Michael Baigent, Richard Leigh, and Henry Lincoln.[9] In their *Holy Blood, Holy Grail,* these writers suggested, on the basis of what can be described only as the flimsiest of historical evidence, that Jesus of Nazareth had married Mary Magdalene, and that they had a child. Their book documented the alleged attempts of the Catholic Church to suppress the bloodline ever since. Brown's book fictionalizes that theory, even including a character named "Sir Leigh Teabing," alluding to both Leigh and Baigent ("Teabing" is an anagram of "Baigent").[10]

The relevance of Brown's novel to popular perceptions of the origins and significance of heresy can be seen in his character Teabing's confident assertion that "almost everything our fathers taught about Christ is false." Jesus of Nazareth was never thought to be divine by Christians, Teabing declares, until the Council of Nicaea in 325, when the matter was put to the vote. It only just scraped through. Brown's cryptologist character Sophie Neveu is shocked by these words: "I don't follow. His divinity?"

> "My dear," Teabing declared, "until *that* moment in history, Jesus was viewed by His followers as a mortal prophet . . . A great and powerful man, but a man nonetheless. A mortal."
>
> "Not the Son of God?" [said Sophie].
>
> "Right," Teabing said. "Jesus' establishment as 'the Son of God' was officially proposed and voted on by the Council of Nicaea."
>
> "Hold on. You're saying Jesus' divinity was the result of a *vote*?"
>
> "A relatively close vote at that," Teabing added.[11]

The risible inaccuracy of this dialogue (it was a landslide vote, for example) is not the point.[12] A perception has become the reality, given plausibility by its resonance with the cultural mood.

The Da Vinci Code declares that the divinity of Christ was a fabrication, a deliberate ploy on the part of a corrupt church determined to secure its social status by any means and at any cost. Teabing goes on to argue that this was all a cynical and shrewd move on the part of the emperor Constantine (274–337), the date of whose conversion to Christianity is uncertain. Constantine had decreed that Christianity should become the official faith of his empire. What could be more natural, Teabing suggests, than that Constantine should upgrade Jesus from a mere mortal to the eternal Son of God?

> "To rewrite the history books, Constantine knew that he would need a bold stroke. From this sprang the most profound moment in Christian history. Constantine commissioned and financed a new Bible, which omitted those gospels which spoke of Christ's *human* traits and embellished those gospels that made him godlike. The earlier gospels were outlawed, gathered up and burned. But fortunately, some of these gospels survived and were found in 1945 at Nag Hammadi, Egypt."[13]

Happily for historians, Teabing declares, Constantine failed to eradicate all the rival Gospels. We now know, he tells us, that the modern Bible was "compiled and edited by men who possessed a political agenda—to promote the divinity of the man Jesus Christ and use his influence to solidify their own power base."

Brown's narrative is an illuminating example of how fiction shapes perceptions of reality. Its equation of "power" and "orthodoxy" has become so influential that it has become the default option for many today. Yet as we shall see, it is open to serious challenge, not least because the idea of orthodoxy began to emerge within Christian communities while they were still marginal groups on the fringes of Roman imperial culture. The reality is much more complex than Brown's stereotypical account of Christian history—just as it is also more interesting and intellectually satisfying.

Brown's brilliant work of fiction plays up to the postmodern suspicion of power, and especially its privileging of certain favored ideas. Like the television series *The X Files,* which came to an end in 2002, *The Da Vinci Code,* with its ingenious historical fabrications, coincided with that era's widespread mistrust of governments, interest in conspiracy theories, and spirituality (as opposed to religion). Yet in many ways it also sets the context for contemporary discussions of heresy.

For many, heresy is now seen as a theological victim, a set of noble ideas that have been brutally crushed and improperly suppressed by dominant orthodoxies and then presented as if they were devious, dishonest, or diabolical. In this romanticized account of things, heresy is portrayed as an island of freethinking in the midst of a torpid ocean of unthinking orthodoxy enforced more by naked ecclesiastical power than by robust intellectual foundations. This is certainly the account of heresy that is firmly embedded in Brown's *Da Vinci Code.* Brown's plot centers on the post-Constantinian church's perennial attempts to guard, frequently violently, its gospel proclamation by hiding the truth that would subvert it. The discovery of this suppressed truth is thus held out as the postmodern equivalent of the classic quest for the Holy Grail. The possessor of this truth could destroy the perpetrator of one of the great institutional deceptions of all time—the Catholic Church. It is, of course, a fantasy—yet it is a fantasy that commands much popular support and attention, and is in itself an important indicator of recent cultural concerns and agendas.

Heresy now has a new appeal, through its emerging associations with the lure of secret knowledge, the transgressing of sacred boundaries, and the eating of forbidden fruit.[14] The Christian Bible opens with two accounts of transgression—the eating of the forbidden fruit (Genesis 3), and the building of the Tower of Babel (Genesis 11). Significantly, both represent challenges to the limits fixed for humanity by God. Boundaries, we are now told, are constructed by those with vested interests in preserving them; by transgressing them, we establish our own identity and authority, and confront and contest an illiberal establishment. Like Prometheus stealing the fire of the gods, transgression is about challenging power and bringing freedom. The forbidden has now become ennobled and made the legitimate object of desire. Heresy is a Promethean liberator of humanity from theocratic bondage. The outcome of this significant shift in cultural mood is obvious. Heresy cannot now simply be seen as an academic historical or theological problem. It has become a *cultural* issue.

Why? A major factor here is the growing emphasis upon choice as a defining characteristic of authentic human existence. As we shall see presently, the Greek term *hairesis,* which gave rise to our term "heresy," has strong associations with "choosing" or "choice." To choose is to express our freedom, to assert our capacity to create and control our own worlds.

This development is directly linked with the availability of religious alternatives. It is no accident that the appeal of heresy increased significantly in the rapidly developing society of twelfth-century Europe. People were becoming increasingly conscious of the choice available in material goods and education, and these wider horizons were reflected in their attitudes to religion. The monopoly of medieval Catholicism was eroded as the laity turned to explore alternative religious options such as those offered by the Cathars and Waldensians.[15] Here as elsewhere, the institutional church's response to this threat took the form of the enforcement of uniformity, thus denying individuals the critical element of choice. Yet the modern period has seen both the rise of religious diversity in much of the West and the erosion of the church's legal capacity to enforce uniformity.

The sociologist Peter Berger drew out the implications of this development in his landmark *Heretical Imperative* (1979). Berger here argues that in traditional primitive cultures, individuals are exposed to only a single set of fundamental assumptions. Each culture is based on, and to some extent defined by, a "myth"—that is, a foundational and legitimizing narrative or set of assumptions. To challenge this foundational mythology amounts to heresy, and traditionally would lead to death or banishment. Yet now we are confronted with a plethora of religions, philosophies, and paradigms. There is no single, fundamental, controlling metanarrative. We are free to choose, to pick and mix—which, for Berger, is the essence of heresy.

> In the matter of religion, as indeed in other areas of human life and thought, this means that the modern individual is faced not just with the opportunity but with the necessity to make choices as to his beliefs. This fact constitutes the heretical imperative in the contemporary situation. Thus heresy, once the occupation of marginal and eccentric types, has become a much more general condition; indeed heresy has become universalized.[16]

We are not required to accept a prepackaged worldview but are able to create one that resonates with our own perceptions of how things ought to be. Heresy is about being master of our own universe, choosing the ways things are—or at least the way we would like them to be.

Yet perhaps the ultimate appeal of heresy in our times lies in its challenge to authority.[17] Religious orthodoxy is equated with claims to absolute authority, which are to be resisted and subverted in the name of freedom. Heresy is thus to be seen as the subversion of authoritarianism, offering liberation to its followers. It is virtually impossible to take this account seriously from a historical perspective, especially as some heresies were at least as authoritarian as their orthodox rivals. The belief that heresy is intellectually and morally liberating tells us far more about today's cultural climate in the West than about the realities of the first centuries of Christian existence. Yet, as any account of the cultural reception of ideas concedes, the present-day relevance of any ancient idea has at least as much to do with what contemporary human beings are looking for as with what ancient ideas have to offer. The significance of heresy is thus not inherent within the heresy itself, but is rather *constructed* within the relationship between the original heresy and its contemporary interpreter.[18]

This suspicion of authority can easily be transferred from orthodoxy itself to its biblical foundations. For some writers, the New Testament canon is to be seen as the authoritarian endorsement of those early Christian writings that were acceptable to the establishment. The New Testament documents are regarded as if they were unconvincing press releases from some official source, designed to conceal the truth about the origins of Christianity. Anything that looks like an official version is automatically suspect. In this view, potentially subversive texts—above all, those associated with Gnosticism—were repressed and marginalized. The theologian and cultural observer Garrett Green has brought out the importance of this point: "Under the suspicious eye of (post)modern critique, every faith in scriptural authority appears as a form of false consciousness, every sacred text as a surreptitious rhetoric of power."[19] To subvert ecclesiastical authoritarianism, it is necessary to undermine the authenticity of the texts on which it is based.

The recent media excitement about the Gospel of Judas in 2006 illustrates this trend. Here, we were told, was an alternative to the traditional Christian Gospels, suppressed by the early church because of the threat it posed to its authority.[20] This document seemed to be a perfect fit for the postmodern template of heresy—a forbidden account of the origins of Christianity, deliberately concealed by anxious church leaders, which was uncovered by bold journalists determined to unearth the truth. A leading British newspaper declared it to be the "greatest archaeological discovery of all time," which posed a "threat to 2000 years of Christian teaching."[21]

The reality seems to have been rather more banal. The Gospel of Judas is a relatively late document, almost certainly originating within a marginalized sect within Christianity that was convinced that everyone else had got Jesus of Nazareth seriously wrong. There was no documentary evidence within the body of literature accepted as authoritative by Christians at this time (including some works that never made it into the New Testament canon) that supported the case they wished to make. They remedied this situation by writing their own gospel. Only Judas *really* understood Jesus, we are told; the other disciples got him wrong and passed on hopelessly muddled accounts of his significance.

The Gospel of Judas represents Jesus as inviting Judas to intimate personal dialogues, from which the other disciples are excluded, in which secret knowledge is imparted to the disciple. This rhetoric of exclusion shapes the ensuing discussion: only Judas was included in the magic circle of the initiated to which the true secrets of the kingdom were entrusted. The Gospel of Judas portrays Jesus of Nazareth as a spiritual guru similar to the Gnostic teachers of the second and third centuries yet bearing little relation to the portrait of Jesus found in the synoptic Gospels. Christianity becomes a kind of mystery cult based on an immense bureaucracy that runs the cosmos, which Jesus is portrayed as explaining in exquisite and disquieting detail to Judas. It is difficult to avoid the conclusion that Jesus of Nazareth has been reinvented as a Gnostic teacher with Gnostic ideas. The Gospel of Judas has indeed the potential to illuminate our understanding of Gnosticism in the mid–second century and beyond, especially its often-noted parasitic relationship to existing worldviews.[22] But it seems to have nothing historically credible to tell us of the origins of Christianity or the identity of Jesus of Nazareth.[23] And it certainly poses no significant "threat" to traditional Christianity.

Nor is the Gospel of Judas even a radical document. The British New Testament scholar N. T. Wright dismisses the widespread belief that Gnosticism was innovative, providing a surge of creative intellectual energy that threatened to sweep away traditional ideas.[24] If anything, Wright argues, it is the Gnostics who are better seen as the cultural conservatives, echoing many of the themes of the mystery religions of the age. In contrast, the orthodox Christians "were breaking new ground," and encountering opposition for doing so.

Where some suggest that the Gnostic Gospels represent radical alternatives to the "conservative" canonical Gospels, Wright argues that quite the opposite is true. It is the message of the New Testament that is truly radical. Yet centuries of cultural familiarity with Christianity, together with the relative novelty of a rediscovered Gnosticism, have created a somewhat different cultural perception. Religious orthodoxy has become the victim of a familiarity fatigue, which creates a yearning for novelty.[25]

This book is a work of synthesis that tries to weave together important recent studies in the field and explore their contemporary relevance for our understanding of the idea of heresy. It does not set out to break new ground in our understanding of the concept of heresy in general, or of any specific heresy in particular. Nor is it a detailed, comprehensive account of the many heresies that have arisen within Christianity. Certain heresies are singled out for detailed discussion, partly because they are of particular importance in their own right, and partly in that they illustrate some more general principles that seem to underlie the origins and development of heretical movements.

The growing body of academic literature casting new light on how heresies originally emerged and developed down the centuries challenges many stereotypes of heresy. The picture that is emerging from this intense scholarly examination of early Christianity endorses neither the view of some Christian writers that heresy is a fundamentally malignant attack on orthodoxy, nor that of those who see it as a principled alternative to orthodoxy that was suppressed by the institutional church. I shall attempt to offer an account of heresy that takes full account of the best modern scholarship. At the same time I shall try to understand why so many important early Christian writers regarded it as dangerous, and to do so without demonizing those who explored avenues of thought that eventually turned out to be heretical.[26]

So what is heresy? Heresy is best seen as a form of Christian belief that, more by accident than design, ultimately ends up subverting, destabilizing, or even destroying the core of Christian faith. Both this process of destabilization and the identification of its threat may be spread out over an extended period of time. A way of making sense of one aspect of the Christian faith, such as the identity of Jesus of Nazareth—an aspect that may initially be welcomed and find general acceptance—may later have to be discontinued on account of the potential damage it is subsequently realized to be capable of causing.

An analogy may help make this difficult idea clearer. The Parthenon is widely regarded as one of the architectural wonders of the ancient world. By 1885, this once-glorious classic Greek building was in an advanced state of decay and was in need of restoration. Iron clamps and rods were used to hold together the building's great slabs of white marble, originally quarried from nearby Mount Pentelicus. Yet the restorers failed to realize that iron expands and contracts with changes in temperature, thus placing the stonework under pressure. More important, they also failed to rustproof the ironwork. As the iron began to corrode, it expanded, cracking the stones it was intended to preserve. A measure that was aimed at saving the building thus actually ended up accelerating its decay, requiring future generations to undertake even more radical restoration work than was originally needed. The correction of critical mistakes is often a costly and time-consuming business; nevertheless, it needs to be done. Heresy represents certain ways of formulating the core themes of the Christian faith—ways that are sooner or later recognized by the church to be dangerously inadequate or even destructive. What one generation welcomes as orthodoxy another may eventually discover to be heretical.

While all attempts to put the realities of God into human words will fall short of what they try to represent, some are much more reliable and trustworthy than others. "Orthodoxy" and "heresy" (or "heterodoxy"; the terms are often seen as interchangeable) are best seen as marking the extremes of a theological spectrum. In between these extremities lies a penumbra of views,[27] which range from adequate without being definitive to questionable without being destructive. Heresy lies in the shadow lands of faith, a failed attempt at orthodoxy whose intentions are likely to have been honorable but whose outcomes were eventually discovered to be as corrosive as Nikolaos Balanos's iron clamps.

Although I shall focus on Christianity, it is important to appreciate that the concept of heresy has wide applicability outside Christianity. Functionally equivalent concepts can be found across the religious spectrum, even in Eastern religions.[28] It has also found growing acceptance in secular contexts to refer to potentially dangerous or destabilizing ideas and approaches that pose a threat to dominant orthodoxies.

Yet heresy extends beyond the realm of ideas. For reasons we shall explore in this volume, the debate between heresy and orthodoxy is all too easily transposed to the social and political realms. As a result, any discussion of heresy must acknowledge the darker side of this discussion—the enforcement of ideas by force, the suppression of liberty, and the violation of rights. This theme is of major importance in western Europe during the Middle Ages, and is of growing importance in the Islamic world today.

Even this brief account of the nature of heresy raises huge questions. Two obvious examples may be noted. Who decides what is definitive and what is dangerous? And how are such decisions made? These questions lie at the heart of this book, and we shall begin to explore them immediately. A good point from which to set out on this journey of exploration is the nature of the Christian faith itself—to which we now turn.

part one

What Is Heresy?

one

Faith, Creeds, and the Christian Gospel

If there is a heartbeat of the Christian faith, it lies in the sheer intellectual delight and excitement caused by the person of Jesus of Nazareth. Here is one whom the church finds to be intellectually luminous, spiritually persuasive, and infinitely satisfying, both communally and individually. While Christians express this delight and wonder in their creeds, they do so more especially in their worship and adoration. Worship proclaims that the Christian faith has the power to capture the imagination, not merely to persuade the mind, by throwing open the depths of the human soul to the realities of the gospel. It sustains an incandescence of enthusiasm for Jesus Christ that nourishes the theological task while at the same time calling into question its capacity to live up to the brilliance of its ultimate object.

Yet while the appeal of the Christian vision of Jesus of Nazareth to the imagination must never be neglected or understated, there remains an intellectual core to the Christian faith. In his essay "The Will to Believe" (1897), the celebrated psychologist William James (1842–1910) argued that human beings find themselves in a position where they have to choose between intellectual options that are, in James's words, "forced, living, and momentous."[1] We all need working hypotheses (James's term) to make sense of our experience of the world. These working hypotheses often lie beyond total

proof, yet they are accepted and acted upon because they are found
to offer reliable and satisfying standpoints from which to engage
the real world. Whether the movement is religious or political,
philosophical or artistic, a group of ideas, of beliefs, is affirmed to
be, in the first place, true and, in the second place, important.[2]
Thinking people need to construct and inhabit mental worlds, from
which they discern ordering and patterns within experience and
make at least some sense of its riddles and enigmas.[3] As the philosopher Michael Polanyi (1891–1976) put it, a defensible framework of
beliefs enables us to hear a tune where otherwise we would hear
only a noise.[4]

Yet this is not to say that Christianity is simply or even fundamentally a set of ideas. For many Christians, an experience of God
lies at the heart of the religious dynamic.[5] This experience may subsequently lead to theological formulations ("What must be true if
this was a genuine experience of God?"), yet these formulations are
ultimately secondary to the experience that precipitated and shaped
them. Indeed, many would argue that an experience of God is irre-
ducible to verbal or conceptual forms.

The American theologian Stanley Hauerwas (b. 1940) is one of
many recent writers to emphasize that treating Christianity simply
as a collection of doctrines or creedal statements leads to a serious
distortion of its character. Rather, it is to be seen as a distinctive way
of life, made possible by the gracious action of the Holy Spirit, that
orients its adherents to the Father through Jesus Christ. Hauerwas
argues that we need a framework or lens through which we may
"see" the world of human behavior. This, he insists, is provided by
sustained, detailed, extended reflection on the Christian narrative:

> The primary task of Christian ethics involves an attempt to
> help us see. For we can only act within the world we can see,
> and we can only see the world rightly by being trained to see.
> We do not come to see just by looking, but by disciplined skills
> developed through initiation into a narrative.[6]

Hauerwas thus stresses the importance of the Christian faith to allow things to be seen for what they really are, and for this true vision of reality to be declared and announced: "The church serves the world by giving the world the means to see itself truthfully."[7]

The Christian faith thus gives us a way of "seeing" the world, which helps us to make sense of it and operate within it. Christianity makes sense in itself, while at the same time making sense of the world. It offers us a way of seeing things that both reflects and creates cohesion. C. S. Lewis made this point well in the conclusion of his essay "Is Theology Poetry?" when he commented: "I believe in Christianity as I believe that the Sun has risen, not only because I see it, but because by it I see everything else."[8] The point here is that the Christian faith makes possible a transformation of the mind that allows us to see things in a new, more exciting, and above all more coherent way. Christianity makes sense in itself; it also makes sense of everything else.

How we "see" things shapes how we behave toward them. Christian theology aims to tell the truth about what it sees—and it sees the world in a specific way: as God's creation. Thus Paul urges his readers not to "be conformed to this world," but rather to "be transformed by the renewing of [their] minds" (Rom. 12:2). The human mind is not replaced or displaced by faith; rather, it is illuminated and energized through faith, understood as a transformed disposition of the knower, which leads to a new way of thinking that enables the discernment of deeper levels of reality than unaided human reason or sight permit.[9] The world thus takes on a new significance. It has been *transsignified,* in that it now points to something beyond itself.[10]

This idea of the transmutation of the world, whether in reality or in perception, has long been associated with the potent image of the "philosopher's stone." This possessed the ability to transmute lesser things into something precious and was ardently sought throughout the Middle Ages. Other sources spoke of an "elixir"—a liquid derived from this mysterious stone—that possessed the power to bring about physical and spiritual regeneration. Although medieval in origin, the image captured the imagination of Renaissance writers.[11] Its potential for theological exploration was developed by the English poet George Herbert (1593–1633) in his poem "The Elixir." Christ is the "philosopher's stone," who transforms the base metal of human existence into the gold of redemption.

> *This is the famous stone*
> *That turneth all to gold:*
> *For that which God doth touch and own*
> *Cannot for less be told.*[12]

Herbert thus points to the power of the Christian vision of God to transform the way we see things. The world is transmuted from a base metal to something that God "doth touch and own," which cannot be "told"—an older way of expressing the idea of "reckoned" or "valued"—for anything less.

Faith thus gives us a viewpoint, a set of spectacles, from and through which we may see things in a Christian way. As the great Yale philosopher of science N. R. Hanson (1924–67) pointed out, the process of observation is always "theory-laden": we see things through theoretical spectacles, which help us to bring things into focus.[13] In one sense, the Christian and secularist "see" the same world; in another sense, however, they see something quite different, because they interpret and value things in very different ways. They wear different sets of spectacles. The Christian faith can thus be thought of in William James's terms as a trusted and trustworthy working hypothesis, or in Hanson's terms as a set of spectacles that allow us to "see" the world in a reliable and trustworthy manner.

The Nature of Faith

To believe in God is to trust in God. This is not an adequate definition of faith, but it is an excellent starting point for further exploration. God is the one who may be trusted in the midst of life's turbulence, confusion, and ambiguities. Trusting someone leads to commitment. It is a pattern that is found throughout the narratives of calling and response that we find in the Christian tradition. One of the great examples of faith is the patriarch Abraham. Abraham trusted God and left behind his family home in order to go to a distant land (Genesis 15, 17). To believe in God is to believe that God may be trusted, leading us to entrust ourselves to God. To believe in God goes far beyond the mere factual acceptance of God's existence; it is to declare that this God may be trusted. It is a familiar theme and has been explored by just about every major Christian writer through the ages.[14]

Similarly, to believe in Christ goes far beyond accepting his historical existence. In its full-blooded sense, faith in Christ is about recognizing him as one who may be trusted. When Jesus of Nazareth asked a man whom he had just healed whether he "believes" in the Son of Man (John 9:35), the healed man was quite clear that he was not being asked whether he believed that Jesus existed. He knew that he was being asked whether he was ready to *trust* Jesus and commit himself to him.

It is therefore no accident that the Gospels of the New Testament go to such trouble to help us understand *why* Jesus of Nazareth may be trusted, and what shape this trust takes. The calling of the first disciples is of especial importance here. In Mark's account of this dramatic event (Mark 1:16–20), Jesus spoke these simple words: "Come, follow me." No explanation or elaboration is offered. Yet the fishermen left everything immediately and followed Jesus. No reason is given for their decision to follow this stranger who has so dramatically entered into their lives. Mark leaves us with the impression of an utterly compelling figure who commands assent by his very presence. They left behind their nets—the basis of their meager existence as fishermen—and followed this strange figure into the unknown. He does not even tell them his name. Yet they choose to entrust themselves to him.

That is where their faith in Jesus Christ began; it is not where it ended. For the Gospels enable us to see the disciples growing in their faith as they gradually come to understand more about the identity and significance of Christ. To begin with, they trusted him; as time passed, they also came to understand something of who he was and why he mattered. Even in the New Testament, this leads to personal trust in God and Christ being supplemented with beliefs concerning their identity—in other words, with doctrinal statements. For example, John's Gospel provides an account of the things that Jesus said and did, in order to bring its readers to the point at which they can commit themselves to him, both personally and intellectually. The narrative of the words and deeds of Jesus has been written so that "you may believe that Jesus is the Christ, the Son of God, and that by believing you may have life in his name" (John 20:31).

This brief foray into Christian terminology allows us to make an important distinction between *faith* (which is generally understood *relationally*) and *belief* (which is generally understood *cognitively* or *conceptually*). Faith primarily describes a relationship with God that is characterized by trust, commitment, and love. To have faith in God is to place one's trust in God, believing him to be worthy of such trust. Beliefs represent an attempt to put into words the substance of that faith, recognizing that words are often not up to the task of representing what they describe, yet recognizing also the need to try to entrust to words what they ultimately could not contain. Words, after all, are of critical importance in communication, argument, and reflection. It is simply unthinkable for Christians not to try to express in words what they believe. Yet these creedal formulations are, in a sense, secondary to the primary act of trust and commitment.

Early Christian statements of faith were often short, even terse.[15] The confession that "Jesus is Lord!" (Rom. 10:9; 1 Cor. 12:3) represents the most compact form of creedal statement.[16] Longer statements of faith include affirmations that clearly embed the core themes of later creeds. An excellent example is found in the Corinthian correspondence:

> For what I received I passed on to you as of first importance:
> that Christ died for our sins according to the Scriptures, that
> he was buried, that he was raised on the third day according to
> the Scriptures, and that he appeared to Peter, and then to the
> Twelve. (1 Cor. 15:3–5)

Paul here weaves together historical narrative and theological interpretation in a manner that became characteristic of early Christian creeds. The historical narrative of Jesus of Nazareth is reaffirmed, but it is interpreted in a particular way. For example, Jesus did not just "die," which is a purely historical statement; he "died *for our sins,*" which is an interpretation of the significance of the historical event of the death of Jesus of Nazareth.[17] History is thus not denied or displaced; rather, it is *interpreted,* being seen in a particular way.

This observation helps us appreciate that Christians do more than simply trust in God or in Christ. They also believe certain quite definite things about them. This does not, however, mean that the Christian faith can be thought of simply as a checklist of beliefs. In a sense, Christianity is a profoundly *relational* faith, which rests on the believer's trusting acceptance of a God who has been proved worthy of such trust in the first place. As Samuel Taylor Coleridge once remarked, "[F]aith is not an accuracy of logic, but a rectitude of heart."[18] Yet despite this relational emphasis within Christianity, there remains a cognitive dimension to faith. Christians do not just believe in Jesus of Nazareth; they believe certain things about him as well. The emergence of the notions of both heresy and orthodoxy during the second century are to be set against an increasing recognition of the importance of developing and sustaining a secure doctrinal core for the maintenance of Christian identity and coherence.

The Consolidation of Faith

One of the challenges confronting the early church was the consolidation of its beliefs. The historical evidence suggests that this was not initially seen as a priority. Even by the middle of the second century, most Christians appear to have been content to live with a certain degree of theological fuzziness. Theological imprecision was not seen as endangering the coherence or existence of the Christian church. This judgment is to be seen as reflecting the historic context of that age: the struggle for survival in a hostile cultural and political environment often led to other issues being seen as of lesser significance.

Yet the rise of controversy forced increasing precision of definition and formulation. And with this increasing concern for theological correctness came an inevitable tightening of the boundaries of what was considered as "authentic" Christianity. The periphery of the community of faith, once relatively loose and porous, came to be defined and policed with increasing rigor. Views that were once regarded as acceptable began to fall out of favor as the rigorous process of examination accompanying the controversies of the age began to expose their vulnerabilities and deficiencies. Ways of expressing certain doctrines that earlier generations regarded as robust began to appear inadequate under relentless examination. It was not necessarily that they were wrong; rather, they were discovered not to be good enough.

A good example of this development can be seen in early Christian reflection on the doctrine of creation. From the outset, Christian writers affirmed that God had created the world. However, there were several ways of understanding what the notion of creation entailed. Many early Christian writers took over existing Jewish notions of creation, which tended to see the act of divine creation primarily as the imposition of order on preexisting matter, or the defeat of chaotic forces. Such views remained dominant within Judaism until the sixteenth century.[19]

Other Christian theologians, however, argued that the New Testament clearly set out the idea of creation as the calling into being of all things from nothing—an idea that later came to be known as creation ex nihilo. As this idea gained ascendancy, the older view of creation as the ordering of existing matter came to be seen initially as deficient and subsequently as wrong.[20] An idea that was once regarded as mainstream thus gradually became sidelined, and eventually rejected altogether. Similar processes can be seen taking place in other areas of Christian thought, especially in relation to the church's understanding of the identity and significance of Jesus Christ.

Sometimes what seem like quite radical shifts in thought take place. A good example of this concerns the question of whether God can be said to suffer. The predominant (but not exclusive) view of the early church was that God could be said to know about suffering, but not to experience this personally. In the twentieth century, an increasing number of Christians came to the view that God did indeed experience suffering personally, above all as a consequence of the Incarnation. "Our God is a suffering God" (Dietrich Bonhoeffer). In part, this growing modern interest in the notion of a suffering God reflects a heightened sensitivity toward pain and suffering in the world, and a new concern to relate the suffering of Christ to the anguish of the world on the one hand and to the nature of God on the other.[21]

One of the most important examples of doctrinal development is found in the Christian doctrine of the Incarnation, which was given formal expression in the fourth century. This affirmation can be seen as the climax of a long, careful, and exhaustive process of theological reflection and exploration.[22] The church had always recognized that Jesus of Nazareth embodied God, making his face visible and his purposes and character accessible to humanity. Yet the intellectual exploration of what this implied took more than three centuries, involving the critical examination of a wide range of intellectual frameworks for making sense of what the church had already discovered to be true. In one sense, the church already knew what was so significant about Jesus of Nazareth. The problem was constructing an intellectual framework that did justice to what was already known about him. And so, inevitably, wrong turns were taken.

The final consensus on the best way of formulating the significance of Jesus of Nazareth—the Council of Nicaea—is perhaps better thought of as a holding formula rather than a final theory, making use of some Greek metaphysical notions that were widespread in the educated world of that age. Some have suggested that this process of development represented a distortion of the original simplicity of the Christian faith. Why should the church have used Greek metaphysical notions to witness to Christ when these are conspicuously absent from the New Testament? The Anglican theologian Charles Gore (1853–1932) set out in some depth a classic account of the relation between the biblical witness to Christ and the more developed understandings of his identity and significance found in the Christian creeds.[23]

Responding to those who argued that the simplicity of the biblical witness to Christ had been compromised and distorted by theoretical development within the history of the church, especially during the first centuries of faith, Gore insisted that these later theoretical formulations are to be seen as "the gradual unfolding" of ideas and themes that were already present, if not explicitly formulated, within Christian thought and worship.[24] Gore pointed out that the motivation to express the church's witness to Christ in increasingly theoretical terms lay partly in the human desire to understand and partly in the desire to protect or safeguard a mystery. For Gore, "Christianity became metaphysical simply and only because man is rational."[25] The development of complex ideas, going beyond the simple language and imagery of the New Testament, is to be seen in part as an inevitable outcome of human intellectual curiosity.

Yet there is clearly more to the development of such ideas than a human desire to probe, or to challenge limits. One of the themes to emerge from the early church exploration of the Incarnation is the need to challenge existing understandings of faith to ensure that they are capable of adequately accommodating and representing the mystery of faith. This means exploring intellectual options, not simply out of curiosity but out of a deep conviction that the survival and health of the church depend upon securing the best possible account of faith. The patristic quest for orthodoxy did not proceed on the assumption that this best account had yet been found, even though it assumed that some reasonable approximations had been developed. In a certain sense, writers such as Athanasius of Alexandria held that orthodoxy had yet to be discovered.[26] The fundamental claim of Christian orthodoxy to tell the truth about things cannot be maintained without asking whether the truth is being fully and properly articulated through existing doctrinal formulations.

We have already used the language of mystery to refer to the realities that stand at the heart of the Christian faith. It is clear that this idea needs considerable expansion if its relevance to the concept of heresy is to be understood.

Preserving the Mysteries of Faith

Early Christian doctrinal development can be compared to an intellectual journey of exploration in which a range of possible ways of formulating core ideas were examined, some to be affirmed and others to be rejected. This process should not really be thought of in terms of winners and losers; it is better understood as a quest for authenticity—a "productive *conflict* about goals and priorities between Christians"[27]—in which all options were examined and assessed.[28]

Yet this process of exploration was both natural and necessary. Christianity could not remain frozen in its first-century forms as it entered the second century and beyond. It faced new intellectual challenges that demanded that it prove itself capable of engaging with religious and intellectual alternatives to Christianity, especially Platonism and Gnosticism. This process of the conceptual expansion of the contents of the Christian faith was extended in time and cautious in execution. The final crystallization of this process of exploration can be seen in the formation of creeds—public, communal authorized statements of faith that represented the *consensus fidelium,* the "consensus of the faithful," rather than the private beliefs of individuals.[29]

This voyage of intellectual exploration involved investigating paths that ultimately turned out to be barren or dangerous. Sometimes wrong turnings were taken at an early stage and corrected later. It is easy to understand why many might believe that early patterns of faith are the most authentic. Yet recognizable forms of views that the church later declared to be heretical—such as Ebionitism and Docetism—can be identified within Christian communities as early as the late first century. Although many early Christian writers, such as Tertullian, held that the antiquity of a theological view was a reliable guide to its orthodoxy, this is simply not correct. Mistakes were made, right from the beginning, that later generations had to correct.

So does this mean that the early church misunderstood or misrepresented Jesus of Nazareth? We need to be clear about one centrally important point. Right from the beginning, Christians knew what really mattered about God and about Jesus of Nazareth. The difficulty was finding a theoretical framework to make sense of this. An intellectual scaffolding needed to be developed to preserve the mystery, to safeguard what the church had discovered to be true—a process that entails both discernment and construction. The critical point to appreciate is that such an intellectual scaffolding is not itself entirely disclosed through divine revelation. Doctrine is something that is at least partly constructed in response to revelation, in order to safeguard what has been revealed. The Arian controversy of the fourth century can be seen as a messy though ultimately productive debate about which of a series of such constructed doctrinal frameworks was best adapted to securing and exhibiting the mystery of Christ. Which framework offered the best integration of the complex biblical witness to his identity and significance?

The church knew that the nature and purposes of God were disclosed in Jesus of Nazareth, even though debate raged about how to make the most sense of this. Christian writers were perfectly aware that the death and resurrection of Jesus of Nazareth had transformed the human situation; their task was to explore patiently and thoroughly every conceivable way of making sense of this. When the Council of Nicaea stated that Jesus was "truly God and truly human" and that he was "consubstantial" with the Father, it was simply safeguarding what Christians already knew to be true. Doctrine thus at one and the same time preserves the central mysteries at the heart of the Christian faith and life while allowing them to be examined and explored in depth.[30]

The use of the technical word "mystery" needs comment. Its fundamental sense is "something that is so vast that it cannot be grasped by the human mind." The human mind is overwhelmed by the vastness of its experience of God—a point expressed, for example, in Rudolf Otto's famous notion of a "tremendous mystery."[31] In a classic discussion of this point, Augustine asked why people were surprised that they could not fully understand God. "If you understand it," he remarked, "it isn't God."[32] Augustine is not suggesting that belief in God is irrational; he is rather making the point that the human mind struggles, and ultimately fails, to cope with the grandeur of God.

This being the case, theology will always prove inadequate to doing justice to the realities that lie at the heart of the Christian faith. We may aim at theological precision, yet our attempts are thwarted by the limitations of the human mind to grapple with the reality of God and the Christian gospel. As the patristic scholar Andrew Louth points out, the gospel cannot be reduced to human words or ideas:

At its heart is the understanding of Christ as the divine *myste-rion:* an idea central to the epistles of the Apostle Paul. This secret is a secret that has been told; but despite that it remains a secret, because what has been declared cannot be simply grasped, since it is *God's* secret, and God is beyond any human comprehension.[33]

A similar point is made by Gore, who also emphasizes the inabil-ity of human words to do justice to divine realities:

Human language never can express adequately divine reali-ties. A constant tendency to apologize for human speech, a great element of agnosticism, an awful sense of unfathomed depths beyond the little that is made known, is always present to the mind of theologians who know what they are about, in conceiving or expressing God. "We see," says St Paul, "in a mirror, in terms of a riddle;" "we know in part." "We are compelled," complains St Hilary, "to attempt what is unattain-able, to climb where we cannot reach, to speak what we cannot utter; instead of the mere adoration of faith, we are compelled to entrust the deep things of religion to the perils of human expression."[34]

Gore thus argued that doctrinal formulations set out the New Testament statements of the mystery of Christ "in a new form for protective purposes, as a legal enactment protects a moral princi-ple."

Doctrine, then, preserves the central mysteries at the heart of the Christian faith and life. Though not necessarily part of divine rev-elation, the doctrines in question are validated partly through their grounding in such revelation, and partly on account of their capac-ity to safeguard and comprehend revelation. The mystery is and remains there, before any attempt to make sense of it and express it in words and formulas. But what happens if a particular doctrine turns out *not* to protect such mystery but in fact undermines it? What if the theoretical framework intended to shield and shelter a central insight of faith is found to erode or distort it? These questions point us to the essence of heresy. *A heresy is a doctrine that ultimately destroys, destabilizes, or distorts a mystery rather than preserving it.* Sometimes a doctrine that was once thought to defend a mystery actually turns out to subvert it. A heresy is a failed attempt at orthodoxy, whose fault lies not in its willingness to explore possibilities or press conceptual boundaries, but in its unwillingness to accept that it has in fact failed.

As we noted earlier, doctrinal frameworks emerge as making sense of the definitive Christian encounter with and experience of God, especially in and through Jesus of Nazareth.[35] Christian theology tries to throw a protective and enfolding net over the fundamental Christian experience of God's disclosure and activity in the life, death, and resurrection of Jesus of Nazareth. Doctrinal statements were developed to preserve and defend the core of the Christian vision of reality. This process, already under way in the New Testament, was consolidated and extended during the patristic era. But what if a doctrinal statement that was originally intended to defend and preserve, and was initially believed to do so, is subsequently discovered to weaken and corrupt? This, I argue throughout this work, is the distinctive feature of heresy.

The threat posed by heresy to the Christian community was often expressed using imagery drawn from the life of ancient Israel, especially its concern to maintain purity and avoid defilement or "uncleanness." Heresy was seen as a contaminant, something that polluted and defiled the purity of the church. This is expressed particularly clearly by Jerome (c. 347–420), who emphasized the importance of maintaining the purity of the church:

> Cut off the decayed flesh, expel the mangy sheep from the fold, as otherwise the whole house, the whole paste, the whole body, and the whole flock, will burn, perish, rot, or die. Arius

was but one spark in Alexandria, but as that spark was not extinguished at once, the whole civilized world was devastated by its flame.[36]

There are clear echoes here of the Levitical code, which demanded the exclusion of contaminating or "unclean" individuals from the community on account of their potentially destructive impact.[37]

The human construction of walls, fences, and ditches can be seen as expressing the importance of establishing barriers to protect community identity.[38] It is well understood that group identity is maintained by the exclusion of those who are held to pose a threat to its ideas or values. Yet although the process by which communities exclude individuals or groups that they regard as intellectually polluting or morally impure can be described by using the categories of social psychology, it is important to appreciate that this exclusion results from the judgment that certain ideas are dangerous to the stability of the community itself.

This brief analysis of the nature of belief has laid the background for a more detailed account of the phenomenon of heresy, to which we shall now turn.

two

The Origins of the Idea of Heresy

Concepts die when they cease to correspond to perceived needs or an experienced reality. Others persist because they express ideas that continue to be meaningful, resonating with the experience of individuals and communities. Heresy belongs to this second category of concepts. Although some regard it as tainted and discredited by its past associations with the enforcement of religious orthodoxy, most recognize that heresy expresses an important idea, essential to all who reflect on the deeper questions of life. Every movement based on core ideas or values has to determine its center on the one hand and its boundaries on the other. What is the focus of the movement? And what are the limits of diversity within the movement?

The essential feature of a heresy is that it is not unbelief (rejection of the core beliefs of a worldview such as Christianity) in the strict sense of the term, but a form of that faith that is held ultimately to be subversive or destructive, and thus *indirectly* leads to such unbelief. Unbelief is the outcome, but not the form, of heresy. Heresy is not, as the historian Fergus Miller notes, a "simple report on observable realities";[1] rather, it is a judgment that a certain set of ideas pose a threat to the community of faith. Heresy is not an empirical, but an evaluative, notion. At one level, it is a *constructed* notion, in that it is the outcome of a judgment or evaluation of a set of ideas by a community—in this case, the Christian church.

From what has just been said, it will be clear that it is not possible to understand the phenomenon of heresy in general, or specific individual heresies, simply at the level of heretical ideas. It is necessary to explore how and why these ideas were judged, often over an extended period of time, to be a threat to faith by the Christian community itself. To understand the nature of heresy, we therefore need to consider both the ideas designated as heretical and the social processes by which they were thus recognized and condemned. Furthermore, heresy is a socially embodied notion, designating communities of discourse as much as ideas, and raising the question of the social or political threat posed by heretical communities to their orthodox counterparts.

One of the more persistent themes in early Christian accounts of heresy is that it smuggles rival accounts of reality into the household of faith. It is a Trojan horse, a means of establishing (whether by accident or design) an alternative belief system within its host.[2] Heresy appears to be Christian, yet it is actually an enemy of faith that sows the seed of faith's destruction.[3] It could be compared to a virus, which establishes its presence within a host, ultimately using its host's replication system to achieve dominance. Yet whatever the ultimate origins of heresy might be, the threat comes from *within* the community of faith.

For example, consider the recent debate in Indonesia over whether the Al-Qiyadah Al-Islamiyah Islamic sect should be recognized as Islamic or treated as another religion.[4] Many Indonesian Islamic organizations are hostile toward Al-Qiyadah Al-Islamiyah because its views deviate from mainstream Islam, most notably in asserting that the hajj, fasting, and the five daily prayers are not compulsory, as well as in its expectation that a new prophet would appear after Muhammad. The central issue is whether the sect's views are to be regarded as representing *ikhtilaf* (legitimate differences in opinion within Islam) or whether these are in fundamental conflict with basic Islamic beliefs and practices.[5] Al-Qiyadah Al-Islamiyah unquestionably regards itself as Islamic, and its adherents would react with horror to any suggestion that they are *kuffar* ("infidels"). Yet their critics within Indonesian Islam argue that their ideas ultimately subvert and undermine the core beliefs of Islam.

Heresy thus poses a threat to faith, arguably more serious than many challenges originating from outside the Christian church. Heretics were insiders who threatened to subvert and disrupt. Lester Kurtz speaks of the "intense union of both nearness and remoteness" in heresy, in that the movement is simultaneously an insider and a stranger to its host.[6] The social theorist Pierre Bourdieu (1930–2002), in offering a sociological account of the significance of heresy, points to its potential to undermine or destabilize core assumptions of a worldview from within, or to identify some instability within that worldview that leads to its radical modification. In each case, Bourdieu argues, the outcome is the same: unintentionally assisting the movement's external opponents.[7]

Every worldview, whether religious or secular, has its orthodoxies and heresies.[8] Although the concepts of heresy and orthodoxy had their origins within early Christianity, they have been found to be useful by other religious traditions on the one hand, and political and scientific ideologies on the other. The development of Darwinism, for example, has witnessed the rise and fall of ways of thinking and schools of thought, with the terms "heresy" and "orthodoxy" being widely used within the field to identify friends and foes.[9] For example, Motoo Kimura's concept of neutral evolution (by which inconsequential amino acid replacements in proteins may account for the bulk of sequence differences between species) was regarded as heretical by many biologists when it was first introduced in the late 1960s.[10] Today it is a part of Darwinian orthodoxy. The appropriation of religious language to describe such controversies is an indication both of the seriousness with which all sides take their positions and of the feeling that certain positions within the Darwinian spectrum are downright dangerous. If evolution can be regarded as a religion, then it has both its orthodoxies and heresies.[11]

The same pattern of development can be seen in modern medical science. Considered from a sociological point of view, modern medicine has arisen through a complex interaction of competing accounts of the origins of illness and how they are to be managed. Dominant ideologies regularly arise, sustained in part by their scientific credentials and in part by significant social factors.[12] The contemporary debate over the relationship of HIV and AIDS, for example, is regularly typecast in terms of "orthodox" and "heretical" schools of thought.[13] Ideas die when they cease to be useful. Heresy lives on—as both a theological and a secular notion.

So how did the term "heresy" come to refer to destabilizing or destructive forms of faith? Words are fluid, shifting their meanings and associations over the years. The English language offers us many examples of words whose meaning seems to have changed so radically over a few centuries that they now signify more or less the opposite of their earlier meaning. The verb "to let," for example, meant "to prevent" or "to hinder" in the sixteenth century; it now means "to permit" or "to allow." The word "urbanize" originally meant "to make someone urbane"—in other words, to educate them in the manners of polite society. Today, it refers to the conversion of the world's diminishing open spaces into the sprawl of the cities. A word with an originally positive association became degraded, coming to refer to what most now regard as a negative development.

The same process can be seen in the development of the Greek language. The word *hypocrites* originally meant "an actor," and was often used in the fifth century before Christ to refer to the specific actor who took a prominent role in a drama.[14] Yet over time the word gradually developed a darker meaning: someone who pretended to be what they were not—in other words, a liar or what we now call a "hypocrite." An originally neutral word thus acquired a strongly negative association.

A more complex shift of meaning is found with the Greek word *hairesis,* from which the term "heresy" is derived. This word originally meant an "act of choosing," although over time it gradually developed the extended senses of "choice," "a preferred course of action," "a school of thought," and "a philosophical or religious sect."[15] Stoicism, for example, is often referred to as a *hairesis* (in other words, a "school of thought") by Greek writers of the late classical period, as are the various medical schools of the age. The first-century Jewish historian Josephus refers to the Sadducees, Pharisees, and Essenes as examples of Jewish *haireses,* by which he means "parties," "schools," or "groupings."[16] In no way is Josephus implying that any of these groups are unorthodox; he is simply noting that they constitute separate, identifiable groups within Judaism. The Greek term *hairesis* is clearly understood to be a neutral, nonpejorative term, implying neither praise nor criticism, referring to a group of people who have common views. The term is descriptive, not evaluative.

It is in this sense that the Greek term *hairesis* is used in the New Testament. If the word has any negative associations at this stage, these appear to be linked to the social divisiveness and intellectual rivalry that these schools of thought sometimes created. The formation of factions was clearly seen as a threat to the unity of Christian communities.[17] Yet at this stage there is no suggestion that a "faction" or "group" is itself dangerous or possesses the subversive or destructive capacity that Christian writers later came to associate with "heresy." The concern is that factionalization is destructive of Christian unity and encourages rivalry and personal ambition. It is not the emergence of "groups" or "parties" that is the issue; it is the negative consequences of this development for the unity of churches if the development is managed badly by church leaders.

This point has been obscured by influential translations of the New Testament, which have created the impression that heresy was a routine problem for Christian communities of the first century. The most significant early English translation of the New Testament was published in 1526 by William Tyndale (c. 1494–1536). Tyndale demonstrated a linguistic competency and a sociological insight that were ahead of his time. He translated the Greek term *hairesis* as "sect," thereby accurately conveying its factionalizing and fissiparous tendencies.[18] Yet the hugely influential King James Bible of 1611, often known as the Authorized Version and praised for its accuracy as a translation, routinely translated the same Greek term as "heresy," thus creating the historically incorrect perception that the later phenomenon that came to be known by this name was present in the New Testament itself. To illustrate the importance of this point, we shall compare the Tyndale and King James translations of 2 Peter 2:1, using the original English spelling found in these sources:

Tyndale (1526): "Ther shal be falce teachers amonge you: wich prevely shall brynge in damnable sectes even denyinge the Lorde."

King James (1611): "There shall be false teachers among you, who privily[19] shall bring in damnable heresies, even denying the Lord."

Heresy may not have emerged as a significant issue in apostolic Christianity, even though there are clear signs of the emergence of views that would later be regarded as heretical. These ideas may have originated during the apostolic era; their heretical nature emerged only during the second century. During this formative period, Christian writers developed a very specific sense of the term *haeresis* (the Latin spelling of the Greek work *hairesis*). No longer did it have the neutral sense of an intellectual option or a school of thought. The term began to develop strongly negative associations, designating those whose views forced them either to withdraw from the church or to be expelled from it.[20] As we have emphasized, some of these views were known, often in early forms, to New Testament writers. The judgment that these were *heretical*—rather than merely inadequate or unacceptable—reflects the ecclesiological situation of the second century, not the first, especially in the Roman church. *Haeresis* now designated a "choice," in the sense of giving private speculative theological ideas (such as those noted in emergent form by New Testament writers) preference over the mind of the Christian community as a whole.[21] Although imperial legal documents continued to use the Latin word *haeresis* in this neutral sense as late as the fifth century (for example, to designate a "guild" or "association" of professional workers),[22] the specifically Christian use of the term was now tinged with associations of religious controversies and their political outcomes.

Heresy rapidly came to be a pejorative, not a descriptive, term. Sociologists have often noted how certain sets of "binary oppositions"—such as "male-female" and "white-black"—play a key role in the social construction of the category of "the other." The notion of "the other," regularly used in the rhetoric of exclusion or denigration, is essentially the devalued or stigmatized half of a binary opposition, and it is chiefly used to refer to groups of people who are seen as inferior or who are believed to constitute a threat. Group identity is often fostered by defining "the other"—as, for example, in Nazi Germany, with its controlling binary opposition "Aryan-Jew." The same point is made, playfully yet seriously, by George Orwell in *Animal Farm,* in which the controlling binary opposition is formulated as "four legs good, two legs bad."

In the second century, the binary opposition "heresy-orthodoxy" began to emerge as a way of excluding certain groups and individuals from the Christian church. *Hairesis* now meant a school of thought that developed ideas that were subversive of the Christian faith, which was to be opposed to *orthodoxia*—an authentic and normative version of the Christian faith.[23] It is this development and the questions it raises that are the subject of this book. How did this happen? Is it a legitimate development? Who decides what counts as heresy and what as orthodoxy? And does the idea of heresy have any continuing relevance for anyone? We shall explore these matters in detail in the following chapters, beginning with the question of the relationship of heresy to early Christian diversity.

part two

The Roots of Heresy

three

Diversity: The Background of Early Heresy

Why did early Christianity invent the idea of heresy? And how—if at all—can a distinction be drawn between the *diversity* that is invariably found within any worldview, whether religious or secular, and the more specific notion of *heresy*? Perhaps the most helpful way of understanding both the nature of heresy and its historical emergence is to reflect on the nature of Christianity during the first century of its existence, as this new and largely misunderstood religious movement began to emerge from within Judaism and establish itself as a significant presence in the Roman Empire. A set of orthodoxies—note the advised use of the plural—began to emerge, representing variations on central themes concerning the identity and significance of Jesus of Nazareth.[1]

As we noted earlier, at the heart of the Christian movement lay a series of reports and interpretations of the words and deeds of Jesus of Nazareth. His significance was presented in terms of both his identity and his function, using a rich range of Christological titles and images of salvation, often drawn from the Jewish roots of Christianity.[2] Initially, Christian groups appear to have been established in leading urban centers, such as Jerusalem, by individuals who had personally known Jesus of Nazareth or who were familiar with his immediate circle.[3] Other Christian communities were established by others with more complex associations with the Jerusalem church, most notably Paul of Tarsus.[4] According to the New Testament itself, Paul was responsible for establishing Christian churches in many parts of the Mediterranean world. At first Christianity would almost certainly have been seen simply as one more sect or group within a Judaism that was already accustomed to considerable diversity in religious expression. Judaism was far from being monolithic.

Yet despite Christianity having its origins within Judaism, which was viewed as a "legal religion" (*religio licita*) by the Roman authorities,[5] these Christian communities were not recognized as entitled to legal protection. The reasons for this are unclear; Pliny, for example, while governor of Bithynia (c. 110–12), appears to have persecuted Christians on the basis of precedent without entirely understanding the reasons for doing so. The churches thus existed under the constant shadow of possible persecution, forcing them to maintain a low public profile. They had no access to power or social influence, and were often the object of oppression by the secular authorities. The early Christian communities were simply not in the position to enforce conformity, even if they had wished to do so.

These Christian communities were scattered throughout the Roman Empire, each facing its own distinctive local challenges and opportunities. This raises two questions, each of which is of major significance for understanding the origins and significance of heresy. First, how did these individual Christian communities maintain their identity with regard to their local cultural context? It is clear, for example, that early Christian worship served to emphasize the distinctiveness of Christian communities, thus helping to forge a sense of shared identity over and against society in general.[6] Second, how did individual Christian communities understand themselves as part of a larger, more universal community? To put this second question another way: how did individual local communities see themselves as connected with a larger universal community, increasingly referred to as "the church" in later writings? For example, there is evidence that these communities maintained contact with each other through correspondence and traveling teachers who visited clusters of churches, and especially through the sharing of foundational documents, some (but not all) of which were later incorporated into the canon of the New Testament.[7]

There is no doubt that the early Christian communities believed that they shared a common faith, which was in the process of spreading throughout the civilized world. Individual churches or congregations saw themselves as local representatives or embodiments of something greater—the church.[8] While it is possible to argue that early second-century Christianity possessed a fundamental theological unity based on its worship of Christ as the risen Lord, the early Christians expressed and enacted their faith in a diversity of manners.

While it is correct to speak of early Christianity as a single tradition, it is perhaps best thought of as a complex network of groups and individuals who existed in different social, cultural, and linguistic contexts. These groups sought to relate their faith to those contexts and to express it in terms that made sense within those contexts. While it is potentially misleading to speak of these groups as "competing," it is certainly fair to suggest that they possessed more autonomy at this early stage than is often appreciated. Early Christianity, as we shall emphasize later, did not possess any authority structures that allowed for the imposition of any kind of uniformity. Indeed, many patristic scholars prize the sheer intellectual excitement of the era, evident in the way in which the early Christians explored and expressed their faith.

However, this historical observation does not in itself negate the idea that there was a fundamental unifying strand in early Christianity. The sociological diversity of early Christianity was not matched by anything even remotely approaching theological anarchy. In an important study, the British scholar of early Christianity H. E. W. Turner argued that it was possible to identify a pattern derived from the apostolic witness and maintained across time as the "deposit of faith" (*depositum fidei*), referred to in the New Testament as "the faith once delivered to the saints."[9] This pattern is embedded, like a genetic code, in the writings and worship of the early church, as well as in the texts of the New Testament. Yet despite this core "pattern of truth" that united them, early Christian communities clearly show diversity as well as unity. We must be careful not to rush to speak of the "emergence of diversity" as if this was a later development. There are reasons for thinking it may have been there from the outset, even if later developments exacerbated it in certain situations.

So what led to this diversity? Five important factors can be identified as contributing to this situation:

1. Early uncertainty over which resources were to be regarded as authoritative by all Christian communities.

2. Diversity concerning aspects of the Christian faith within the documents that would later be gathered together as the New Testament.

3. Divergent interpretations of these documents, leading to different ways of thinking emerging within the Christian church.

4. Diversity of patterns within early Christian worship. These are now known to have been considerably more diverse than was once thought, with important implications for how some core aspects of faith were understood within early Christianity.

5. An inability to enforce uniformity. In its early phase, Christianity was a minority group on the fringes of society, without proper legal status, and with no access to power until the conversion of Constantine in the fourth century. This prevented any enforcement of uniformity until a relatively late stage, by which point considerable diversity existed.

We shall consider each of these points individually, as they are of major importance to our theme.

Uncertainty over Authoritative Resources

The second-century writer Lucian of Samosata noted that one of the most distinctive features of Christians was a penchant for writing and interpreting books. Christianity appeared to him to be a textual community, whose life and beliefs were shaped by its writings.[10] Perhaps it was for this reason that pagan Roman criticism of Christianity often focused on its writings, just as attempts to eliminate it often took the form of confiscation of its books.[11] This does not necessarily mean that Christians were more literate than their contemporaries within Judaism or classical culture.[12] It is simply to note how important texts were to the early Christian communities, even if their impact primarily concerned their leaders.

Yet many early Christian manuscripts include more than texts that were later recognized as canonical New Testament writings. For example, some early Christian manuscripts take the form of collections of writings drawn from the Old Testament, early extra-canonical writings such as the Gospel of Thomas and the Shepherd of Hermas, and fragments of other, unknown writings, as well as liturgical and theological texts.[13] Christians seem to have drawn on a variety of resources in developing their faith, some of which would have appeared strange to those familiar with the settled canon of Scripture. A variety of texts jostled for the attention of their readers, including Gnostic Gospels, accounts of martyrdoms, pastoral works, and apocryphal acts.[14] It is becoming increasingly clear that the early Christian communities had complex theological and devotional loyalties, which is clearly expressed in their reading preferences.

As the antiheretical writings of Irenaeus of Lyons make clear, an issue that emerged as significant as early as the second century was the question of *apocrypha*—writings whose origins and provenance were regarded as suspect, lacking historical or theological continuity with the apostolic church.[15] As Jerome darkly commented, *caveat omnia apocrypha*—beware of all apocrypha.[16] The formation of an established canon of Scripture was an integral part of the early church's efforts to eliminate writings of dubious provenance from theological discussion.[17] The appeal to the continuity of use of a given book within the churches was of particular significance, as this was seen as witnessing both to its antiquity and to its authority.

The point here is that the texts being so widely read within Christian communities offered quite divergent views about the nature and characteristics of Christianity, sometimes reflecting the concerns of their authors to address particular social or religious groups. There was a clear need to identify a group of such writings as possessing universal, as opposed to local, authority. While Christians were free to read what they liked, there was a growing recognition of a need to identify which works possessed a normative status for the church as a whole. Without wishing to prevent Christians from reading their favorite authors, Christian leaders began to identify a group of texts that transcended local preferences. Athanasius of Alexandria played a particularly significant role in assessing criteria of authenticity for the purposes of canonical evaluation.[18] This process of crystallization gradually led to the formation of the New Testament canon.[19]

Christianity, in its formative stages, was subject to influence from a surprisingly wide variety of textual sources, with no clear agreement at this stage concerning their authenticity and authority. For example, "apocryphal" literature posed a particular challenge to the early church, on account of the diversity of materials recognized as potentially authoritative in different regions of the Christian world. Heresy could thus arise from basing one's theology on apocryphal sources,[20] whereas orthodoxy gave priority to those works that were, or would be, included in the New Testament canon.

While this is an important point, it is important to appreciate that a degree of diversity can be found even in the limited range of texts eventually accepted as canonical. We shall therefore consider the significance of the theological diversity of the New Testament for any account of the origins of heresy.

Diversity Within the New Testament Documents

The collection of documents that we now know as the New Testament clearly presupposes that there is some basic unity among and across Christian communities, yet it presents a subtly variegated range of ways of understanding the fundamental themes of the Christian faith and how these are to be applied to issues of practical conduct. While some writers offer somewhat facile harmonizations of the New Testament, others have appreciated the importance of identifying and respecting differing emphases and nuances,[21] not least on account of the New Testament's implications for diversity within contemporary Christianity.

A recognition of the polyphony of the New Testament is ultimately little more than an indirect acceptance of the diversity that existed within early Christianity. The term "diversity" must be used with caution, and surrounded with qualifications. In the first place, concession of diversity does not entail the notion of a fundamental unity. As Stephen Neill pointed out many years ago, Jesus of Nazareth is a central focus of the New Testament; nevertheless, his significance is articulated in terms that are adapted to the audiences and communities served by the authors of the New Testament books.[22] And in the second, the diversity in question is actually quite limited. We must avoid speaking carelessly, as if to suggest that the New Testament offers an unbridled multiplicity of visions of the Christian faith.[23] It is perfectly possible to identify a "core" set of ideas within the New Testament, as follows:

1. The God of Israel can be loved and trusted as Creator of all.

2. Jesus is the one sent by God, to reveal God and redeem humanity.

3. In spite of human failure, trust in God's redemptive work through Christ is the way to salvation, a redemptive process begun in this life and completed in the life beyond.

4. A person who has salvation is expected to love others and care about them, and to follow the ethical standards laid down by Jesus.

5. The body of believers is an extended fellowship.[24]

While being critical of the idea of an early crystallization of Christian orthodoxy, the leading British New Testament scholar James Dunn also argues that a "unifying strand" can be discerned within the New Testament. Dunn uses the Greek work *kerygma,* best translated as "proclamation," to refer to New Testament interpretations of the significance of Jesus of Nazareth. Where Rudolf Bultmann and others once spoke of the New Testament *kerygma,* in the *singular,* Dunn suggests that the evidence points to a group of New Testament *kerygmata,* in the *plural,* held together by certain core themes.[25] Dunn argues that there "was no standardized pattern, no extended outline of Christian proclamation" in the New Testament, but a range of such proclamations, adapted to the particular circumstances of the situation. For example, Paul's proclamation of the gospel "took diverse forms as circumstances determined, and it developed over the years, altering in emphasis in tone."[26]

The question is one of interpretation and synthesis: of allowing the inherent unity of the New Testament to be perceived, while respecting its diversity. Whether the New Testament is perceived as a cacophony or symphony depends in part on how it is interpreted, especially how its diverse voices are allowed to relate to one another. Richard Hays, for example, argues that the multifaceted vision of the Christian faith found in the New Testament can be set out in terms of a complex narrative with three focal points: community, cross, and new creation.[27] Yet the point is clear: the intrinsic diversity of the New Testament is such that it potentially gives rise to a corresponding diversity of interpretations. We shall explore this point further in what follows.

Divergent Interpretations of the New Testament

The long history of Christian interpretation of the New Testament makes it abundantly clear that certain texts are interpreted in very different ways by different individuals and groups. This poses the critically important question, Who is authorized to adjudicate between such interpretations of the New Testament? The growing emphasis upon the Catholic Church as the supreme authority in the interpretation of the New Testament began to proceed apace in the second century and is especially evident in the writings of Irenaeus of Lyons.

To understand the importance of Irenaeus's appeal to the institution of the church as the interpreter of the New Testament, we may consider some difficulties in biblical interpretation that affect Protestantism—a religious movement that does not acknowledge any authority above Scripture.[28]

Consider the question, Are Christians meant to evangelize? The predominant interpretation of the gospel imperative to "make disciples of all nations" (Matt. 28:19) in the first phase of Protestantism during the sixteenth century was that this command was addressed to the apostles, not to subsequent generations. While the first apostles were therefore under an obligation to spread the gospel, this responsibility was restricted to their age. It was not until the late eighteenth century that this view began to be challenged successfully, particularly through the growing influence of missionary societies in England. By the end of the nineteenth century, most Protestants considered that the obvious and clear meaning of the passage was that all Christians were called to evangelize, and to support the work of missions. The predominant way of interpreting a biblical text had undergone a major shift. But which of the two options was right? And who had the authority to decide?

The problems that Protestantism faced here were famously set out by John Dryden (1631–1700) in his satirical poem "Religio Laici" (A Layperson's Religion) (1682). Dryden here argued that the great Protestant emphasis on the Bible merely led to the proliferation of heresy, due to the absence of any universally acknowledged, authoritative interpreter. The attitude toward biblical interpretation found within Protestantism, Dryden argues, not merely leaves it powerless to resist heresy, but actually encourages the emergence of heresy, through Protestantism's naive idea that ordinary Christians will be led, inerrantly and inevitably, to orthodoxy as they browse the scriptural pages. The text of Scripture was open to all; but what of the rule by which it was to be interpreted? Protestants agreed on and respected a common authority, but they had no shared notion of a meta-authority.

Dryden invites us to imagine an orthodox Protestant convinced that the Bible clearly teaches the divinity of Christ, yet disturbingly confronted with another Protestant who interprets those same passages purely in terms of Christ's humanity—the Socinian heresy,[29] which emerged in the sixteenth century and held that Christ was a human being devoid of divine identity. Thus Dryden writes, in "Religio Laici":

We hold, and say we prove from Scripture plain,
That Christ is God; *the bold Socinian*
From the same Scripture urges he's but man.
Now what appeal can end th' important suit;
Both parts talk loudly, but the Rule is mute?

Dryden's point is that Scripture did not disclose, clearly and unambiguously, the rule by which it was to be interpreted. And as there was no authority higher than Scripture, how could Protestantism discriminate between orthodoxy and heresy? If any norm or institution outside or apart from the Bible is recognized as authoritatively determining its meaning, that norm or institution is in effect superior to the Bible. This was a dangerous vulnerability, which many believe remains at best incompletely resolved within Protestantism.

Irenaeus appears to have anticipated this difficulty in arguing for the role of the church as the authoritative interpreter of Scripture. For some scholars, Irenaeus was motivated primarily by a desire for uniformity, which according to Elaine Pagels and Karen King led to his laying down that "all true Christians must confess the same things, joining together to say a common creed that states what all believe." The driving force behind Irenaeus's approach was an institutional agenda that would set the church over and above individual Christians, intended to "consolidate scattered groups of Jesus's followers into what he and certain other bishops envisioned as a single, united organization." Heresy could therefore be understood as those teachings that were "antithetical to the consolidation of the church under the bishops' authority."[30]

Yet this is only one way of interpreting Irenaeus's approach. Most Christian theologians would argue that Irenaeus's concern was neither for ecclesiastical uniformity for its own sake, nor for the empowerment of the episcopacy. Irenaeus wanted to maintain continuity with the apostolic era, ensuring that what was taught in that formative age continued to characterize his own age. For this reason, he placed emphasis on the importance of historical continuity between the present church leadership and the apostles. The church represented a community of memory, capable of aligning its interpretation of the Bible with its recollection of the apostolic witness and teaching.

A further attempt to limit diversity developed later. Vincent of Lérins (d. 450), increasingly concerned about theological innovation, developed a checklist to limit the spread of new and potentially dangerous ideas. Every doctrine needed to conform to three criteria. It had to be shown to have been accepted (1) everywhere, (2) always, and (3) by all believers. In this way, Vincent hoped to limit Christian teaching to those teachings that had always commanded universal assent.[31] Yet the historical evidence suggests that Vincent's efforts did not succeed in checking the growth of doctrinal diversity in the church at the time.[32]

In this section, we have emphasized the diversity of interpretations of the Bible found within the Christian tradition. So who decides which interpretation of the Bible is orthodox and which heretical? It is an important question. Every major heresy within the Christian faith has presented itself as offering a legitimate interpretation of the Bible and has criticized its orthodox opponents as deficient in the art of biblical hermeneutics.[33] Appealing to the Bible was not the exclusive preserve of the orthodox. Indeed, many views that would later be regarded as heretical had their origins in a close reading of the biblical text.[34] The Arian controversy of the fourth century, which pitted the arch-heretic Arius against his orthodox opponent Athanasius, can be seen as fundamentally concerning how best to interpret the statements found in John's Gospel concerning the identity and significance of Jesus Christ.[35]

Up to this point, we have considered a number of factors concerning Christian texts that appear to have led to increasing diversity of belief within the church. Yet it is important to appreciate that diversity also seems to have developed in relation to another aspect of the church's life—its worship.

Diversity in Early Christian Worship

Traditional liturgical scholarship has generally assumed that a single, coherent line of evolution of Christian worship can be traced from the apostolic age to the fourth century. Even by the early second century, Christian worship had developed considerably beyond what is described in the New Testament, characterized by a tendency to invent new symbolism not directly present in Scripture.

In some cases, the continuity between early Christian liturgies and the practice of the New Testament church is obscure.[36] In recent years, there has been a growing realization that early Christian worship may have been more diverse and variegated than this simple model suggests.[37]

Why is this so important? Because the way in which Christian communities worship both reflects and affects their doctrinal beliefs.[38] According to Prosper of Aquitaine (c. 390–c. 455), "the law of prayer determines the law of belief [*legem credendi lex statuat supplicandi*]."[39] The Latin slogan *lex orandi, lex credendi* ("the way you pray shapes the way you believe") is often cited here as indicating the way in which doctrine and worship are interconnected.[40] Differences in worship would thus be expected to further increase the degree of diversity already present in early Christian communities.

Christian Orthodoxy in the Fourth Century

The early church was socially fragmented, disconnected from influence and power within the imperial structures. There was no question of some centralized church authority "imposing" its views on other congregations, as the church was denied access to political or military power. No mechanism for preventing diversification or enforcing orthodoxy existed. The Roman state was generally hostile to Christianity, often seeing it as subverting traditional religious views. Occasionally, periods of repression developed, such as the Decian persecution (250–51). Until the conversion of Constantine and the issuing of the Edict of Milan (313), the Christian churches had no significant social status or access to power. The convening of the Council of Nicaea by Constantine in 325 can be seen as the first step in the attempted creation of an essentially uniform imperial church, whose doctrines would be publicly defined by creeds. By this stage, however, a considerable degree of diversity had become established within the church.

The comparison with early Islam is instructive. Following the death of the Prophet Muhammad in 632, a political structure for ruling the new Muslim state emerged. Known as "the caliphate," it grew both in power and territory during the centuries following Muhammad's death, conquering the lands of the Fertile Crescent to the north. Within this expanding territory, often referred to as the *ummah,* Islam was enforced as the official state religion. During the period of the first two caliphs, Abu Bakr (632–34) and Umar (634–44), the codification of the Qu'ran was carried out as the number of individuals who had committed it to memory (the "Companions of the Prophet") began to diminish. Yet the process of committing the Qu'ran to writing led to textual divergencies. Thus the codex of Abdullah ibn Mas'ud became the standard text for the Muslims at Kufa in Iraq, while the codex of Ubayy ibn Ka'b was widely used in Damascus in Syria. Aware that this situation might lead to factionalization and disunity within the emergent Islamic state, Umar ordered the production of an official, authorized text of the Qu'ran. All other texts, whether complete or fragmentary, were ordered to be destroyed.[41] We see here a strategy devised to achieve uniformity within early Islam—one that had, and could have had, no parallel within early Christianity.

This point is of no small importance in connection with the argument of Walter Bauer, to be considered in more detail in the following chapter, that orthodoxy arose through the gradual and expanding imposition of the views of the Roman church on its neighbors in the second century. This suggestion has proved very difficult to defend, given that Rome's influence over other churches in the region began to become significant only in the third century.[42] Bauer seems to have retrojected the later influence of the Roman church onto an earlier period, when, it is perfectly clear, the Christian communities at Rome did not have the power or authority that later emerged.

All these factors combined to lead to a significant degree of doctrinal diversity within early Christianity, particularly in the late first and early second centuries. Even in the New Testament documents, concerns are expressed at some of the outcomes of such diversity— most notably, the tendency to form factions within Christian communities, which was seen as a threat to the unity of churches. Theological latitude is not identical with heresy; nevertheless, it may be argued that it provides a context within which heresy may arise. All this tends to confirm the judgment of H. E. W. Turner in his landmark 1954 study of the relationship between heresy and orthodoxy in the early church:

> During the formative period of the Christian Church orthodoxy resembles a symphony composed of various elements rather than a single melodic theme, or a confluence of many tributaries into a single stream rather than a river which pursues its course to the sea without mingling with other waters. Already within the New Testament itself there exists a considerable variety of theological traditions.[43]

Yet despite this obvious diversity of early Christian expression, the historical evidence clearly points to a shared sense of identity, expressed and maintained in the face of considerable geographical distance and cultural differences. Early Christians clearly saw themselves as belonging to the same extended family, characterized by a minimal "basic kit" of beliefs, values, and attitudes toward worship.[44] The core Christian rituals or sacraments of baptism and Eucharist provided a focus of identity, which was supplemented by emerging creedal statements.[45] Diversity generally arose over what was to be added to this "basic kit," or how some of its key elements were to be interpreted or applied. This identity was not sustained simply by internal means; external agencies, including representatives of the Roman state, came to see Christianity as a coherent entity—in the case of the Roman state, as a potential threat—and solidified its sense of shared identity through various repressive measures.[46] Despite its internal diversities, Christianity came to be

seen as a coherent entity by outside observers who felt threatened
by its increasing numerical strength. Christian identity can thus be
seen to have been enhanced by processes of social negotiation, involving at least some degree of social construction, that reinforced
an internally generated Christian sense of corporate identity.

These reflections on the complex character of early Christianity
set the context for any discussion of heresy. It is very difficult to
speak of "Christian orthodoxy" in the late first century or early
second century as this would later be understood as an "authorized"
or "official" statement of faith. Christian orthodoxy was emergent
at this time, characterized by an exploration of intellectual options,
without any decisive control by authoritative figures or institutions.
It is perfectly possible to speak of the beginnings of a process of
"crystallization" of orthodoxy, as various theological formulations
of faith were proposed and examined, some to be affirmed and
others rejected. In the former, we see the beginnings of orthodoxy;
in the latter, of heresy. From the outset, heresy had its origins within
the church, as part of an ongoing process of explorations of the
center and boundaries of faith.

It is important to appreciate that many of those who came to be
regarded as heretics were active and committed participants in
Christian communities who were genuinely concerned to enable
the gospel to be understood and presented faithfully and effectively.
The impression created by some patristic writers is that heretics
were outsiders who sought to subvert or destroy the church. The
origins of this inaccurate stereotype of heresy are now reasonably
well understood. In recent years, increased attention has been paid
to the strategies devised by Irenaeus of Lyons to exclude certain individuals and teachings from the church.[47] A new "heresiology"
emerged in the late second century as a way of portraying heresy
that attempted to mask the fact that heresy had its origins within
the church, occasionally even remaining present within it.[48]

Making use of established forms of "philosophical invective,"[49]
Irenaeus and others argued that heretics were impostors, wolves in

sheep's clothing, who pretended to be members of the church yet were ultimately bent on its destruction. Where the heretics based their views on a reading of Scripture, it was argued that their exegesis was merely a pretext for developing views that had their origin outside the tradition of Christ and his apostles and were intended to subvert the church. Such studies suggest that Irenaeus wanted to convert difference into exclusion, as a means both of isolating heretics from the community of faith and of maintaining the idea that heresy was a contaminant of faith that had its origins outside the church, being smuggled in by imposters or traitors. Yet to understand the importance of heresy, we must confront the fact that every major heresy began as an exploration of the dynamics of faith within the church.

So where might we begin this exploration? The most obvious point is to consider how the phenomenon of heresy came to emerge within the early church, and its potential significance. We shall consider this in the chapter that follows.

four

The Early Development of Heresy

In the summer of 144, a wealthy Christian shipowner called a meeting of church leaders in Rome. By this time, Christianity had gained a significant following in the imperial capital.[1] Marcion of Sinope (c. 110–60) wanted to propose a fundamental change in the way in which the church positioned itself in relation to Judaism, not least its use of the Hebrew Bible.[2] Marcion held that Christianity ought to be discontinuous with Judaism, appealing to biblical texts such as Luke 5:37: "[N]o one puts new wine into old wineskins; otherwise the new wine will burst the skins and will be spilled, and the skins will be destroyed." Christianity, he argued, should have nothing to do with the God, beliefs, and rituals of Judaism. A clean break was necessary.

Sadly, the full details of Marcion's theological proposals have been lost to history; his views, like those of so many who became embroiled in ecclesiastical controversies of this age, we know only through the writings of his opponents. The most detailed account of what happened in Rome is in the writings of Epiphanius of Salamis (c. 315–403).[3] It seems clear that what Marcion was proposing represented a radical break with both the established tradition of the church and the writings of the New Testament. The majority position within the church, at Rome and elsewhere, was that Christianity represented the fulfillment of the covenant between God and Abraham, not its rejection or abrogation. The God whom Christians worshipped was the same as that worshipped by Abraham, Isaac, and Jacob, the God whose will was disclosed through the Law and the Prophets.[4] In marked contrast, Marcion proposed breaking with Judaism completely, seeing Christianity as a new faith concerning a new God.

We shall consider Marcion's views in more detail later in this work. Our concern at this point, however, has to do with the reaction of the assembled Christian leaders to Marcion's proposals, as related by Epiphanius. They declined to follow him in his views, and they returned his earlier gift of two hundred thousand sesterces, a very substantial sum by the standards of the day.[5] There is no evidence that Christian leaders at Rome were particularly hostile toward Marcion. They unquestionably regarded him as being wrong in his beliefs. Yet they did not expel him from the church. Epiphanius makes it clear that Marcion dissociated himself from them, believing that they were not properly Christian in their beliefs, and went on to establish his own organization. Marcion saw himself as the defender of true orthodoxy and came to the conclusion that the only way to defend it was to break with the doctrinally suspect church of Rome and found his own society of true believers—a *sect,* to use the language of a later age.

The point here is that Marcion was perfectly clear about who was orthodox and who was heretical in this matter. Marcion was quite persuaded that his own views were correct, and that by failing to endorse them the Roman church had compromised its theology and thus lost its claim to be the true church. The Roman church leaders, of course, took a rather different view on the matter of which ecclesial group was heretical. Everyone wanted to be a champion of orthodoxy, Marcion included. Marcion did not see himself as a heretic but rather as a stalwart defender of what Christianity ought to be. But his prescription for what Christianity ought to be did not find significant support.

This observation that there were competing accounts of orthodoxy helps us appreciate that heresy is not a neutral concept but is determined by prior understandings of what Christianity ought to be. It is an evaluative notion, one that cannot be confirmed or disconfirmed by historical analysis. It is this factor that makes the historical study of heresy so difficult, in that the historian is obliged to describe what others have prescribed. The judgment as to what is heretical and what is orthodox is not one that the historian can make using the legitimate tools of historical method. Rather, history attempts to understand the nature of heretical beliefs and of the processes, motivations, and criteria that led to the prescriptive judgment on the part of the church that these beliefs were heretical in the first place.

Epiphanius's account of Marcion's break with the Roman church is consistent with much of what we know about the history of the church and its circumstances around this time. But there were other ways of spinning this story. There is evidence of an emerging "official" narrative of the origins of heresy, locating its genesis in personal rivalry, ambition, and dishonesty in the late second and early third centuries. Tertullian, who played a significant role in the formulation of this alternative account, tells us that the Roman church threw out Marcion on account of his heretical views.[6] Tertullian portrays the origins of Marcion's heresy as lying in thwarted personal ambitions. According to Tertullian, Marcion was an eloquent and gifted Christian teacher who wanted to become bishop of Rome. When another candidate was appointed, Marcion reacted by leaving the church and establishing his heresy as an act of petulance.[7] Marcion, he asserts, lost his faith, and as a result turned to heresy. He "was a deserter before he became a heretic."[8]

There is little evidence that Tertullian had firsthand knowledge of the situation in Rome. His account is really of theological rather than historical significance, in that it points to a crystallizing "official" narrative of the origins of heresy that came to dominate early Christian heresiology. Significantly, the moral character and motivations of heretics often seem to assume at least as great a significance in these narratives as the theological characteristics of the heresies that they advocated. So what is the "official" or "received" view of the origins of heresy? In what follows, we shall explore the account of the nature and origins of heresy that gained the ascendancy in early Christianity.

The "Received View" on the Origins of Heresy

By the middle of the third century, a narrative of the origins of heresy had become established within the church. Its main features can be summarized as follows.[9]

1. The church founded by the apostles was "unsullied and undefiled," holding firm to the teachings of Jesus of Nazareth and the traditions of the apostles.

2. Orthodoxy took temporal precedence over heresy. This argument is developed with particular vigor by Tertullian, who insists that the *primum* is the *verum*. The older a teaching, the more authentic it is. Heresy is thus regarded as innovation.

3. Heresy is thus to be seen as a deliberate deviation from an already existing orthodoxy. Orthodoxy came first; the decision to deliberately reject it came later.

4. Heresy represents the fulfillment of New Testament prophecies of defection and deviation within the church, and can be seen as a providential means by which the faith of believers can be tested and confirmed.

5. Heresy arises through a love of novelty, or jealousy and envy on the part of heretics. Tertullian regularly portrays heretics such as Valentinus as frustrated and ambitious, and ascribes their views to resentment at their failure to achieve the recognition of high ecclesiastical office.

6. Taken as a whole, heresy is internally inconsistent, lacking the coherency of orthodoxy.

7. Individual heresies are geographically and chronologically restricted, whereas orthodoxy is found throughout the world.

8. Heresy results from the "dilution of orthodoxy with pagan philosophy." Once more, Tertullian is a vigorous advocate of this position, arguing that Valentinus's ideas were derived from Platonism and Marcion's from Stoicism. What, he asked, has Athens to do with Jerusalem?[10]

This "received view" of the origins of heresy was widely accepted within Christianity until the early nineteenth century. Despite their many differences, both Protestant and Catholic theologians held that Christian orthodoxy—to which they both aspired—was to be equated with the teaching of the early church. Heresy was a later deviation from this original pure doctrine. Thus the influential early Lutheran theologian Philip Melanchthon (1497–1560) argued that the Protestant Reformation was a return to the *primum et verum,* the "first and the true," which had become distorted and confused by the medieval church. "Ancient doctrine, original doctrine and true doctrine are thus one and the same thing."[11] Theological orthodoxy is identical with the earliest teachings of the church. Melanchthon's Catholic opponents agreed with him in asserting that the church's earliest teachings were the most authentic, but they argued that Catholicism preserved these teachings whereas Protestantism introduced innovations. And was not innovation one of the distinctive features of heresy?

This regnant theory began to be challenged in the nineteenth century, largely on account of the growing recognition that Christian doctrine had undergone development or evolution. Rather than having been fixed in the earliest period of the church's history, doctrinal formulations had emerged over an extended period of time through a process of reflection and negotiation. The emergence of heresy, it seemed, was part of the greater process of the development of Christian doctrine itself, in which the seeds of the New Testament began to grow into the more sophisticated and extended vision of reality that is often styled "orthodoxy." Where once heresies were seen as the deliberate flouting of a well-established set of beliefs, they came to be seen more as byways opened up for exploration through the process of doctrinal development.

The classical view of the origins of heresy was put under even greater pressure in the twentieth century, when historians suggested that the causal relationship of heresy and orthodoxy was not quite as straightforward as was once thought. In what follows, we shall consider these challenges to the "received view" of the origins of heresy and explore their implications for our understanding of the notion.

The Development of Doctrine

In his influential study of the nature of heresy, H. E. W. Turner identified a number of pressures that led to heretical outcomes. One of the most intriguing is what Turner terms *archaism*—a refusal to accept that development in Christian thinking is necessary.[12] Turner's point is significant, as it draws attention to the fact that the church gradually found the repetition of earlier formulas to be inadequate as a means of ensuring continuity, except at the purely formal level, with the apostolic church. An instinct to preserve tradition by reiteration gradually gave way to the realization that the church must continue its history by restatement and interpretation of those traditions. The dynamism of the New Testament traditions concerning Jesus was simply compromised through such a process of preservation, in that this involved what amounted to petrification.[13] The wooden repetition of biblical formulas proved inadequate as a means of safeguarding and consolidating the Christian faith as new challenges to its identity and integrity emerged.

The importance of this point can be seen through a close reading of Athanasius of Alexandria (c. 293–373). One of Athanasius's most significant insights is that loyalty to the Christian tradition actually demands innovation. As the inadequacy of traditional concepts and formulas to do justice to God's self-revelation became increasingly clear, Athanasius argued for the need to explore fresh ways of expressing the fundamental themes of faith. For Athanasius, the critical question concerned what specific forms of doctrinal innovation were required if the integrity of the Christian faith was to be preserved.[14] The stolid and unimaginative repetition of doctrinal formulas of the past offered no guarantee that the living tradition of the Christian faith was being adequately or authentically transmitted.

Yet the question of whether Christian doctrine can be said to "develop" caused many considerable unease in the nineteenth century. The issue was particularly sensitive for Catholics. Earlier generations of theologians had asserted the unchangeability of the fundamentals of faith with complete confidence. Thus the influential Catholic theologian Jacques-Bénigne Bossuet (1627–1704) insisted that the catholic "deposit of faith" remains the same— yesterday, today, and forever. The innovations of Protestants and heretics, Bossuet argued, could easily be identified because they represented change to a hitherto static and unchanged body of teaching.[15]

Yet evidence was mounting that pointed to the development of doctrine—that the teaching of the church had undergone evolution over a period of several centuries before crystallizing into the mature belief system expressed at the Council of Chalcedon (451). During the 1830s and 1840s, a group of Catholic theologians based at the University of Tübingen, including Johann Sebastian Drey (1777–1853) and Johann Adam Möhler (1796–1838), developed an organic approach to doctrinal development that likened the process to the natural growth of a biological seed.[16] This simple biological analogy, which had its roots in the New Testament itself, became increasingly popular in German theological circles. It allowed for doctrinal development while at the same time suggesting that the pattern of growth was predetermined rather than arbitrary or random. To concede that doctrine had developed was therefore not necessarily a cause for theological concern.[17]

This approach was developed in the English-speaking world by John Henry Newman (1801–90). In a university sermon at Oxford in 1843, Newman used the text of the day—"But Mary kept these things, and pondered them in her heart" (Luke 2:19)—to draw a pointed distinction between "new truths" and "further insights."[18] The church, he argued, was engaged in a process of reflection, through which new insights emerged. This did not, he insisted, result in innovation; rather, it led to an expansion of the church's understanding of what it believed.

In 1845, Newman set out his ideas more fully in his celebrated *Essay on the Development of Christian Doctrine.* Its most important contribution to the study of the development of doctrine was arguably not a theory of how doctrine develops but its acknowledgment that such change had indeed taken place.[19] It is the insistence upon the observable *fact* of doctrinal development, not any specific *theory* or model of this process, that is probably the distinguishing feature and most significant achievement of Newman's seminal work. For Newman, "development," or the attainment of "further insights" in matters of doctrine, was an entirely orthodox idea.

> From the necessity, then, of the case, from the history of all sects and parties in religion, and from the analogy and example of Scripture, we may fairly conclude that Christian doctrine admits of formal, legitimate, and true developments, that is, of developments contemplated by its Divine Author.[20]

Newman's idea was not well received in more traditional Catholic circles, which were alarmed at signs of growing secularization in Europe and regarded any dilution or diminution of traditional standpoints as anathema in such a dangerous context. The First Vatican Council (1869–70) had little time for the idea of doctrinal development, reasserting the notion of the "immutability of doctrine"[21] alongside that of papal infallibility. Yet the historical evidence for this process of development was accumulating inexorably, laying the groundwork for a reconsideration of the traditional notion of a static doctrinal heritage. Perhaps the "faith once delivered to the saints" was not a full-fledged set of dogmas but the basic kit for the construction of such dogmas under God's providential guidance.[22]

The idea of the "development of doctrine" was given a new injection of intellectual energy with the publication of Charles Darwin's *Origin of Species* (1859). If one could speak of evolution within the biological world, could not the same—or at least an analogous—process be discerned within the world of ideas? Given the growing impact of Darwinism throughout the Western world in the late nineteenth century and beyond, it was perhaps inevitable that the phenomenon of doctrinal development would begin to be thought of in Darwinian terms.

So, was the "faith once delivered to the saints" (Jude 3) itself a fully developed system of doctrine, or was it rather the seed from which such a system might grow?[23] Most Christian writers would now give broad assent, with inevitable qualifications, to the general position mapped out by Charles Gore in 1891. Dealing with the question of the relationship of the New Testament witness to Christ and the subsequent elaboration and consolidation of those ideas in the doctrines of the church, Gore argues for a natural, organic emergence of the Chalcedonian definition.[24] The whole process is governed by the gradual emergence of what Gore termed "a corporate consciousness" that is in a continual process of "gaining clearer expression" using the language and conceptualities of its environment.

The idea of doctrinal development is now widely accepted by most theologians, whether Protestant or Catholic, and is no longer seen as causing any particular difficulties. Most theologians would now argue that the Christian church has constantly been engaged in a process of self-criticism and self-evaluation as it interrogates itself as to whether its existing modes of thought are indeed adequately grounded in the realities of divine revelation or whether they are indeed the best possible representations of a divine self-disclosure that is ultimately resistant to being reduced to human words and concepts.[25]

It is not difficult to see how this demand for constant theological vigilance is intimately connected with the notion of the development of doctrine, in that the church's internal dialogue and self-critique inevitably (if slowly) lead to a realization that, in some cases, yesterday's attempts to conceptualize the essence of faith need improvement, the need perhaps arising through their being too closely tied to the prevailing assumptions of the day, or perhaps through their focusing excessively on only one aspect of a complex question. Doctrinal development is the inevitable and proper outcome of the theological watchfulness demanded by the church. There is thus a sense in which Christian orthodoxy is something that is *made* as succeeding generations inherit ways of speaking about God and Christ that they rightly respect yet equally rightly wish to subject to examination. And, conversely, it follows that certain approaches, even those once regarded as positive and helpful, may have to be set aside as unacceptable or even heretical.

Rather than passively accepting the ways that previous generations interpreted a particular biblical passage or dogmatic concept, the church is called to "put everything to the test, and hold on to what is found to be good" (1 Thess. 5:21). This is most emphatically not being disrespectful toward the past; rather, it is about maintaining the dialogue that began in the past, continues today, and will not end until the close of history. Is this really the best way of telling the truth of faith? Is this really the most comprehensive account of who God is and what God has done? Is this really the least conceptually extravagant way of representing the identity of Christ? These questions must be asked *and answered* as part of the church's "discipleship of the mind."

The acceptance of the idea of the development of doctrine has important implications for the classical model of the origins of heresy. For Tertullian, heresy was about innovation, change, or modification of the pristine doctrinal truth of antiquity. Yet if it is accepted that orthodox doctrine develops over time, Tertullian's method of identifying and accounting for heresy is left stranded. This clearly raises difficulties for the traditional account—difficulties that are compounded through a growing realization of the complexity of the interconnection of orthodoxy and heresy, as we shall see presently.

Outsider or Insider? The Origins of Heresy

Traditional Christian accounts of the origins of heresy generally depict heresy as an invader or external contaminant. Heresy arises when alien ideas become influential within the church. Tertullian, for example, argued that a naive Christian willingness to make use of the ideas of the Platonic Academy in theological reflection led to the church's falling victim to a series of heresies. What has Jerusalem to do with Athens? What has the Christian church to do with the Platonic Academy?[26] Heresy is the inevitable outcome of the contamination of the purity of the Christian faith by external influences.

This received account of the origins of heresy is now generally regarded as incorrect. While certain forms of heresy may represent responses to wider intellectual or cultural movements in society, heresy nevertheless appears to originate from inside the church. The stimulus for the development of heresy may come from outside the church; the development of heresy takes place within the community of faith. Tertullian and others are correct to suggest that wider cultural and intellectual influences may play a role in catalyzing the emergence of a heresy. Yet it is important to appreciate that the heresies in question seem to have been developed by Christians, particularly those who felt the need to ensure that the church remained culturally engaged.

To illustrate these issues, we may consider the origins of Montanism, a movement that originated in Phrygia, in Asia Minor, during the late second century. Montanism was noted for its moral rigorism, and it developed ideas concerning ecstatic prophesying that are often seen as anticipations of modern Pentecostalism.[27] It has been argued for some time that there are important points of contact between Montanism and Phrygian paganism, suggesting that the movement was influenced, at least to some extent, by its immediate context.[28] Yet while a good case can be made for arguing that from its outset Montanism exhibited characteristics that are more compatible with aspects of pagan religions prominent in Phrygia at the time than with contemporary traditional Christianity, this does not mean that Montanism is to be seen as an essentially pagan corruption of Christianity. Other scholars have emphasized how Montanism, despite its distinctive emphases, remains an essentially Christian movement.[29]

Montanism is perhaps best understood as a local form of Christianity that adapted itself to its local cultural environment, developing emphases that can be seen as representing accommodations to local Phrygian culture. Although the influences that shaped its emergence originated from outside the church, Montanism is not to be thought of as representing a pagan takeover of Christianity. It clearly arose within a church, or group of churches, as some church members sought to develop what they regarded as an authentic form of Christianity capable of engaging with the pagan culture of its day.

Similar narratives can be offered in the case of most of the other classical heresies of Christendom. The common pattern is the development, *within the churches,* of movements that were later regarded as heretical but that were considered by their originators as authentic forms of Christianity, superior to their alternatives in that they were better adapted to the cultural environment or more effective in avoiding certain weaknesses of their rivals. The subsequent fate of these approaches depended heavily upon the long-term reliability of that judgment.

The Relation of Orthodoxy and Heresy: The Bauer Thesis

The twentieth century witnessed the discovery of significant documents at Nag Hammadi and other locations that opened up new
debates about the interaction of orthodoxy and heresy. The Nag
Hammadi library consisted of a collection of thirteen ancient codi-
ces containing over fifty texts in a sealed glass jar that was discovered by agricultural workers in upper Egypt in December 1945.
The discovery of these documents led to the reopening of many
questions concerning the context in which early Christianity developed. One of the most significant of these discussions involved re-
visiting the issues originally raised by Walter Bauer in his *Orthodoxy
and Heresy in Earliest Christianity* (1934).[30] In this work, published
before the discovery of the Nag Hammadi library, Bauer set out
two principal theses defining the relationship between orthodoxy
and heresy in the second century.

In the first place, Bauer argued that Christianity was, from its
outset, a loose coalition of different groups that differed considerably in their understanding of the significance of Jesus of Nazareth
and in their history of religious provenance. What would later be
called heresies were not to be seen as illegitimate deviations from an
originally unified and orthodox mainstream, but as direct descen-
dants of earlier forms of Christianity that differed from those from
which second-century orthodoxy is derived. In other words, what
would later be termed "heresy" and "orthodoxy" were present from
the earliest of times in the church.

In the second place, Bauer argued that the predominant form of
Christianity in most places down to the end of the second century
was heretical rather than orthodox. Early Christianity was thus
dominated by what was later termed "heresy" by the orthodox, but
which was not regarded as such at this stage. Bauer makes a significant exception in the case of Rome, which he concedes to have been
dominated by orthodoxy. From the end of the first century onward,
Rome gradually extended its orthodox influence eastward, until it

achieved dominance by the end of the third century. Bauer's assertion has, it must be said, puzzled most historians of this period, who
correctly note that the early Christian communities were simply
not in a position to coerce anyone. (See the earlier discussion on
pp. 55–57.)

Bauer went on to argue that a variety of views that were tolerated in the early church gradually began to be regarded with
suspicion by the later church. Teachings that were accepted in the
earliest decades of the church's existence were later condemned,
particularly from the end of the second century onward, as an
orthodox consensus began to emerge. Bauer's hostility to the idea
of doctrinal norms can be seen particularly clearly in his conviction
that these were a late development within Christianity. Opinions
that had once been tolerated were now discarded as inadequate.

So how was this distinction between heresy and orthodoxy
drawn? Bauer argued that the shared sense of fellowship within
the early Christian churches was not initially located at the level
of doctrines but lay primarily in the worship of the same Lord
rather than in any formal statement of doctrine (which is how
"orthodoxy" tends to be defined). The notion of orthodoxy, he
suggested, was a direct result of the growing political power of
Rome, which increasingly came to impose its own views upon
others, using the term "heresy" to designate and disparage those
views it rejected or found threatening. The rhetoric of the Roman
church created a climate of hostility and suspicion toward earlier
forms of orthodoxy that the church found threatening or uncon-
genial.

For Bauer, the distinction between orthodoxy and heresy was
thus essentially arbitrary, reflecting the sociological and political
predominance of power groups rather than anything intrinsic to
the ideas themselves. Bauer's ideas were taken up and developed in
the writings of the Harvard scholar Helmut Koester[31] and enjoyed
at least a degree of acceptance within the scholarly community until
as late as the 1960s.[32] Koester lauded Bauer's achievement, declaring

that he had "demonstrated convincingly" that "Christian groups later labeled heretical actually predominated in the first two or three centuries, both geographically and theologically. Recent discoveries, especially those at Nag Hammadi in Upper Egypt, have made it even clearer that Bauer was essentially right, and that a thorough and extensive revaluation of early Christian history is called for."[33]

Today, Bauer's thesis looks decidedly shaky.[34] While fully conceding that Bauer demonstrated that early orthodoxy was a more fluid and less rigidly defined notion than some had supposed, his critics have called most of his conclusions into question, expressing particular concern over his extensive argumentation from silence.[35] For example, Bauer's argument that early Christianity did not understand its unity in doctrinal terms received early support from some writers, such as Martin Elze;[36] however, others had been arguing that a fundamentally doctrinal understanding of Christian unity was already present in the writings of Clement of Rome, Ignatius of Antioch, and Justin Martyr.[37]

Further, Bauer's assertion that, in most geographical regions, what would later be stigmatized as heresy was actually the earliest form of Christianity has been firmly rebutted on the basis of both literary and archaeological evidence.[38] A growing awareness of the ease of communication within the Roman Empire has led to an increasing understanding of how relatively easy it was for a widely flung faith to sustain a network of interlocking and interrelating communities with a shared sense of identity and purpose.[39]

The accuracy of Bauer's account of certain heresies has also been challenged. For example, Bauer held that Valentinism was a form of Christianity that was essentially independent of orthodoxy in terms of its origins. Yet in a careful study of Valentinian sources, James McCue suggested that the origins of Valentinism were best understood as lying within second-century orthodoxy. In particular, McCue noted the following:

1. The role of orthodoxy in Valentinism is such that it seems to
    be part of the self-understanding of the moment rather than
    its antithesis.

2. Valentinian sources at several points explicitly and clearly
    identify the orthodox as a large group, compared with a
    relatively small number of Valentinians.

3. The Valentinians of the decades prior to Irenaeus and
    Clement of Alexandria use the books of the orthodox New
    Testament in a manner that is best accounted for by
    supposing that Valentinianism developed within a mid-
    second-century orthodox matrix.[40]

A similar conclusion was reached by Birger Pearson, who noted
that pre-Valentinian Gnosticism in Alexandria seemed to have
emerged in a context in which orthodox faith and practice were already established.[41] Valentinism here conforms to the general pattern, which we noted earlier, in which heresy has its origins within
the community of faith rather than outside the church.

In his influential study of the relationship of Christianity and
paganism in this formative era, Robin Lane Fox shows that Bauer's
historical approach to heresy fails on the grounds of precisely those
historical criteria that he chooses to deploy in its support. While it is
difficult to make firm historical judgments on many issues relating
to the history of early Christianity, on one issue a clear verdict is
possible:

An older view that heretical types of Christianity arrived in
many places before the orthodox faith has nothing in its
favour, except perhaps in the one Syrian city of Edessa. In
Lyons and North Africa, there is no evidence of this first heretical phase and the likelier origins are all against it. In Egypt,
the argument has been decisively refuted from the evidence of
the papyri. Details of practice and leadership did differ widely,

but the later existence of so many heresies must not obscure the common core of history and basic teaching throughout the Christian world.[42]

Instead, there has been a renewed appreciation of the merits of a more traditional view, which holds that second-century Christianity ought to be viewed essentially as an orthodox core surrounded by a penumbra within which the borderline between orthodoxy and heresy was still somewhat blurred and open to further clarification through controversy and debate.[43] One can speak of a "pool of acceptable diversity" without raising any fundamental theological or historical difficulties.[44] In any case, the historical observation that heresy existed prior to orthodoxy in a given location does not amount to saying that heresy exists on historically equal terms to orthodoxy.[45]

For most scholars, Bauer's thesis is now to be seen as being of relatively little historical value. It rests on a series of assumptions that subsequent scholarship has found unsustainable. Yet there is one point at which Bauer is unquestionably correct—namely, that early Christianity was much more complex and diverse than some of its leading representatives of the time appear to wish us to believe. That, however, is now widely accepted and is no longer seen as controversial—or problematic.

The most significant legacy of Bauer's thesis is the view that heretical visions of Christianity have just as much claim to legitimacy as their orthodox alternatives. An example of this approach is found in Elaine Pagels's writings, beginning with *The Gnostic Gospels*.[46] Pagels is an important witness not only to the lingering influence of the Bauer thesis within sections of academia but to the curious belief that Gnosticism offers a more liberating vision of reality, especially for women.[47]

Pagels's revisionist account of heresy, especially her advocacy of Gnosticism as an egalitarian movement that encouraged the participation of women in sacred rites,[48] can be sustained only through a policy of selective attention to the sources, filtering out or marginalizing those aspects of heresy that are inconveniently inconsistent with her approach. One obvious example will make this point clear. Let us consider the ending of the Gnostic Gospel of Thomas, which Pagels seems to regard as an early feminist manifesto. It is clearly nothing of the sort. This work's dramatic conclusion sets out its view on women vigorously and forcefully. It is worth citing in its totality.

According to this Gnostic document, Jesus ends his ministry with a proclamation that the "kingdom of the Father" is spread throughout the world. So who will enter this kingdom? What are the preconditions of membership?

> Simon Peter said to them: "Let Mary go out from among us, because women are not worthy of the Life."
>
> Jesus said: "See, I shall lead her, so that I will make her male, in order that she too may become a living spirit, resembling you males. For every woman who makes herself male will enter the Kingdom of Heaven."[49]

The Gospel of Thomas proclaims that entrance to the kingdom of Heaven is restricted to males and to a select few females who are willing to sacrifice their gender identity. Egalitarian? Hardly. As the feminist scholar Kathryn Greene-McCreight rightly points out, Gnostic writings "abound in antifemale statements that make the 'problematic' New Testament passages about women pale in comparison to their own misogyny."[50]

It needs to be made clear from the outset that it is historically indefensible to contrast a liberal, relaxed, gender-neutral, and generous heresy with a narrow, dogmatic, patriarchal, and rigid orthodoxy. It makes for a neat and winsome antithesis, ideally attuned to the contemporary cultural mood. Yet it is not compatible with the historical data. To mention some obvious difficulties: Montanism and Pelagianism were strongly disciplinarian heresies, while Marcionism was unpleasantly anti-Semitic. If heresy is to be dealt with seriously as a historical phenomenon, we need to abandon the curious presumption that it is a victim of some kind of theological oppression. To designate a movement as heretical does not imply that it was egalitarian or libertarian in a patriarchal and authoritarian age. Heresies could be even more patriarchal and authoritarian than orthodoxies. Sometimes heresies were rejected because they needed to be rejected.

So where do these reflections take us? The essential point that has been established by modern scholarship is that orthodoxy is an *emergent phenomenon.* It was not delivered as a ready-made package but grew, as a seed, over an extended period of time. All the fundamental themes that would be woven into the fabric of orthodoxy were there from the beginning; as time progressed, however, they came to be expressed in ways that sometimes involved moving beyond the language and imagery of the documents that would later be incorporated into the canon of the New Testament.[51] A core orthodoxy was in the process of emerging and being passed on within a culture that was accustomed to oral transmission. Even without a functioning and authoritative New Testament, the patterns of teaching and worship that we know to have been operational in early Christianity would have been sufficient to create what some are now calling a *proto-orthodoxy.* Larry Hurtado defines this notion as follows:

> By "proto-orthodox," I mean early examples and stages of the sorts of beliefs and practices that, across the next couple of centuries, succeeded in becoming characteristic of classical, "orthodox," Christianity, and came to be widely affirmed in Christian circles over and against the alternatives.[52]

Hurtado points out that a study of the second-century Christianity shows its tendency to affirm, preserve, promote, and develop what were by then becoming traditional expressions of belief that had originated in earlier years of the Christian church.[53]

Heresy

The crystallization of doctrinal formulations and that of the canon of the New Testament are thus to be seen as related processes, two sides of the same coin of the firming up of a Christian community that was increasingly confident about its identity, vision, and place. As Christian communities came under increasing pressure, internal and external, to define themselves and to defend themselves against their alternatives, so there was growing interest in clarifying what were acceptable and unacceptable expressions of the faith—without enforcing a rigid, restrictive, and monochrome view of the essence of Christianity.[54] And this program involved *doctrines*—attempts to express central themes of the Christian vision of reality in words.

This was a highly significant development, one that could stabilize and safeguard the core reality of the Christian faith. Doctrines were like protective, enfolding intellectual cocoons spun around the larva of faith. When constructed properly, they had the potential to give added resilience and stability to Christian life and thought. Yet a defective cocoon had the potential to disfigure, distort, and damage the life of faith. Heresy can be considered as an inadequate, distorting, or damaging conceptualization of faith—a faulty cocoon that damages rather than protects its larva.

These musings on how heresy is to be understood naturally lead us to ask whether it is possible to identify the "essence" of heresy, and if so, what this might be.

five

Is There an "Essence" of Heresy?

What, if anything, is the essential feature of heresy? What defines a heresy and distinguishes it from something that is simply wrong or questionable? We have already noted that early Christianity was characterized by a diversity of views on some issues. Yet this diversity was not seen in itself as an intellectual threat to the fundamental idea of Christian unity, even if it may have occasionally generated a degree of dissent and factionalization within or between Christian congregations. We have also reflected on Walter Bauer's view that many visions of Christianity existed in its first phases, often associated with specific geographical regions and each of which was regarded as orthodox by its followers. Some early versions of Christianity that were accepted as orthodox at the time, he argued, were later demonized as heresies as the Roman church tried to impose its own version of Christianity on other cities in the region.

In this view, a heresy is basically an earlier orthodoxy that has fallen out of favor with those who possess power and influence in the Christian world. What determines whether a set of ideas is heretical or not is whether those ideas are approved and adopted by those who happen to be in power. Orthodoxy is simply the set of ideas that won out; heresies are the losers.[1] While this idea of lost or suppressed Christianities has a deep appeal to some, it is historically very difficult to sustain. The process of marginalization or neglect of these "lost Christianities" generally has more to do with an emerging consensus within the church that they are inadequate than with any attempt to impose an unpopular orthodoxy on an unwilling body of believers.

Others have rightly pointed out that it is impossible to offer an account of the "essence" of heresy in that it would necessarily represent a socially constructed or negotiated entity. Such accounts of heresy often are written from some supposed position of objective historical truth that is held to exist apart from and independently of Christian evaluation and interpretation. This "view from nowhere" of the phenomenon of heresy cannot even begin to encompass the distinct identity or significance of heresy. Increasing emphasis within early Christian scholarship on how social identities are constructed and maintained has drawn attention to how certain movements are designated as heretical as a means of safeguarding the identity of a community. Heresy is thus not an observable or empirical reality but a socially constructed entity.[2] To speak of the "essence" of heresy is thus to make a fundamental category error. What makes a heresy is not so much its ideas as the way it is characterized and categorized by others.[3] Underlying this approach is a rhetoric of separation similar to that which served to sharpen the emerging distinction, soon to become a fissure, between Jew and Christian.[4]

There is undoubtedly merit in recognizing the importance of the strategies and mechanisms by which certain groups were designated as or determined to be heretical. Orthodoxy is indeed a "discursive institution,"[5] concerned with "naming" the other, the outsider, and potential threats. Yet such a judgment is not predicated solely on the will of the one who names, but also on the characteristics of what is named. It is about one group's assessment of another group's significance for its own identity and security. This immediately entails that *heretical* is not an empirical characteristic; it is negotiated or constructed. But it does not follow that this is an arbitrary or invented conclusion. It represents an act of discernment on the part of the church that a certain set of ideas are ultimately destabilizing or destructive. It is thus entirely appropriate to inquire as to what general patterns or characteristics are shared by movements or sets of ideas that were designated as heretical. This is especially the case when the issue is approached from a Christian perspective, as in the case of this work.

So what is the characteristic feature of heresy, distinguishing it from other variants of Christianity? By the fourth century, the term "heresy" was generally being used regularly to designate a teaching that emerges from within the community of faith on the one hand yet is ultimately destructive of that faith on the other. The central defining paradox of heresy is that it is *not unbelief*; it is rather a vulnerable and fragile form of Christianity that proves incapable of sustaining itself in the long term. Nor can heresy be characterized in terms of questionable practices or ethics.[6] Orthodox Christian writers were perfectly aware that moral ambivalence and failure were a common human concern and could not defensibly be argued to be exclusive to heretics or unknown among the orthodox.

Heresy is thus to be understood to refer to an intellectually defective vision of the Christian faith, having its origins within the church.[7] This assertion may cause distress to some Christians, who might find the notion of heresy as originating within the church unacceptable. This is a perfectly understandable reaction. Yet to understand why heresy is such a dangerous notion for Christian churches, the question of its relationship with the church must be addressed firmly and fairly. The seeds of heresy may come from outside the church, but they take root in her garden. Heresy is not unbelief. Nor is the term used to refer to a non-Christian belief system. Neither atheism nor Aristotelianism are heresies. To use a biological analogy, heresy shares a lot of the theological DNA of orthodoxy. Or to use the sociological categories of Pierre Bourdieu (1930–2002), heresy and orthodoxy share a common *doxa*—the "taken-for-granted" assumptions of an age or community.[8] Yet they diverge at points of critical importance, despite holding so much in common. From an orthodox perspective, the divergence creates incoherence and instability within the *doxa* as a whole.

The early church regarded heresy as dangerous not so much on account of any challenge it posed to contemporary church authority figures or structures, but on account of its implications for the future of Christianity itself. While orthodox Christian theologians often used extravagant and inflated language when referring to heresy, there is no doubt that their strident tone and their aggressive vocabulary reflected their concerns about the survival potential of Christianity itself if it was contaminated or damaged by what they considered to be impoverished and emaciated versions of Christianity. Heresy was a flawed, deficient, anemic, and inauthentic form of Christian faith that was inevitably doomed to extinction in the pluralist and intensely competitive world of late classical antiquity. Orthodoxy had greater survival potential, prompting a "search for authenticity" as a means of safeguarding its future.[9] To understand this point, we must consider the threats to Christian faith in its early period, which prompted this concern on the part of theologians to marginalize what they regarded as its deficient variants.

Threats to Early Christianity

Christianity faced three major threats during its first centuries. The first was physical—the constant possibility of persecution, with its implications for the suppression of Christian communities, and the threat of violence against its leaders.[10] Since the Roman authorities generally had little interest in making fine theological distinctions between various forms of Christianity, the notions of heresy and orthodoxy proved to be of relatively minor importance in confronting this challenge. From a Roman outsider's perspective in the second century, Christian heresy and Christian orthodoxy were just different forms of Christianity; both were unauthorized.

The second was the danger of intellectual or religious assimilation.[11] For example, Christianity had emerged from within Judaism; there was a risk during its earliest phases that it might simply revert to its roots, in effect becoming a new Jewish group (a *hairesis,* in the neutral sense of the term). More significantly, as Christianity became a growing presence within Greco-Roman culture, there was a corresponding danger that it would become assimilated to cultural or religious groups that were already well established, thus losing its distinctive identity. Cultural assimilation is all too often the prelude to ecclesial extinction.

While many theologians of the early church may have overstated the case for suggesting that heresy represented a form of Christianity that had been diluted by secular ideas, the potential danger that such a process represented was clear. If the salt of the Christian faith were to lose its saltiness, what would remain? The church had to maintain its identity by safeguarding its distinctiveness. Tertullian (c. 160–c. 220) was one such writer to express a deep concern that an uncritical importation of secular ideas might ultimately lead to the secularization of the church and the loss of its identity and integrity.

> For philosophy provides the material of worldly wisdom, in boldly asserting itself to be the interpreter of the divine nature and dispensation. The heresies themselves receive their weapons from philosophy. It was from this source that Valentinus, who was a disciple of Plato, got his ideas about the "aeons" and the "trinity of humanity." And it was from there that the god of Marcion (much to be preferred, on account of his tranquility) came; Marcion came from the Stoics.[12]

Tertullian here interprets philosophy not in a neutral sense, as a quest for wisdom, but in a sense of *"worldly* wisdom," thus creating the conditions for the inevitable secularization of Christian ideas and values. For Tertullian, heresy made the church porous to ideas that would rob the church of its stability, leading to a situation comparable to a ship that was slowly sinking through taking in (secular) seawater. In much the same way, Hippolytus of Rome (c. 170–c. 236) likened the church to a boat: "The world is a sea in which the Church, like a ship, is beaten by the waves, but not submerged."[13]

A third danger was the fragmentation of Christianity through intellectual incoherence. As Christianity became more deeply embedded in late classical culture, it was subjected to increased criticism by its intellectual and cultural opponents. Some of the most formidable of these criticisms concerned the coherence of Christianity's ideas. Leading critics of Christianity, such as Celsus (fl. c. 175–80) and Galen of Pergamum (129–200), argued that its leading doctrines could not be taken seriously by cultured people.[14] Any intellectually defective form of Christianity was vulnerable in this critical environment. Heretical conceptions of faith, it was argued, lacked the rigor of their orthodox equivalents.

It can be seen that the second and third of these factors are of importance to any attempt to understand the notion of heresy. It will also be obvious that these factors are in tension with one another. Tertullian, for example, argued that any attempt by Christian theologians to be intellectually respectable by the standards of their day merely led to their becoming contaminated and seduced by pagan philosophy. Although Tertullian's argument that engagement with secular philosophy leads to a heretical understanding of Christianity is widely regarded as something of an overstatement, there is nevertheless a grain of truth in his concerns.

Similarly, in the fourth century Arius (256–336) offered an understanding of the relationship between God and the creation that was regarded as philosophically rigorous by the standards of the time. Yet for his opponents, such as Athanasius of Alexandria (c. 293–373), the understanding of the identity of Jesus Christ that resulted from this philosophically driven approach was incapable of reconciliation with the orthodox faith, especially its worship. Arius introduced radical inconsistency into the Christian understanding of its core identity, leaving it seriously vulnerable to intellectual criticism on the one hand and cultural erosion on the other. As Thomas Carlyle once commented: "If the Arians had won, [Christianity] would have dwindled away into a legend."[15] The accuracy of this judgment may, of course, be contested. Yet it is reasonable to suggest that, had certain forms of Arianism gained the upper hand, Christianity might have transmuted into something akin to Islam. This is not to criticize Islam; it is simply to point out the importance of certain fundamental ideas in shaping the life, worship, and witness of communities of faith. The vision of faith offered by Arianism is quite different from that offered by orthodox writers such as Athanasius of Alexandria.

Heresy and Orthodoxy as Doctrinal Concepts

Although Christianity emerged from within Judaism, it rapidly developed its own distinctive identity. One of the most striking differences between the two faiths, evident by the early second century, is that Judaism tended to define itself by correct practice, whereas Christianity appealed to correct doctrines. Many Jewish writers continue to argue that the essence of Judaism is *halakhah,* an attempt to organize human life around the fundamental principles of the Torah.[16] One should therefore speak of Jewish *orthopraxy* rather than *orthodoxy.*

While the New Testament is critical of certain aspects of Jewish orthopraxy, such as circumcision, the emerging Christian response to Judaism takes the form of a shift toward orthodoxy as much as a rejection of existing orthopraxy. Christians declined to adopt the cultic rituals of Judaism (such as food laws, Sabbath observance, and circumcision) that served to identify Jews within a Gentile community; on the other hand, Marcion's proposal that Christianity should be declared utterly distinct from Judaism failed to gain support.[17] There was an obvious polarity within the relationship of Christianity and Judaism. As a result, Christian self-definition was initially directed toward clarification of the relationship of Christianity and Judaism, centering upon the identity of Jesus and subsequently upon the role of the Old Testament Law.[18] It is thus perfectly acceptable to suggest that the Pauline doctrine of justification by faith represents a theoretical justification for the separation of Gentile Christian communities from Judaism.[19]

Yet the emerging Christian communities found themselves obliged to distinguish themselves from other communities as well. The church was not to be identified with Judaism on the one hand, nor with "the world" on the other. Even in the New Testament, a sharp distinction can be seen emerging between "church" and "world." The distinction was initially understood, at least in part, in terms of separation from the world. Perhaps encouraged by an expectation of an early end to all things, the first Christians appear to have formed communities based on shared loyalties and specific commitments rather than explicitly theoretical notions.

Early Christian communities do not appear to have regarded precise and elaborate doctrinal formulations as essential to their self-definition, in that they were already distinguished from the world by sharing in their meetings and worship. In the words of R. A. Markus, "Their doctrinal distinctiveness, however defined, was reinforced, sustained, perhaps even eclipsed, by their sociological distinctness as groups set, literally, apart from the world."[20] Thus, on the basis of one understanding of the Johannine community, this group regarded its circumstances as a group set apart from the world as being explained and legitimated by the accounts of Jesus Christ's words and actions transmitted within the fourth Gospel.[21]

The very early Christian communities, although clearly bearing a "family resemblance" on account of their beliefs concerning Jesus of Nazareth and their ways of worshipping him, did not require doctrinal formulations to distinguish themselves from the world: that distinction was already forced upon them by the world, which isolated them as visible and readily identifiable social groups.[22] To become a Christian was (at least potentially) to be liable to a visible change in social location, which in itself was adequate for the purposes of being demarcated from society.

Yet there were limits to social and physical approaches to demarcation. The early Christians, unlike the Essenes, did not withdraw into the wilderness; they remained in the world of the cities and their institutions, gradually developing means of existing in the world without being of the world.[23] "We Christians," Tertullian wrote to his pagan audience, "live with you, enjoy the same food, have the same manner of life and dress, and the same requirements for life as you."[24] So how were they distinguished from other communities of the period?

Doctrine came increasingly to represent a means by which Christian individuals and communities might be distinguished from the world around them—especially as the beliefs, values, and actions of the Christian community came to converge. Controversy with Gnostic and other communities forced the Christian communities to develop their understanding of self-definition and led to increased pressure for creeds and other authorized statements of faith.[25] Although the contribution of Irenaeus of Lyons to this process during the late second century was pivotal, the importance of Tertullian in urging self-definition and the maintenance of self-identity within the Christian communities must not be overlooked. Yardsticks—such as the canon of the New Testament and adherence to the apostolic rule of faith—were agreed upon by which the claims of religious communities to be Christian churches could be tested.[26] Doctrine came to be of increasing importance in distinguishing the church from secular culture at large and in increasing a sense of identity and cohesion within its ranks.

Doctrine thus came to be a significant factor in shaping Christian identity. So how did the early Christian communities define and identify themselves? In the first phase of Christianity, there existed none of the precise normative doctrinal formulations—such as the Nicene Creed—that became so pervasive and influential in the late fourth century. It is certainly true that some later writings in the New Testament, especially the Pastoral Epistles, show a clear concern about the danger of "false teaching"[27] and recognize the importance of developing institutional structures capable of responding to these threats. However, while such writings emphasize the importance of "sound teaching,"[28] this is not defined or illustrated extensively by using creedal statements.[29]

The historical evidence suggests that both the New Testament and early Christian writers tended to emphasize the center of the Christian faith rather than focusing on policing its periphery. Jesus Christ was widely regarded as defining and marking the core of Christianity. Paul sets out what seems to have been a prototypical Christian creed when he places the affirmation "Jesus is Lord" (Rom. 10:9) at the heart of the Christian confession.[30] Paul links the confession that "Jesus is Lord" with the call to believe that God raised Jesus from the dead (Rom. 10:9–10). Here, as throughout the New Testament, "Jesus is Lord" is inseparably linked with Jesus's resurrection, and so identifies him as the "living one"; he is not a dead, though revered, figure from the past, nor does his appeal lie merely in his ideals or his inspiring life. When Paul speaks of Christ as the head of the body,[31] his language clearly points to a central role for Christ in both communal and personal Christian existence. This is evident, for example, in both prayer and worship. Jesus Christ stands at the heart of early Christian worship as both its agent and object.[32] Indeed, the worship of a Christian community may be regarded as underlying its capacity to be a local church while at the same time participating in a more universal reality.[33]

Yet the focus of a Christian community does not determine its limits.[34] Historical developments soon made it necessary to address the question of whether there were indeed boundaries to the Christian church; and, as this question came increasingly to be answered in the affirmative, it was followed by two equally pressing successors: who had the right to set such limits, and how were they to be determined? Hedges had to be placed around the pasturelands in order to safeguard those who had found sanctuary there.[35] These "hedges" appear to have taken three forms: cultic, ethical, and theological.

In the first place, Christianity sought to distance itself from those who insisted on cultic practices that would amount to a reversion to Judaism—such as the need for circumcision for male believers and rituals concerning unclean foods. Second, Christians who behaved in certain unacceptable ways were regarded as having transgressed certain boundaries. Third, and most important for our narrative, Christianity came to place an increased emphasis upon certain theological ideas that were held to be essential to the faith. Yet despite this growing recognition of the importance of Christianity's boundaries, Christian communities appear to have regarded its center as being of greater importance well into the second century. There appears to have been relatively little interest in policing the periphery of faith; churches appear to have preferred to accentuate the importance of their central focus, especially in worship. Yet from the middle of the second century onward, the policing of the perimeter appears to have been regarded as increasingly important if the identity and authenticity of the Christian faith were to be maintained.

As the churches increasingly defined themselves using doctrinal terms, so they identified threats to their integrity using the same categories. Orthodoxy and heresy were both conceived in terms of "right thinking," with other possible means of definition being marginalized. Ways of maintaining Christian authenticity, as well as threats to that authenticity, were now conceived of doctrinally. "Sound" doctrine was edifying to the church, just as corrupt or deformed doctrine was destructive.

So how are we to understand the threat posed by heresy? One theoretical model, developed in the early nineteenth century, has some potential to help us appreciate both the distinctive character of heresy on the one hand and its threat to faith on the other. In what follows, we shall consider the theory of heresy developed by the noted Protestant theologian Friedrich Daniel Ernst Schleiermacher (1768–1834).

A Model of Heresy

Schleiermacher is widely regarded as one of the most significant liberal Protestant theologians. Writing in response to the rise of the Enlightenment, Schleiermacher subverted any attempt to reduce theology to rationalist platitudes. There is more to the Christian faith, and hence to Christian theology, than the exercise of the mind. Religion is not a particular body of knowledge nor a specific variety of action, but is rather a form of consciousness. There is a deep experiential dimension to faith that reason cannot fully apprehend. Doctrines, creeds, and other statements of belief are thus to be seen as a form of second-order reflection on the immediate experience of faith, which is of primary importance. Although Schleiermacher's distinctive approach to theology is of interest in its own right, it is his model of heresy that we shall consider here.

What is heresy? For Schleiermacher, heresy is anything that contradicts the essential identity of Christianity, even though it retains the formal outward appearance of Christianity. Heresy is therefore to be thought of as a deficient form of Christian belief that preserves the *appearance* of Christianity while contradicting its *essence*.[36] This immediately locates the sphere of heresy as lying within, not outside, the church. Yet this definition also requires us to define the "essence" of the Christian faith. Without an understanding of the "essence" of Christianity, it proves impossible to define what heresy actually is. Schleiermacher's definition places Jesus of Nazareth at the center of things:

> Christianity is a monotheistic faith, belonging to the teleological type of religion, and is essentially distinguished from other such faiths by the fact that in it everything is related to the redemption accomplished by Jesus of Nazareth.[37]

For Schleiermacher, the rejection or denial of the principle that God has redeemed us through Christ is tantamount to the rejection of Christianity itself. To deny that God has redeemed us through Jesus Christ is to deny the most fundamental truth claim that the Christian faith dares to make, and thus amounts to unbelief. The distinction between what is *Christian* and what is not, between faith and unbelief, lies in whether this principle is accepted; the distinction between what is *orthodox* and what is *heretical,* however, lies in how this principle, once conceded and accepted, is understood. In other words, to reiterate the point we made earlier, heresy is not a form of unbelief; it is something that arises within the context of faith itself.

Heresy thus results, Schleiermacher argues, when it is affirmed that "everything is related to the redemption accomplished by Jesus of Nazareth," but this statement is interpreted in such a way that it is reduced to incoherence. If Jesus of Nazareth's central and fundamental place is asserted, yet interpreted in such a way that it is implicitly denied or rendered inoperable, the outcome is heresy.

This approach can be found earlier in the history of Christian thought. For example, the great Anglican theologian Richard Hooker (1554–1600) noted how a series of basic heresies arose through misunderstanding the identity of Christ. In his *Laws of Ecclesiastical Polity* (1593–97), Hooker wrote as follows.

> There are but four things which concur to make complete the whole state of our Lord Jesus Christ: his Deity, his manhood, the conjunction of both, and the distinction of the one from the other being joined in one.[38]

According to Hooker, a failure to affirm each of these, coherently and responsibly, leads to a distortion of the core teachings of the Christian faith: Arianism, by denying the divinity of Christ; Apollinarianism, by "maiming and misinterpreting" his humanity; Nestorianism, by "rending Christ asunder" and dividing him into two persons; and Eutychianism, by "confounding what they should distinguish."

Schleiermacher follows Hooker in identifying four "natural types" of heresy that arise from an incoherent understanding of Jesus of Nazareth.

> If the distinctive essence of Christianity consists in the fact that in it all religious emotions are related to the redemption wrought by Jesus Christ, there will be two ways in which heresy can arise. That is to say: this fundamental formula will be retained in general . . . but *either* human nature will be so defined that a redemption in the strict case cannot be accomplished, *or* the Redeemer will be defined in such a way that he cannot accomplish redemption.[39]

Schleiermacher thus notes how it is possible to affirm that "all religious emotions are related to the redemption wrought by Jesus Christ" while at the same time to deny that humanity needs redemption (which is Pelagianism) or that humanity can be redeemed (which is Manicheanism). Or one could make this affirmation while understanding Jesus of Nazareth as being so different from us (Doceticism), or else so like us (Ebionitism), that he cannot truly bring us redemption.[40]

Schleiermacher's model of heresy is an important tool in making sense of both the nature of heresy and its potential threat to the Christian faith. It posits that a heresy is fundamentally a theology that maintains the outward appearance of faith while contradicting or rendering incoherent its inner identity. This locates heresy as arising within the community of faith while at the same time identifying its potential danger to that community's identity. Heresy amounts to a counterfeit faith lacking the intellectual coherence of orthodoxy.

There are, however, some difficulties with Schleiermacher's approach. In the first place, it restricts heresy to areas of doctrine that are closely connected with the identity and significance of Jesus of Nazareth. As we shall see in the following chapter, heresies can arise in a number of areas of Christian doctrine. So what of Trinitarian heresies such as Sabellianism? Or ecclesiological heresies such as Donatism? Although this is a legitimate criticism of Schleiermacher, its force could be blunted by arguing that Sabellianism and Donatism must both ultimately be recognized as heretical views that at least touch on the identity of Jesus of Nazareth. The doctrine of the Trinity, for example, is often interpreted as a means of expressing the significance of Jesus as much as the nature of God. Similarly, Donatism could be argued to concern the question of the conditions under which the "benefits of Christ" are transferred to believers.

Second, and perhaps more significantly, Schleiermacher tends to treat heresy as a purely intellectual phenomenon and fails to take account of its historical and social dimensions. His analysis of the four "natural heresies" is detached from any account of their origins and specific historical forms. It is well known that many heresies arose within specific communities, often in response to specific cultural pressures.[41] For example, Donatism can be interpreted as a cultural movement representing an indigenous Berber reaction against the Roman imperial presence in North Africa.[42] Schleiermacher's somewhat abstract and unhistorical approach fails to account for the social factors that may give rise to certain heresies under quite specific conditions, tending instead to present heresy as a timeless matter of intellectual incoherency. More significantly, tensions between powerful individuals or ecclesiastical centers of power could easily lead to a power struggle being conceptualized as a conflict between heresy and orthodoxy. Schleiermacher's view of individual heresies seems both inattentive to and disinterested in the real historical movements, of which he offers a theological silhouette rather than a full historical image.

Third, Schleiermacher's account of heresy suggests that heresy is identified primarily through its intellectual incoherence. Yet an adjudication of incoherence raises questions that are not properly addressed by Schleiermacher's model. At what point does incoherence become heretical? Who makes the decision that a viewpoint is heretical? The decision that a given theology is to be regarded as heretical is corporate, not individual, reflecting the judgment of the church. Heresy is a social reality reflecting the judgments of networks of individuals.[43] As studies of the Arian controversy have made clear, the fourth century in particular witnessed significant changes in the ecclesiastical structures and processes through which "right belief" was assessed.[44]

So who decides what is heresy? Schleiermacher appears to assume that it is self-evident from the incoherence of heretical ideas. Yet this fails to do justice to the historical evidence, which points to the importance of the community of faith in judging and declaring certain views to constitute heresy. As Malcolm Lambert famously pointed out, "[I]t takes two to create a heresy; the heretic, with his dissident beliefs and practices; and the Church, to condemn his views and to define what is orthodox doctrine."[45] Heresy represents a judgment by the church that a certain set of ideas are unacceptable. Any account of heresy must therefore take account both of the core ideas of a heresy, and of the *reasons* that, and the *procedures* by which, they came to be held to be dangerous and destructive.

Developing this concern further, it may be pointed out that the early church saw heresy as dangerous and potentially destructive of faith. While a threat to the coherence of faith would have been an important contributing cause to this concern, there are more fundamental issues at stake. Schleiermacher's model of heresy does not appear well adapted to dealing with the idea of heresy as a "Trojan horse" that covertly smuggles the elements of alternative worldviews into the church. Theological destabilization may indeed arise from internal inconsistencies; yet there are other potential causes of such instability, including the intrusion of alien ideas, that duly give rise to incoherence within the Christian worldview.

The questions raised in this chapter suggest that it is both difficult and possibly even somewhat unhelpful to attempt to develop a general theoretical approach to heresy without looking in some detail at individual historical heresies, taking due account of their historical emergence. In the two chapters that follow, we shall consider some of the great classical heresies of Christianity and attempt to understand their origins, the concerns of those who developed them, why the church regarded them as dangerous, and the processes by which they were declared to be heretical.

part three

The Classic Heresies of Christianity

six

Early Classic Heresies: Ebionitism, Docetism, Valentinism

Christianity had its origins in the region of Judea, especially the city of Jerusalem. It initially regarded itself primarily as a continuation and development of Judaism and hence flourished in regions with which Judaism was traditionally associated, supremely Palestine. However, it rapidly spread to neighboring areas, partially through the efforts of early Christian evangelists such as Paul of Tarsus. By the end of the first century, Christianity appears to have become established throughout the eastern Mediterranean world and even to have gained a significant presence in the city of Rome, the capital of the Roman Empire.[1]

This expansion, however, was intellectual as much as geographical. As Christianity developed throughout the civilized world of the late classical period, it encountered ways of thinking that posed challenges to, yet also offered opportunities for, its proclamation of the gospel. Although Christianity initially found itself having to negotiate its identity in relation to Judaism, it soon found itself confronting other cultural and intellectual movements in the area, such as the various Greek religious and philosophical traditions that were firmly embedded in cities such as Antioch and Alexandria. The result was growing intellectual pressure to identify the most authentic and reliable ways of articulating and explaining the Christian faith. This "quest for authenticity" involved exploring ways of understanding and expressing the gospel, some of which proved to be powerful and resilient. Others, however, turned out to be dead ends, whose drawbacks outweighed their advantages. The process of developing and evaluating these approaches was slow, often extending over many decades precisely because it was thorough and extensive. The crystallization of the notions of orthodoxy and heresy was thus generally measured and cautious.

The first five centuries witnessed the crystallization of the notions of orthodoxy and heresy through this process of intellectual exploration. It soon became clear that the task of Christian theology could not be limited simply to the loyal and uncritical repetition of formulas derived from the past—such as biblical verses. Simply repeating early Christian formulas and ideas was found to be inadequate to meet the church's need for mature, reliable statements of faith. These statements, which were occasionally in tension with one another, needed to be woven together into a coherent tapestry of faith. But what pattern did they reveal?

In recent years there has been a growing interest in the patristic interpretation of the Bible, partly reflecting an increased awareness of how significantly doctrinal formulations rest upon biblical foundations.[2] This scholarship has illuminated many points—such as the way in which patristic authors use individual biblical books.[3] Yet for our purposes, the most important point concerns how biblical passages were woven into more complex dogmatic statements, resolving (or at least holding in tension) the complex New Testament witness to central gospel themes.[4] This process of interpretation was contested, leading to multiple outcomes, each of which required careful testing against an emerging sense of what constituted "authentic" Christianity.[5] Which seemed to represent the "best fit" between theological formulations and the actual experience of Christian living?

It must be emphasized that this journey of conceptual exploration was undertaken with the best of motives and intentions. While some early Christian heresiologists portrayed writers such as Valentinus in dark and somber colors, the evidence suggests that most of those who would later be regarded as heretics undertook their theological quests out of a genuine concern to ensure that the Christian faith was represented and articulated in the most authentic and robust forms. The inevitable outcome of the early Christian community's corporate quest for theological excellence was that a variety of manners of conceiving the gospel were initially proposed and subsequently subjected to rigorous examination, leading to some being rejected. The problems really began when movements eventually regarded as inadequate or as theological liabilities refused to accept this status, seeing themselves instead as suppressed orthodoxies.

As emphasized earlier, the classic heresies of the Christian faith all emerged during the first five centuries of faith, often referred to as the *patristic period*. Although the term "heresy" was applied to many movements in the Middle Ages, it was clearly used in a legal or juridical sense to stigmatize a movement that was seen as a challenge to the authority of the pope. We shall consider this point later (pp. 205–8), when we examine medieval heresies in much greater detail. However, it is appropriate to expand these comments further at this earlier stage.

It is clear that medieval movements such as the Hussites, Waldensians, and Lollards were seen as threats to the church not so much on account of their ideas as on account of their popular appeal.[6] They had the potential to become alternative centers of power and influence, bypassing or challenging the centralized structures of the church. It has been realized for some time that it is not appropriate to use the term "heresy" to refer to such movements. This point was first made in 1935 by Herbert Grundmann,[7] who argued that the notion of heresy was here being defined from an inquisitional rather than a theological perspective. *Heresy* was being defined in terms of challenges posed to the political authority of the church rather than in terms of the actual ideas of these movements.

A purely historical account of the notion of heresy in the Middle Ages is obliged to define *orthodoxy* in terms of papal teaching and *heresy* in terms of dissent from such teaching. Given this context, heresy will inevitably be understood primarily as a legal or juridical notion.[8] Where the patristic period conceived heresy in terms of a deviation from the Catholic faith, the church lawyers of the twelfth and thirteenth centuries succeeded in redefining the notion in terms of the rejection of ecclesiastical authority, especially papal authority. As Robert Moore has argued, the extension of the category of heresy became an increasingly important instrument of social control,[9] by means of which the papacy was able to claim religious justification for suppressing what were essentially political and social movements. This medieval redefinition of heresy locates its essence in challenging papal power rather than in deviating from Christian orthodoxy. Heresy became the means by which a society subsumed its endemic tensions under a notionally religious category. It ceased to be a theological notion and was now defined legally or sociologically. We shall return to consider medieval heresies in chapter 9.

Our concern in this chapter and that which follows, however, is with the heresies that emerged during the great theological voyages of discovery and exploration that took place during the patristic age. While each of the heresies to be considered has its own special points of interest, in each case we shall explore how the heresy emerged, identify its distinctive features, and consider how and why it came to be regarded as inadequate. In the following chapter, we shall consider three of the later heresies, which came to be of importance after the Christianization of the Roman Empire: Arianism, Donatism, and Pelagianism. In the present chapter, we shall consider three early heresies, all of which developed during the second century. We open our discussion by considering Ebionitism.

Ebionitism: A Jewish Model for Jesus of Nazareth

Most of the heresies to be described in this and the following chapters are named after the individuals who are especially associated
with them—such as Arius, Marcion, Pelagius, and Valentinus. Our
first heresy, however, is not associated with any specific person but
represents a general trend in some Christian circles in the first and
early second centuries to limit the interpretation of the identity of
Jesus of Nazareth to categories inherited from Judaism. The terms
"Ebionite" and "Ebionitism" are used to refer to such models of
Jesus, which typically interpret him as a prophet.[10] Frustratingly
little is known about this movement, despite the fact that it represents such a significant theological landmark.[11] While uncertainties
remain concerning the origins of the name of the movement, and
some significant historical questions still await clarification in the
light of the Qumran documents,[12] it is nevertheless widely accepted
that the beliefs of the Ebionites are to be positioned firmly within
the matrix of contemporary Judaism.

The early church fully recognized the importance of articulating
the importance of Jesus Christ for the human mind, imagination,
emotions, and behavior. In the course of its development, the church
had to deal with a number of interpretations of the identity of Jesus
Christ that it regarded as failing to do justice to his significance. An
improper location of Jesus Christ on a conceptual map would be fatal
to Christian evangelism and discipleship. Yet it was clear that this
process of identifying the best conceptual framework within which to
locate Jesus Christ was intensely difficult. The initial tendency was to
take existing categories, inherited from the social matrices to which
early Christians belonged, and treat these as appropriate to the task of
conceptualizing the significance of Jesus Christ. The origins of such a
trend can be seen inside the New Testament itself, in that the Gospels
record attempts to make sense of Jesus that are drawn from contemporary Judaism—such as interpreting Jesus of Nazareth as a second
Elijah, a new Jewish prophet, or a high priest of Israel.[13]

Recent scholarship, while affirming that Ebionitism represents an essentially Jewish way of thinking about Jesus of Nazareth, has raised some concerns about the historical use of the term. The problem arises partly because of our indirect knowledge of the movement, which often derives from its critics, such as Irenaeus of Lyons and Hippolytus of Rome.[14] Most scholars consider that early second-century Ebionitism was characterized by a "low Christology"—that is, an understanding of Jesus of Nazareth that interprets him as spiritually superior to ordinary human beings but not otherwise distinct.[15] In this approach, Jesus of Nazareth was a human being who was singled out for divine favor by being possessed by the Holy Spirit in a manner similar to, yet more intensive than, the calling of a Hebrew prophet. Yet it is possible that the term later came to be used to refer to a somewhat different set of beliefs, influenced to various extents by Gnosticism (on which more later).[16] For this reason, we shall focus on the early phase of Ebionitism, in which it clearly has the features of an essentially Jewish Christology.

So what is the problem with Ebionitism? Why was it rejected as inadequate by the church? One simple answer is that it was perceived to be inadequate to do justice to the full significance of Jesus of Nazareth. An incident from the Gospel accounts of the ministry of Jesus casts some light on this point: the healing of a paralytic (Mark 2:1–12).[17] On hearing that Jesus is in the vicinity, four people bring their paralyzed friend to be healed by him. All the evidence we possess suggests that those who witnessed Jesus in action initially tried to interpret him in terms of existing models and categories—for example, as a healer.[18] It was entirely natural to do so. After all, the Old Testament contained many references to God's way of acting in the world, and it was entirely reasonable to try to assimilate Jesus to one of these familiar patterns. So why not regard Jesus as a new Elijah who was able to heal the sick?

Yet as the narrative proceeds, it undermines and ultimately subverts such attempts to assimilate Jesus to prevailing Jewish models of divine endorsement or inhabitation.

When Jesus saw their faith, he said to the paralytic, "Son, your sins are forgiven." Now some of the scribes were sitting there, questioning in their hearts, "Why does this fellow speak in this way? It is blasphemy! Who can forgive sins but God alone?"

In line with Jewish orthodoxy, the scribes point out that Jesus was claiming to be able to do something—forgive sins—that is to be regarded as an exclusively divine prerogative.[19] Yet the Gospel narrative presses traditional ways of thinking about God's presence in the world to their absolute limits by intimating the outcome of Jesus of Nazareth's intervention:

> "But so that you may know that the Son of Man has authority on earth to forgive sins"—he said to the paralytic—"I say to you, stand up, take your mat and go to your home." And he stood up, and immediately took the mat and went out before all of them; so that they were all amazed and glorified God, saying, "We have never seen anything like this!"

The healing of the paralytic may be dramatically primary within the narrative; nevertheless, it is theologically secondary. The amazement of the crowds resulted primarily from their realization of the theological implications of what they had just seen and heard. Someone had implicitly claimed authority to act as God and for God. The outcome of this intervention appeared to imply that God had honored—even endorsed—this astonishing claim. Traditional Jewish ways of thinking about God's presence and activity in the world seem subverted when confronted with the ministry of Jesus of Nazareth.

It is significant that the Gospels follow their account of this remarkable incident by citing Jesus of Nazareth's words about the failure of old wineskins to contain new wine (Mark 2:22). The coming of Jesus into human history is understood to have introduced

something new, something dynamic, that traditional ways of thinking within Israel's prophetic and wisdom traditions alike were not
capable of grasping. This theme is of especial importance in Matthew's Gospel, which is generally regarded as the most concerned
to establish parallels between Israel and the church.[20] The inescap-
able failure of Israel's traditional rationalities of faith to enfold Jesus
of Nazareth forced a revision of existing models of God's presence
and activity in this specific individual. Ebionitism can be regarded
as an attempt to constrain innovation by insisting that Jesus of
Nazareth be interpreted only within the traditional paradigms of
theological rationality inherited from Israel. In the end, these
proved inadequate to the challenge that they faced. Innovation was
clearly demanded.

Ebionitism has been widely criticized by leading orthodox theologians. For example, the Swiss Protestant theologian Karl Barth
argued against any Ebionite account of the identity of Jesus that
treats him essentially as a heroic human being or as a human being
who was "adopted" by God.[21] Barth's approach corresponds to the
widespread tendency to interpret Ebionitism as an approach to
Jesus of Nazareth characterized by a refusal to concede his intrinsic
divinity, affirming only his humanity. While this is partly true, it is
far from representing a full account of Ebionitism as a historical
movement. Furthermore, it makes Ebionitism difficult to distinguish from Arianism, which can also be characterized as a denial of
Christ's divinity. The historian of Christian thought will agree that
both Ebionitism and Arianism denied the essential and intrinsic
divinity of Jesus of Nazareth, yet will point out that they denied it
for significantly different reasons.

This brings home the importance of studying heresies in their
historical contexts rather than reducing them to a theological head-
line. Despite a superficial theological similarity, Arianism and
Ebionitism are historically and sociologically distinct. One origi-
nates within the world of Alexandrian Hellenistic philosophy,
the other within the world of Judaism. It is indeed true that both

Arianism and Ebionitism deny the divinity of Jesus Christ. But they do so for very different reasons. As we shall see, Arianism insists that Christ is to be seen as a human being on account of a philosophical commitment to the absolute unity of God. God is utterly distinct from the created order, and it is unthinkable that any hybrid or intermediate being can exist. Jesus Christ must therefore be seen as a creature, as the alternatives are philosophically incoherent.

Ebionitism, in contrast, did not arise as a result of philosophical concerns. Indeed, it could be argued that it did not really *deny* the divinity of Christ; it simply saw no reason to assert it. Ebionitism chose to situate Jesus of Nazareth within the context of Judaism and to interpret his importance using its categories. Jesus was thus to be understood as analogous to the great prophets of Israel—human beings who were in some way given special insight or wisdom through the Holy Spirit. The suggestion that Jesus of Nazareth *was* himself divine does not really enter into consideration, given the Jewish context within which Ebionitism arose.

So why did the church reject Ebionitism as a heresy? The process by which this rejection took place is not clear, although the perception that Ebionitism was unacceptable had certainly crystallized in Roman Christian circles by about 135. The reasons for this perception cannot be established with complete certainty, partly because early patristic reports concerning Ebionitism—such as that provided by Irenaeus—may conflate a number of distinct groups.[22] Nevertheless, it is possible to identify the main concerns that appear to have led to the exclusion of Ebionitism.

The most important of these was the perception that Ebionitism was a form of Jewish Christianity.[23] The position of Jewish Christianity within an increasingly Gentile church became increasingly difficult with the passage of time, especially in relation to potentially contentious issues such as circumcision, food laws, and the observation of the Sabbath.[24] Gentile Christians regarded themselves as liberated from these, and cited Paul in support of their position.[25] Although some accounts of the development of Christianity

suggest that these issues were essentially resolved in favor of the
Gentiles by the end of the first century, there is evidence that they
lingered on well into the second century. For example, Justin Martyr's *Dialogue with Trypho,* which dates from around the year 150,
explicitly refers to such tensions.[26]

The problem that Gentile Christians experienced with Ebionitism was that it interpreted Jesus of Nazareth within a Jewish
context, reinforcing the notion that Christianity was essentially a
new form of Judaism. This approach to Christology sat very uneasily with the growing perception that Christianity was distinct
from Judaism, however their present relationship was to be understood. The Ebionites perceived Jesus of Nazareth as a reforming
Hebrew prophet. While Marcion's view that Christianity should
totally dissociate itself from its Jewish origins won few supporters,
it was a telling indication of the way Christianity now saw itself—
as a new universal faith that acknowledged its origins within
Judaism[27] but also transcended its ethnic, cultural, and religious
limitations. Ebionitism trapped the new faith within a Jewish
matrix, making it a prisoner of its own history. The future of
Christianity as a faith in its own right—rather than as a Jewish
sect—depended upon the church's developing new categories for
making sense of Jesus of Nazareth. These categories would acknowledge, even value, his origins within Judaism while at the
same time articulating his significance in terms that emphasized
his global, even cosmic, significance. In the end, Ebionitism became
heretical because it was a symbol of parochialism within a faith
that was clear about its universal significance and calling. Although Ebionitism lingered, in various forms, it finally simply
petered out.

But not permanently. One of the most intriguing religious developments in the last hundred years, generally overlooked by journalists[28] and scholars alike, is a significant stream of conversions from
Judaism to Christianity. While some Jewish converts assimilated
themselves completely to Christianity, abandoning their Jewish cul-

ture, others saw themselves in a very different way. As the anthropologist Juliene Lipson has pointed out, the term "Hebrew Christian" is now widely used to refer to "a Jew who has accepted Christ as the Messiah and his savior, but who nonetheless chooses to retain his identity as a Jew."[29] This Jewish identity is expressed in a number of ways, including observing the Sabbath, but particularly by using the Hebrew term *Yeshua* to refer to Jesus.

The resurgence of Jewish Christianity in recent years has led to a new interest within the movement of articulating the significance of Jesus in essentially Jewish terms. Just as the name Jesus is avoided on account of its Greek roots, so many traditional Christian ways of explaining his significance are also held to reflect Greek metaphysical ideas and hence require restatement in more authentically Jewish ways—such as seeing Jesus as a prophet. This has led to the reemergence of an Ebionite Christology within Jewish Christian circles.

We now turn to consider another early heresy concerning the identity of Jesus of Nazareth, generally known as *Docetism*.

Docetism: The Illusionary Humanity of Jesus of Nazareth

The three letters of John are regarded by some scholars as being among the later works of the New Testament, possibly dating from around the year 90. According to these letters, a new and potentially dangerous idea was in circulation in some Christian churches—that Jesus of Nazareth was not really a human being at all.[30] Jesus only seemed to be human; in reality, he was divine. His humanity was a phantasm, an illusion. The term "Docetism," deriving from the Greek verb *dokein* ("to appear"), rapidly came to be used to refer to this teaching. It is thought that the first person to have used the word "Docetism" in this sense was Serapion, bishop of Antioch (190–203).

According to Irenaeus of Lyons, writing toward the end of the second century, these ideas were associated with Cerinthus, who

was active in the city of Ephesus around the time that the letters of
John were being written.

> Cerinthus, a man who was educated in the wisdom of the
> Egyptians, taught that the world was not made by the primary
> God, but by a certain power far separated from him, and at a
> distance from that Principality who is supreme over the uni-
> verse, and ignorant of him who is above all. He represented
> Jesus as having not been born of a virgin, but as being the son
> of Joseph and Mary according to the ordinary course of human
> generation, while he was nevertheless more righteous, pru-
> dent, and wise than other men. Moreover, after his baptism,
> Christ descended upon him in the form of a dove from the
> Supreme Ruler, and that he proclaimed the unknown Father,
> and performed miracles. But at last Christ departed from
> Jesus, and that then Jesus suffered and rose again, while Christ
> remained impassible, inasmuch as he was a spiritual being.[31]

Cerinthus thus drew a distinction between a human "Jesus" and
a divine "Christ." Jesus differed from the remainder of humanity
only in the extent to which he possessed certain virtues, and to the
extent that the divine Christ descended upon him at the baptism
and left him at the cross.

The first explicit references to what is recognizable as a form of
Docetism are found in some of the letters of Ignatius of Antioch (c.
35–c. 107), bishop of Antioch in Syria, who was martyred at Rome.
Ignatius is remembered mainly on account of seven letters, which
both exercised considerable influence in the early church and bear
important witness to some of its controversies. These letters show
him to be concerned about the teachings of two groups, each of
which clearly had influence within some Christian churches: the
Judaizers, who wished Christianity to remain within the orbit of
Judaism;[32] and the Docetists, who argued that the suffering of Jesus
was illusory. His letters to the churches at Trallia and Smyrna

clearly indicate that some were arguing that Christ merely *appeared* to suffer. Christ, Ignatius maintained in his letter to the Trallians, "really and truly did suffer, just as he really and truly rose again. His passion was no imaginary illusion."[33]

The Docetic refusal to accept the fundamental humanity of Jesus of Nazareth is expressed in a number of intriguing ways. Valentinus, whom we shall consider presently, took a strongly Docetist view of Christ, and extended this to include his digestive system. The idea that Jesus of Nazareth should urinate or defecate was simply inconceivable to Valentinus. These were degrading aspects of being human, something that could not conceivably apply to Jesus. According to Clement of Alexandria, Valentinus taught that Jesus of Nazareth "was continent," in that "he ate and drank in a special way, without excreting his solids."[34]

Despite these clear indications of the influence of Docetic ideas in the early church, it is difficult to find evidence of a coherent movement that could be called Docetism.[35] The earliest sources available to us indicate that some parties held that Jesus had only appeared to suffer; yet these are never explicitly styled "Docetists." Irenaeus, for example, cites a number of unorthodox writers as claiming that Jesus of Nazareth "was a man merely in appearance"; he does not, however, refer to this as Docetism. Hippolytus of Rome, writing in the early third century, clearly encountered a group called Docetists, which he associates with a refusal to allow that Jesus Christ really suffered. However, the forms of Docetism that he encountered often mingled these ideas with some of the concepts from various Gnostic sources, making it difficult to understand what is specifically distinctive about Docetism.

Once more, we are confronted with a complex historical picture of what early Christianity understood by the term "Docetism." Some scholars have suggested that the best way of defining Docetism historically is to limit it to the belief that, in the words of the patristic scholar Norbert Brox, "Jesus was different from what he appeared to be."[36] Two types of Docetism can be identified, which are clearly related but not identical.[37] The first relates to Christ's incarnation. Jesus Christ could not really be properly human, as there was no way in which the divine and the human could coexist in a single being. Christ would therefore have to be totally spiritual in nature. The second relates to his suffering on the cross: even if Christ was indeed truly human, he did not really suffer on the cross. Of these two views, the first appears to have been the more widespread within the early church.

Understanding the origins of Docetism is just as problematic as making sense of its essential ideas. Some have argued that it arose as a result of Greek philosophical influences, particularly difficulties in understanding how God could coexist alongside "matter." Others have suggested that it was the result of Jewish influences or that it reflects the growing influence of certain forms of Gnosticism within early Christianity.[38] Recently, however, another approach has emerged, one that may well cast light on why Docetism proved so attractive to many at this time.

In their study of the historical origins of Docetism, Ronnie Goldstein and Guy Stroumsa note how classical Greek mythology makes reference to heroes and heroines being replaced by "doubles" when their death is imminent.[39] This device is common in Greek tragedy and can be seen in Euripides' account of Helen of Troy, which dates from the fifth century B.C.[40] The figure of Helen of Troy represented a considerable challenge to the dramatists of the classical age in that she had to be recognized as one who was simultaneously to be valued and despised. On the one hand, she was a prize for which countless men were willing to fight and die—the "face that launched a thousand ships";[41] on the other, she was an adulteress and was hence both the source and object of deep shame. Some dramatists portrayed her as heartlessly evil, others as sympathetically chastened, and still others as subject to forces beyond her control. Yet there was a fourth approach, elaborated by authors as diverse and distinguished as Stesichorus, Herodotus, and Euripides. A new myth was constructed, displacing the harsher historical narrative:

Contrary to Homer, Helen herself never went to Troy. A phantom (*eidolon*) took her place.

For those who do not know it, the story is worth repeating. According to Plato, the poet Stesichorus lost his eyesight as a punishment for slandering Helen in a poem, in which he accused her of lewd behavior.[42] Stesichorus then repented and wrote a second, revised version of his poem (*Palinodia*) according to which Helen did not really go to Troy. This solved a theological problem—how to protect the virtue of the divinized Helen in places where she was already the object of a cult, when her behavior in Troy caused such offense and undermined her claims to divinity. How could Helen of Troy be worshipped as divine when she had such a questionable reputation? According to Goldstein and Stroumsa:

> The *eidolon* is systematically used in Greek literature to solve theological problems related to myth and its interpretation. This simple device of the hero's double solves the problem of an unworthy behavior on the part of the (usually divine) hero, or of his (or her) intolerable fate, without suppressing the mythical story altogether.[43]

Was such an approach found in early Christian heresy? A case can be made for suggesting that Jewish Christian groups might have been tempted to assimilate the narrative of the crucifixion of Christ to the story of Abraham and Isaac (Genesis 22), in which the demand for the death of Isaac as a sacrifice is averted at the last moment, as a substitute victim is provided.[44] Irenaeus of Lyons certainly reports this unorthodox view as having been in circulation, attributing it to Basilides.

> [Jesus Christ] did not suffer. Rather, a certain Simon of Cyrene was forced to bear his cross for him, and it was he who was unwittingly and accidentally crucified, being transformed by the other, so that he was taken for Jesus.[45]

This is clearly a form of Docetism, originating within a Gnostic framework.

The influence of this approach within Gnosticism proved to be considerable, as is evident from the body of literature recovered from Nag Hammadi. Consider this extract from the Gnostic Second Treatise of the Great Seth, which offers an alternative account of the crucifixion of Christ, spoken in the first person:

> I did not succumb to them as they had planned. But I was not afflicted at all. Those who were there punished me. And I did not die in reality but in appearance. . . . For my death, which they think happened, [happened] to them in their error and blindness, since they nailed their man unto their death. For their Ennoias did not see me, for they were deaf and blind. But in doing these things, they condemn themselves. Yes, they saw me; they punished me. It was another, their father, who drank the gall and the vinegar; it was not I. They struck me with the reed; it was another, Simon, who bore the cross on his shoulder. It was another upon Whom they placed the crown of thorns.[46]

We see here a studied reluctance to allow that Jesus of Nazareth should have suffered the indignity of death, especially such a humiliating death. The Docetic Christological trends that are so characteristic of such types of Gnosticism here lead to some intriguing historical revisionism.

We have referred to Gnosticism at several points in our discussion without explaining what is to be understood by this term. So what exactly was Gnosticism? And why did it have such an impact on the early church? We shall begin to answer these questions by considering the case of Valentinus, an important figure in the early church's struggle to define its center and limits.

Valentinism: Gnosticism and Christianity

At the end of the first century, the city of Rome was the hub of a vast empire. Yet although Rome had subjugated much of the world of its day, a subtle form of reverse colonialism took root. Religious movements having their origins in Greece, Palestine, and beyond began to gain a following in Rome. One of them, of course, was Christianity, which rapidly found its way to the center of the empire. The evidence clearly suggests that the church to which the apostle Paul wrote was actually a collection of individual congregations meeting in homes, rather than a single coherent Roman church. At this stage, the Roman church possessed little in the way of centralized authorities or organization.[47] It is perhaps best compared to secular Roman clubs or societies (the *collegia*), or to Jewish synagogues. In each case, these were essentially independent associations with no centralized control.

Others derived from other regions of the Roman Empire. The Eleusinian mysteries, which had their origins in Greece, gained many adherents at Rome. These were based on the cults of Demeter and Persephone, and were believed to unite the worshipper with the gods, offering rewards in the afterlife.[48] The Mithraic mysteries also took hold around this time, proving particularly popular within the Roman army. The origins of this cult, and the identity of its central figure of Mithras, remain uncertain,[49] although it probably represents a local adaptation of an Anatolian or Iranian cult.

Yet most scholarly interest has focused on a tradition that is widely known as Gnosticism (a term derived from the Greek word *gnosis,* "knowledge"). If any ancient religious tradition can be said to resonate particularly well with contemporary social and religious fashions in North America, it is Gnosticism. What we know of Gnostic beliefs suggests that they chime in with contemporary ideals of self-discovery, self-awareness, self-actualization, and self-salvation, not to mention a dislike of any kind of authority, especially ecclesiastical. The current fascination with Gnosticism on the part of segments of modern American academia tells us rather more about contemporary cultural anxieties and aspirations than about this religious movement.[50]

Such movements often use the term "Gnosticism" in a loose sense to designate an emphasis on the spiritual side of life and a concern for seeking truth within the depths of human nature rather than being told what is right by authority figures. While these themes are indeed found within Gnosticism, they were so widespread within late classical antiquity that they cannot be regarded as being distinctive of the movement. There is a need for historical precision at this point, not least in trying to understand why the church came to see Gnosticism as constituting a threat rather than—like Platonism—being a congenial dialogue partner.

So what is this Gnosticism? Traditionally, the movement has been held to refer to those groups in the Roman Empire, especially in the first or second century, that advocated knowing God through experience rather than formal doctrines.[51] This creates the impression that Gnosticism is a well-defined movement with a well-formed set of beliefs.

In fact, this religious tradition turns out to be something of a broad church—so broad, in fact, that many are questioning whether it can actually be regarded as a well-defined school of thought with any specific identity.[52] There is a growing consensus that the term "Gnosticism" is misleading in that it gathers together a number of quite disparate groups and presents them as if they represented a single religious belief system. There is growing sympathy for the view that the idea of Gnosticism as a coherent entity is largely the invention of modern scholars of religion,[53] who have perhaps been unduly influenced by early Christian writers such as Irenaeus of Lyons, who had their own reasons for wanting to portray it as a homogenous, well-organized group—an evil empire that posed a real threat to the fledgling Christian church.[54]

There is now a clear consensus that it is very difficult to use the category of Gnosticism in any meaningful way.[55] According to

Karen King, "The variety of phenomena classified as 'Gnostic' simply will not support a single, monolithic definition, and in fact none of the primary materials fits the standard typological definition."[56] So do we need to give up on using the words "Gnosticism" and "Gnostic"? No. They simply need to be used with caution. A good case can be made for using them to refer to a family of religious doctrines and myths that flourished in late antiquity and that maintain or presuppose two things: (1) that the cosmos is a result of the activity of an evil or ignorant creator; and (2) that salvation is a process in the course of which believers receive the knowledge of their divine origin so that they are enabled to return to the realm of light after having been freed from the limitations of the physical world in general and the human body in particular.

With these cautionary points in mind, let us turn to consider the views of Valentinus, widely regarded as the originator of a form of Gnostic Christianity. We possess enough information to be able to offer a reasonably complete account of his ideas and assess their significance.[57] Valentinus appears to have arrived in Rome around the year 135. His earlier history is difficult to fix with any precision. Traditionally, he is portrayed as originating from Egypt, having been born in the Nile Delta area and educated at Alexandria. (Significantly, Walter Bauer had suggested that Alexandria was a leading center for Gnosticism at this time.) The disciples of Valentinus claimed that he had been educated by Theudas, a pupil of the apostle Paul, from whom he derived his "secret teachings." Also present in Rome around this time was the Christian theologian Justin Martyr, who condemned Valentinus's ideas. Yet Justin had no official position within the Roman church and appears to have existed on its margins, having limited influence at the time.[58]

Although most popular accounts of Valentinus's career routinely report that he was condemned by the church at Rome, there is actually no historical evidence that any figure of authority within the Roman church ever condemned him or his teachings.[59] This has led some to suggest that Valentinus remained active in the church at

Rome, and others to speculate that the disciplinary structures of the
Roman church were tightened up in the second half of the second
century.

So what are the fundamental ideas of Valentinism?[60] It is not
clear to what extent the distinctive doctrines of Valentinism can be
ascribed to Valentinus personally, since at least some of those ideas
were developed by his followers after his death. The easiest way to
make sense of Valentinism is to see it as originating within Christianity yet interpreting or developing essentially Christian ideas in a
Gnostic manner—especially in regard to the imperfection of matter
and the subordinate status of the creator God. It is thought that
Valentinus himself encountered the teachings of Basilides, an Alexandrian teacher who held that the Jewish creator God was not the
same God as that disclosed by Jesus of Nazareth. As Basilides' later
followers were wont to say, believers were "no longer Jews, but still
not yet Christians."[61]

The diversification of Valentinism is partly due to the variety of
its later interpreters and its geographical expansion. The greatest
interpreters of Valentinus are usually thought to be Ptolemy, Theodotus, and Heracleon. Yet both early Christian sources and
modern scholarship have expressed doubts about whether Heracleon was really a representative of Valentinism.[62] Furthermore,
early documentary sources make reference to two "schools" within
Valentinism, one based in Italy and the other in "the east."[63] Interestingly, the texts discovered at Nag Hammadi in 1945 include a
number of Valentinian texts, along with documents representing
another form of Gnosticism that is generally known as "Sethian"
Gnosticism.[64] Yet despite these difficulties, it is possible to provide a
general overview of the Valentinian system while recognizing that
variations exist within the school.

Valentinism used the term "fullness" (Greek: *pleroma*) to refer to
the dwelling place of the true God, the Father of the Universe, as
well as a host of eternal beings who lived in perfect harmony with
each other. This cosmic harmony was destroyed by one of the eter-

nal beings, Wisdom (Greek: *sophia*), which was not prepared to rest content with its own position but wished to imitate the Father of the Universe and do some creating itself. This abortive attempt at creation by Wisdom resulted in the Demiurge (from the Greek term *demiurgos,* "workman"), who was expelled from the divine realm and subsequently attempted to create worlds of his own.

This idea of an inferior creator god, the Demiurge, is found in classical Greek philosophy and plays a significant role in Plato's dialogue *Timaeus.* In general, Gnosticism held that the Demiurge created the physical world without any knowledge of the "true God," falsely believing that he was the only God. Since the Demiurge acted in ignorance of the true God, his creation had to be considered as imperfect or even evil. Gnosticism thus proposed a dichotomy between the visible world of experience and the spiritual world of the true God. Sethian Gnosticism, which shows little Christian influence and is widely thought to derive from Judaism, took a strongly negative view of the creator god, often referred to using the Semitic name *Yaldabaoth,* and occasionally as "the fool" or "the blind god." Yaldabaoth is typically presented, in demonic terms, as the leader of other spiritual beings and as the enemy of humanity. For Sethian Gnosticism, Yaldabaoth was tormented by sexual desire, leading him to rape Eve and to father her two sons, Cain and Abel. Seth is Adam's own son, and is thus to be seen as a prototype of "spiritual" humanity.[65] In contrast, Valentinism understood the Demiurge in more positive terms than in many Gnostic systems, holding that the Demiurge was the mediator for Wisdom in the creation of the world.

So what of the place of humanity within this created order? While the human body was created by the Demiurge, it nevertheless contains a divine spirit that enables it to establish a connection with the highest God. For this reason, human beings may be regarded as being superior to their creator. The divine "spark" within humanity possesses a homing instinct, longing to break free of the body and achieve its true destiny. The aim of the body created by the Demiurge is to function as a prison and cause humanity to re-press or forget the divine spirit within. The Greek slogan *soma sema* ("the body is a tomb") expresses this notion well. Yet this spark can be awakened if and when a divine messenger awakes individuals from their dream of forgetfulness, thus allowing it to illuminate humanity through this esoteric knowledge and reconnect with its divine origins.

For Valentinism, Christ is this redeemer figure who awakens the divine spark within humanity, enabling it to find its way back to its true home. In order to save those who were held captive by the body, the savior "let himself be conceived and he let himself be born as an infant with body and soul."[66] Theodotus taught that the savior, or *Logos*, descended from the *pleroma* to the visible world, where he assumed a "spiritual flesh" in order to allow the spiritual elements trapped in earthly human beings to be reunited with their divine origins.[67]

So why did the church reject such an approach? Why did it feel that Valentinism posed such a threat? The simplest way to under-stand the church's rejection of Valentinism is that it was seen as an attempt, in effect but not intention, to subvert the church from within. Irenaeus of Lyons's polemic against Valentinus reveals how similar his ideas were to those of the mainstream church: both Val-entinians and adherents of the mainstream church went to the same meetings, used the same vocabulary, read and respected the same scrip-tures, and took part in the same sacramental rites.[68] The difference lay in how these were interpreted. Valentinus's use of New Testa-ment books is consistent with the majority view within contempo-rary scholarship, which is that Valentinism originated within the matrix of Christian orthodoxy at a time when the canon was in the process of crystallizing.[69]

It is clear that Valentinus saw himself as enriching Christianity by using Gnostic ideas both as a means of deepening its appeal to con-temporary culture and to give it added intellectual depth. A signifi-cant number of Valentinians thought of themselves as representing a deeper, more spiritual version of Christianity. Yet others saw this as tantamount to the conversion of Christianity to Gnosticism. Instead of making Christianity congenial to Gnostics, it had achieved precisely the opposite result. Valentinian biblical exegesis seemed to involve the imposition of Gnostic meanings upon Christian words. Valentinus offered a version of Gnosticism that seemed highly adapted to Christian sensitivities, especially when compared with its Sethian counterpart. It was, however, still a form of Gnosticism.

In responding to Valentinus and his circle, Irenaeus of Lyons argued for the "economy of salvation." The entire work of salvation, from creation through to its final consummation, was carried out by one and the same God.[70] The creator God was no Demiurge, nor was the redeemer some mere emissary from the heavenly realms. Irenaeus accentuates the importance of the emerging doctrine of the Trinity as a means of articulating divine continuity throughout the history of the world on the one hand and as safeguarding the essential unity of Scripture on the other. Matter is not intrinsically evil; it is God's good creation. It has fallen and is susceptible to restoration and renewal. For Irenaeus, the doctrine of the Incarnation and the Christian use of sacraments represent explicit denials of any Gnostic notion of an intrinsically evil matter. Did not God choose to become incarnate, uniting himself to human nature? Does not the church use water, wine, and bread as symbols of divine grace and presence?

Irenaeus's concern at this point was to place clear blue water between the church and its Gnostic alternatives. Yet it appears that for Irenaeus, underlying differences of substance was a deeper concern about issues of method—above all, the interpretation of Scripture. As he reflected on Valentinus's interpretation of sacred texts, Irenaeus appears to have come to the conclusion that the Gnostics had hijacked the foundational documents of Christianity and interpreted its core terms in a Gnostic manner. The outcome, in Irenaeus's view, was that Valentinus turned Christianity into Gnosticism.

Irenaeus's response to this development is widely regarded as marking a landmark in early Christian thought. Heretics, he argued, interpreted the Bible according to their own taste. Orthodox believers, in contrast, interpreted the Bible in ways that their apostolic authors would have approved. What had been handed down from the apostles through the church was not merely the biblical texts themselves, but a certain way of reading and understanding those texts.

> Everyone who wishes to know the truth should consider the apostolic tradition, which has been made known in every church in the entire world. We are able to number those who are bishops appointed by the apostles, and their successors in the churches to the present day, who taught and knew nothing of such things as these people imagine. . . . The apostles have, as it were, deposited this truth in all its fullness in this depository, so that whoever wants to may draw from this water of life. This is the gate of life; all others are thieves and robbers.[71]

Irenaeus's point is that a continuous stream of Christian teaching, life, and interpretation can be traced from the time of the apostles to his own period. The church is able to point to those who have maintained the teaching of the church, and to certain public standard creeds that set out the main lines of Christian belief.

Tradition is thus the guarantor of faithfulness to the original apostolic teaching, a safeguard against the innovations and misrepresentations of biblical texts on the part of the Gnostics. The New Testament represents the teaching of the apostles, which is to be interpreted as the apostles wished. The church, Irenaeus insisted, safeguarded both text and interpretation, passing both on to future generations. This development is of major importance, as it underlies the emergence of *creeds*—public, authoritative statements of the basic points of the Christian faith. This point was further developed in the early fifth century by Vincent of Lérins, who was concerned that certain doctrinal innovations were being introduced without good reason. There was a need to have public standards by which such doctrines could be judged.

Yet what is particularly interesting about Irenaeus's appeal to the apostolic tradition is his clear sense that orthodoxy is chronologically prior to heresy. Valentinism is clearly understood to be a recent development, one whose very novelty raises questions about its provenance and integrity. A similar argument about the temporal priority of orthodoxy can also be found in the writings of Clement of Rome, Ignatius of Antioch, and Justin Martyr.[72] We have already noted the difficulties that this poses for Walter Bauer's historical account of the origins of heresy.

We noted earlier that later followers of the Gnostic writer Basilides held that so-called Christians were "no longer Jews, but still not yet Christians."[73] We see here a Gnostic notion of a trajectory away from Judaism and toward a purer form of Christianity. The church, for its Gnostic critics, had stalled along this road and was still far closer to Judaism than it ought to be. In what follows, we shall consider the most famous movement in the early church that sought to dissociate Christianity totally from its Jewish roots— Marcionism.

Marcionism: Judaism and the Gospel

What is the relationship of Christianity to Judaism? The model that began to gain the ascendancy in early Christianity was that of the fulfillment of the hopes of pagans and Jews in Christ. Writers such as Justin Martyr were adamant that the story of Jesus of Nazareth could not be told in isolation. To understand the identity and significance of Jesus, it was necessary to tell other stories and explore how they interlocked and interrelated. One of those stories concerns God's creation of the world; another tells of God's calling of Israel; a third tells of the age-old human quest for meaning and significance. For Justin Martyr, the story of Jesus intersects all three, ultimately to provide their fulfillment. Jesus is the focal point from which all other stories are to be seen and on which all finally and decisively converge.[74]

This theme has fascinated theologians throughout Christian history, especially those of the Greek-speaking church of the first five centuries. The great Egyptian city of Alexandria was noted for its philosophical sophistication.[75] Several schools of thought, all basing their ideas on the great classical philosopher Plato, argued for the existence of an ideal world lying beyond the world of appearances. But how could this shadowy and elusive realm be known? Or, more tantalizingly, how might it be *entered*? Growing importance came to be attached to the idea of the *Logos*—a Greek term best translated as "word," referring to a mediator between these two very different, yet apparently interconnected, worlds. But how might this gap be bridged? Who could bring the ideal realm into the everyday world? Or bring people from the present order of things to the ideal world lying beyond it?

Alexandria was also home to a highly cultured Jewish population well aware of the importance of the questions raised by Greek philosophy yet faithful to their own way of seeing the world. For such writers, "Law"—the Torah—was of critical importance. Law represented God's will, the ultimate standard of life, and the true goal of human nature. Yet some within Judaism held that the Law did not represent the final state of things. It was an interim measure, a staging post on the way to something still better. They waited for the fulfillment of the Law—for the culmination of the hopes of Israel in God's anointed one, the Messiah. A new prophet was awaited who would be as Moses and know God face-to-face. A new king was expected who would restore the fortunes of Israel's great monarch David. A new priest would come, in the line of Aaron, who would finally purge the guilt of his people. Early Christian writers proclaimed that the hopes of the ages had been fulfilled through the coming of Christ, which brought to perfection and completion the great aspirations of the seemingly endless human quest for truth. Greek philosophy and the Law of Israel alike were fulfilled and transcended in this one individual, Jesus of Nazareth. Human wisdom and divine promise converged.[76] There was a fundamental continuity between the old and new covenants, with the church as the new Israel.

This idea gradually emerged as dominant within the church of the late first and early second centuries. In his letters, Paul affirmed the divine inspiration of the "writings" or "scriptures"—meaning the Hebrew Bible—and recognized its importance for moral guidance within the church.[77] He represented Jesus of Nazareth as fulfilling the Torah. Later, other writers began to develop schemes for deepening this understanding of the relation of Jesus of Nazareth to the history of Israel. An excellent example of this approach is found in the idea of the *type*—an event or person who is understood as anticipating some aspect of the New Testament, especially Jesus of Nazareth.[78] An excellent example of this approach is found in the writings of Justin Martyr (100–165), who interpreted the story of the bronze serpent (Num. 21:4–9) as a type of Christ. As God could not have intended Moses to set up an idol, the serpent must have had some other, deeper significance. Since a serpent on a pole would be in the shape of a cross, Justin argues that the bronze serpent was a symbol or "type" of the future defeat of the devil through the cross.[79]

But not all shared this vision. Some held that the progress of Christianity was impeded by its connection with Judaism and that the church ought to sever all of its links with the older religion. This view received its classic expression in the writings of Marcion of Sinope, who died around 160. Relatively little is known about him. He was originally from Sinope in Pontus, in Asia Minor, and is believed to have moved to Rome in the late 130s, where he appears to have established a shipping business, becoming wealthy. Perhaps to ensure his acceptance in the Roman church after what appears to have been a slightly questionable past in Asia Minor, Marcion gave the Roman church a very sizable gift—two hundred thousand sesterces—upon his arrival. At first, Marcion appears to have been accepted by the Roman church. However, following his failure to persuade the church to adopt his radical views on Judaism, Marcion severed his connections and set up his own alternative religious community.

Marcion's fundamental argument is that the "God" of the Old Testament was not the same as that of the New Testament. Justin Martyr summarized Marcion's views thus:

> One Marcion, a man of Pontus, who is still alive even now, taught those who believe him to pay honor to a different god, greater than the Creator: and this man has by the assistance of those demons caused many of every nation to utter blasphemies, denying the God who made this universe, and professing that another, a greater than he, has done greater things.[80]

For Marcion, the Old Testament God was to be seen as inferior, even defective, in the light of the Christian conception of God. There was no connection whatsoever between these deities.

Marcion proposed that Jesus had no direct relation to the Jewish creator god and that he was not to be thought of as the "Messiah" sent by this Jewish God. Rather, Jesus was sent from a previously unknown, strange God, characterized by love rather than jealousy and aggression.[81] Irenaeus of Lyons represents Marcion as declaring that the Jewish God "is the creator of evil things, and takes delight in wars, is fickle, and behaves inconsistently."[82] Tertullian tells us that he proposed two gods "of unequal rank, the one a stern and warlike judge, the other gentle and mild, kind, and supremely good."[83] The creator god of the Bible was a Jewish divinity that represented the total antithesis of the very different God who sent Jesus—a view set out in some detail by Marcion in his now-lost *Antitheses*. As Robin Lane Fox comments:

> The creator, [Marcion] argued, was an incompetent being: why else had he afflicted women with the agonies of child-

birth? "God" in the Old Testament was a "committed barbarian" who favored bandits and such terrorists as Israel's King David. Christ, by contrast, was the new and separate revelation of an altogether higher God. Marcion's teaching was the most extreme statement of the newness of the Christian faith.[84]

The stridency of the anti-Jewish tone of Marcion's theology[85] suggests that issues deeper than theology were involved in his hostility toward the Old Testament.

There are possible connections between Marcion and Gnosticism, evident especially in Marcion's strongly negative evaluation of the world and the one who created it.[86] Marcion regarded the material world with intense distaste and had no time for the idea that the world's redeemer should be contaminated through human flesh. Marcion was inclined to a Docetic Christology, which played down the historical and human side of Jesus of Nazareth. Naturally, to minimize or deny the humanity of Jesus was correspondingly to downplay or deny his Jewishness.

Yet Marcion was not prepared to rest content with affirming the radical difference between the God of the Jews and the God of Jesus of Nazareth. Many of the documents that were being widely accepted as authoritative by early Christians—which would later be canonically gathered together as the New Testament—made extensive reference to the Jewish scriptures. Marcion thus developed his own authorized collection of documents, which excluded works that he regarded as contaminated by Jewish ideas and associations. Needless to say, Marcion's biblical canon excluded the Old Testament altogether. It consisted simply of ten of Paul's letters, along with the Gospel of Luke. Yet Marcion was obliged to edit even these works in order to remove contaminating influences that suggested that there was some connection between Jesus and the Jewish God. Marcion thus excised from his version of Luke's Gospel the narratives of the Annunciation and the Nativity; Christ's baptism, temptation, and genealogy; and all references to Bethlehem and Nazareth.[87] Paul's letters also required some editorial work, to remove their associations with Judaism.[88]

So, did Marcion regard himself as having the right to change the contents of Scripture? Irenaeus certainly thought so, and complained bitterly about Marcion's presumption in daring "openly to mutilate the scriptures."[89] Tertullian complained about Valentinus's altering of the scriptures by means of faulty exposition, and Marcion's by textual emendation. One used sophistry, the other a knife.[90] The evidence suggests that Marcion did not see his editorial work in this light, taking the view that Luke's Gospel had already been doctored by Jewish sympathizers, who had also altered Paul's letters. Marcion therefore saw himself as eliminating contaminating additions, restoring the texts to their original condition. To avoid misunderstanding, Marcion also appears to have added "prologues" to the epistles, reinforcing his anti-Judaizing message. For example, a strongly antagonistic attitude toward the Old Testament is easily discerned in his prologue to Paul's letter to Titus: "[Paul] warns and instructs Titus concerning the constitution of the priesthood and spiritual conversation, and heretics who believe in the Jewish scriptures who are to be avoided [*et hereticis vitandis qui in scripturis Iudaicis credunt*]."[91]

So why did Marcion's approach pose such a threat to the church? Most obviously, it attempted to deny Christianity's roots in Judaism and, above all, Jesus of Nazareth's Jewish lineage. Marcion's excision of the genealogy in Luke's Gospel is a powerful symbol of his refusal to accept that Jesus of Nazareth was, in the first place, a human being and, in the second place, a Jew. Judaism, according to Marcion, is a religion with a corrupt view of God. In dealing with such challenges, Christian theologians have developed approaches to the Old Testament that allow them to respect its moral and religious insights while at the same time neutralizing some of its more problematic aspects—such as the ethnic cleansing of Canaan.[92] If Marcion had had his way, this would not have been an issue. Yet other problems would have arisen, not least the total historical dislocation of the Christian faith. For Marcion, the gospel comes from nowhere, without any historical context. There is no sense of its being the climax and fulfillment of God's engagement with humanity, which began with the call of Abraham.

Yet it is easy to see why Marcionism is so appealing. Richard Dawkins's *God Delusion* is one of the most successful works of atheist apologetics in recent years. In this work, Dawkins mounts a ferocious attack on the morality of God. The God that Dawkins does not believe in is "a petty, unjust, unforgiving control freak; a vindictive, bloodthirsty ethnic cleanser; a misogynistic, homophobic, racist, infanticidal, genocidal, filicidal, pestilential, megalomaniacal, sadomasochistic, capriciously malevolent bully."[93] Virtually all of the biblical material that underlies Dawkins's charges is drawn from the Old Testament.[94]

It is not particularly difficult to see why some wonder whether Christianity would have been better off if it had broken with Judaism altogether. Indeed, the famous German liberal Protestant theologian Adolf von Harnack (1851–1930) argued along these lines in a controversial attempt to reinstate Marcion within German Christianity in 1921.[95] While Harnack was opposed to the more strident versions of anti-Semitism that gained ground within Germany from about 1880, his attitude toward Jews has been described as "paternalistic."[96] Sadly, Marcionism is a heresy that seems set to be revived with every resurgence of anti-Semitism. It is not just a heresy about the identity of Jesus of Nazareth; it is a heresy about the dignity and historical significance of the Jewish people.

One final point needs to be stressed. Popular accounts of Marcion's career speak of his being "condemned" or "expelled" by the church at Rome. This never happened. Irritated that the Roman church refused to accept his views, Marcion left the church, which promptly returned a generous gift he had made earlier. It was not that the church decided that Marcion was not a proper Christian;

rather, Marcion came to the view that the Roman church was not properly Christian, and left to found his own pure sect.[97] Marcion excluded himself from the church.

Reflections on Early Heresies

In this section, we have considered three early heresies, two of which have particularly strong links with the churches of Rome. These heresies have some common themes. For example, a belief that matter is fundamentally evil is found in Docetism, Marcionism, and Valentinism. All three involve the relationship between Christianity and other religious groups—Judaism and Gnosticism—that threatened to dilute or distort the essence of Christianity. Yet what is particularly interesting about these three approaches to Christianity is that they emerged and were finally judged to be heretical before the church had evolved any permanent authority structures, before the emergence of creeds as personal or official statements of faith, and before the New Testament canon had been formally agreed upon. Although many studies continue to speak of the church declaring Marcion and Valentinus to be heretics, the situation is much more complex than this suggests, as we noted earlier.

We do not entirely understand how the process of recognizing movements as heretical took place in the church of the first half of the second century. The evidence suggests that a gradual process of crystallization of opinion took place, similar to that which led to the emergence of early canons of the New Testament. The relatively high degree of diversity that was such a characteristic feature of Christian congregations at this stage allowed Marcion to go and establish his own church, separate from existing congregations, and Valentinus to continue ministering in some Roman congregations. The organizational fluidity of the early church was such that it was difficult to organize any campaign against alleged heresies. As far as we can tell, the first action taken by the Roman church against Valentinism dates from the 190s, a generation after the movement came into being.[98]

So how was heresy identified at this time? What processes led to a theological opinion being transformed into a heresy? We probably do not yet know enough about the manner in which a consensus emerged within the early church, which depends upon an understanding of its complex social networks, the growing authority of Scripture (which began to emerge as a coherent entity around this time), and especially the role of opinion makers (such as Justin Martyr) and members of the hierarchy, to answer this question. Yet there can be little doubt that these opinions crystallized, to become the settled opinion of the church.

As we noted earlier, Walter Bauer portrayed the triumph of orthodoxy as essentially an ideological accident. It was the power of institutions that really mattered; which ideas they chose to promote within the diversity of early Christianity was secondary. The decision as to which of the early competing visions of Christianity would be declared orthodox and which heretical reflected the power politics of the age, not the intellectual merits of the ideas in question. Heresy was thus simply an early orthodoxy that failed to gain the support of the power brokers.

Yet the historical evidence does not really fit the picture proposed by Bauer. Furthermore, there are clearly theological issues at stake. The relative weakness of institutional ecclesiastical structures at this time, including those at Rome, suggest that the quality of the ideas themselves played a significant role in their evaluation—especially in regard to their intellectual provenance and their consequences for the identity and mission of the church.[99]

So what of later heresies? What of the ideas that were declared heretical after the church gained its somewhat problematic status as the favored religion of the Roman Empire, when issues of imperial stability and polity came to be interlocked with the life and thought of the church? In the following chapter, we shall consider some of the great heresies of the fourth and fifth centuries, including what many regard to be the greatest of all—Arianism.

seven

Later Classic Heresies: Arianism, Donatism, Pelagianism

In the previous chapter we considered some heresies that emerged at a time when the Christian churches existed on the margins of imperial culture, without robust leadership structures and mechanisms, and with only an emerging sense of what constituted theological and ethical norms. There is, however, clear evidence that a process of crystallization was taking place in the final half of the second century, with agreement beginning to emerge within the Christian world on the group of texts that would be recognized as the New Testament and how these were to be interpreted and applied. If heresy can be regarded as simply the outcome of theological uncertainty or confusion, its causes were steadily diminishing with the emergence of an early form of orthodoxy at this time.

However, as we have emphasized, the roots of heresy lie far deeper than any confusion or ambiguity over theological sources or how they are to be interpreted. The process of emergence of Christian doctrine can be likened to a journey of exploration, in which new pathways were explored—for example, to express the significance of Jesus of Nazareth or the interaction of the divine and human in the process of conversion. Some of these proved to be dead ends and were consequently declared to be out-of-bounds for theological orthodoxy. This process of exploration did not end with the emergence of "proto-orthodoxy" in the second century, but continued well into the fifth century.

Yet a further factor came into play during the fourth century. Christianity ceased to be a movement on the fringe of imperial culture, becoming the official faith of the empire. Orthodoxy and heresy were now more than matters of theological debate; they had significant consequences for social cohesion and unity. Theology found itself caught up in imperial politics, beginning to face pressures for which it was not initially prepared.

Imperial Politics and the Heresies of the Age

To appreciate the importance of this point, we must give thought to the dramatic change in status of the Christian faith in the Roman Empire in the first two decades of the fourth century. Up to this point, Christianity had not enjoyed any favored status. Indeed, it was seen by many as a social problem. Christian refusal to participate in the imperial cult was interpreted as an act of civil disobedience and was thus seen as a threat to the social cohesion of the empire. The Latin term *religio,* as is often pointed out, derives from a root meaning "to bind together."[1] Religion was meant to be the glue that held Roman society together.[2] The Christian refusal to integrate with the official religion was thus seen as subversive. Christians began to be described as "atheists"—in other words, as people who refused to conform to the official religion.[3]

This distrust of Christianity led to sporadic, though not persistent, harassment, often initiated independently by local Roman governors. The accession of the emperor Decius in 249, however, marked a significant escalation in the official Roman hostility toward Christians.[4] The emperor's dislike of Christianity is often held to have arisen from his belief that Rome could recover its former glory only by restoring its ancient pagan religion. This led to repression of movements that were seen to pose a threat to traditional Roman values and beliefs, with Christianity being prominent among them.[5] Christianity may have been an indirect target of Decius's actions; it was nevertheless hit hard.

The Edict of Decius, issued in June 250, ordered provincial governors and magistrates to ensure that there was universal observance of the requirement to offer sacrifices to the Roman gods and to the emperor. A certificate (*libellus pacis*) was issued to those who offered such sacrifices. The edict seems to have been widely ignored, but it was nevertheless enforced in some regions. Thousands of Christians were martyred during this difficult period, which led to many others lapsing or abandoning their faith in the face of persecution. The Decian persecution ended in June 251, when Decius was killed on a military expedition.

A further severe outburst of persecution came about in February 303, under the emperor Diocletian. An edict was issued ordering the destruction of all Christian places of worship, the surrender and destruction of all their books, and the cessation of all acts of Christian worship. Christian civil servants were to lose all privileges of rank or status and be reduced to the status of slaves. Prominent Christians were forced to offer sacrifice according to traditional Roman practices. It is an indication of how influential Christianity had become that Diocletian forced both his wife and daughter, who were known to be Christians, to comply with this order. The persecution continued under successive emperors, including Galerius, who ruled the eastern region of the empire.

In 311, Galerius ordered the cessation of the persecution. It had been a failure and had merely hardened Christians in their resolve to resist the reimposition of classical Roman pagan religion. Galerius issued an edict that permitted Christians to live normally again and "hold their religious assemblies, provided that they do nothing which would disturb public order."[6] The edict explicitly identified Christianity as a distinct religion in its own right, and offered it the full protection of the law. The legal status of Christianity, which had been ambiguous up to this point, was now resolved. The church no longer needed to exist under a siege mentality.

Christianity was now a legal religion; it was, however, merely one among many such religions. Yet the death of Galerius precipitated a fierce battle for the imperial succession, eventually won by Constantine (285–337). Following Maxentius's seizure of power in Italy and North Africa, Constantine led a body of troops from western Europe in an attempt to gain authority in the region. The decisive battle took place on October 28, 312, at the Milvian Bridge, to the north of Rome. Constantine defeated Maxentius and was proclaimed emperor. Constantine attributed his victory to the power of "the God of the Christians" and committed himself to the Christian faith from then onward, although his understanding of the Christian faith at this time appears to have been quite superficial.[7] The Edict of Milan, issued in 313 by Constantine and Licinius, granted religious freedom throughout the Roman Empire and ordered the restitution of property confiscated from Christians during the recent period of suppression.

It is not entirely clear at what point Constantine converted to Christianity. Although Constantine appears to have appreciated the pragmatic virtues of imperial religious toleration, he showed no particular attraction to Christianity in his early period. The implications, however, of his conversion were considerable. Having only just emerged from the margins of Roman society through being recognized as a legitimate religion, Christianity now found itself propelled to the forefront of Roman civic life. The conversion of the emperor Constantine brought about a complete change in the status of Christianity throughout the Roman Empire. It simply did not have time to acclimatize to being a legitimate faith before becoming the religion of the imperial establishment. As a result, it was relatively easy for Constantine to exploit the church as an instrument of imperial policy, impose his imperial ideology upon it, and deprive it of much of the independence that it had previously enjoyed. In 325, Constantine secured control of the eastern domains of the Roman Empire as well as the west and proceeded to establish the imperial capital in Byzantium, which came to be known as Constantinople after his death in 337.

To his obvious dismay, Constantine soon realized that there was a lack of unity within the church, potentially compromising its role as a unifying imperial influence. Events in the province of Africa caused an immediate headache for Constantine. Tensions arose there between two rival groups of Christians, who took very different attitudes toward those who had lapsed in the Diocletian persecution. Diocletian's demands for the suppression of Christianity had met with a mixed response. In eastern cities of the empire, Christianity was too strong numerically to be intimidated in this way. But in Roman North Africa, a particularly efficient administrative structure, linked with the relative weakness of the church, made suppression of the church relatively easy. Many clergy lapsed under threat of death, handed over their sacred texts, and conformed to the Roman imperial cult.

When Constantine declared that Christianity was legal, the question arose over what to do with lapsed clergy (*lapsi*). Should they be readmitted to office, perhaps after an appropriate public apology and retraction? Two positions rapidly emerged: those who took a rigorist position toward the *lapsi,* and those who took a more moderate, forgiving position. (The rigorists eventually became known as the Donatists, named after Donatus, a Berber whom they elected bishop of Carthage in 315.) Following a dispute over the election of Caecilian as bishop of Carthage in 312, the rigorists asked Constantine to intervene on their behalf. In the end, Constantine declined to resolve the matter personally, appointing a synod of bishops to deal with the matter. The ill feeling arising from the Donatist crisis simmered on throughout the fourth century and erupted again at the end of the century. We shall consider the theological issues arising from the Donatist controversy later in the present chapter.

Yet the main point to note here is how Constantine became drawn into ecclesiastical disputes. The new imperial status of Christianity meant that its unity and polity were now matters of significance to the state. Up to this point, heresy and orthodoxy had been concepts of importance within the Christian communities alone.

They now became imperial political concerns, with important legal implications.[8] The significance of this point can be seen from Constantine's role in the Arian controversy (which we shall consider shortly), which threatened to split the church in the eastern region of the empire. Constantine himself convened the Council of Nicaea in 325 to resolve this controversy. Politically, the move failed in the short term, in that disagreement and division broke out again soon afterward.

Given the importance of Arianism for our theme, we shall consider its ideas in some detail in the next section of the chapter. But once more, the important point to note is how the state was now deeply involved in theological disagreements. Heresy was no longer a matter for the church; it became a matter of significance for the empire. As Christianity became the established religious ideology of the Roman Empire, both orthodoxy and heresy began to assume a new status as political, almost legal, entities. The stakes were now much higher, and the problems in dealing with heresy were much greater than they had been in the past.

In this chapter, we shall examine three heresies—Arianism, Donatism, and Pelagianism—that emerged during this era, each of which had the potential to create disunity and potential division within the empire. We begin by considering what is widely regarded as the most significant heresy of the classical period—Arianism.

Arianism: The Identity of Christ

One of the greatest challenges faced by the early church was the weaving together of the threads of the New Testament witness to the identity of Jesus of Nazareth into a coherent theological tapestry. As we noted in the previous chapter, one early attempt to make sense of Jesus of Nazareth—Ebionitism—involved trying to accommodate him within existing Jewish categories. Because so many early Christians were Jewish, it seemed natural to them to explore conceptual frameworks that were already familiar—such as the category of the prophet. It became clear at a very early stage that the new wine of the Christian faith simply could not be contained by the old conceptual wineskins of Judaism. These, the church decided, failed to capture the exhilarating possibilities Christians knew to have been opened up through the life, death, and resurrection of Christ.

Christological models inherited from Judaism seemed to focus on the idea of Jesus of Nazareth as a means of endorsed communication from God. Docetic Christologies, for example, often appear to regard Jesus of Nazareth as an intermediary between humanity and God who passes on to us some signed, sealed, and authorized communication from God. Yet this revelatory emphasis could accommodate only one aspect of the significance of Jesus of Nazareth. What, for example, about his identity as savior of humanity?

Other frameworks were therefore explored to see if they could be adopted or adapted in the quest for the best way of making sense of Jesus of Nazareth *without* reducing him to theological stereotypes. One approach that seemed to hold particular promise involved making use of the notion of the *Logos*—a Greek term, extensively used in contemporary philosophy, that is often translated simply as "word" and yet has far richer associations than this simple translation might suggest. Middle Platonism saw the *Logos* as a mediating principle between the ideal and real worlds, allowing Christian theologians to explore the role of Jesus of Nazareth as mediator between God and humanity. Justin Martyr is an excellent example of a writer who found this approach helpful in communicating the significance of Jesus to secular Hellenistic culture.[9]

In the end, the church reacted decisively against any notion of Jesus of Nazareth as being God's deputy. Even the most honorific ways of thinking of Christ in such terms ended up representing him as an authorized representative of a God who was nevertheless conspicuously absent from the world into which Christ came. This way of thinking about Christ simply would not map onto the New

Testament's witness to him, nor would it map onto the church's experience of him, especially in worship.

The church came to realize that no existing analogy or model was good enough to meet its needs in expressing the significance of Jesus of Nazareth. The situation demanded that the church develop a new way of thinking rather than relying on theological hand-me-downs. So the concept of the Incarnation began to emerge as of central importance to the church's understanding of Jesus Christ.[10] While the idea was developed in slightly different ways by different writers, the basic theme is that of God entering into history and taking on a human nature in Jesus of Nazareth. This idea caused considerable philosophical difficulties for many of the prevailing schools of Hellenistic philosophy. How, many asked, could an immutable God enter into history? Surely this implied that God underwent change. Contemporary philosophers drew a sharp distinction between the unchanging heavenly realm and the changeable created order. The notion of God entering into and dwelling within this transitory and changing order seemed inconceivable, and proved a significant barrier to some cultured pagans' embracing of Christianity.

This process of exploration of religious and philosophical categories suitable for expressing the significance of Jesus of Nazareth reached a watershed in the fourth century. The controversy that forced the issue was precipitated by Arius (c. 270–336), a priest in one of the larger churches in the great Egyptian city of Alexandria. Arius set out his views in a work known as the *Thalia* ("banquet"), which has not survived in its entirety. As a result, we know Arius's ideas primarily through the writings of his opponents. This means that these extracts from his works are presented out of context, so that we do not fully understand the context in which Arius developed his ideas.

In this section, we shall try to answer four questions. First, what did Arius actually teach? Second, what factors led Arius to develop his ideas? Third, why were these ideas seen as being so dangerous that they were branded as heretical? And fourth, what process was used to make the decision that Arius's views were indeed heretical?

The fundamental themes of Arius's teachings are not in dispute, even though they are known primarily through works that cite them in order to critique them.[11] They are traditionally summarized as three basic statements, each of which needs a considerable amount of conceptual unpacking.[12]

1. The Son and the Father do not have the same essence (*ousia*).

2. The Son is a created being (*ktisma* or *poiema*), even though he is to be recognized as first and foremost among created beings in terms of origination and rank.

3. Although the Son was the creator of the worlds, and must therefore have existed before them and before all time, there was nevertheless a time when the Son did not exist.

One of the outcomes of the Arian controversy was the recognition of the futility, even theological illegitimacy, of biblical "prooftexting"—the simplistic practice of believing that a theological debate can be settled by quoting a few passages from the Bible. Arius's theological position was clearly grounded on biblical texts. For example, Proverbs 8:22 speaks of God possessing Wisdom at the beginning of creation. Christ is also described by Paul as the "first born" of the redeemed (Rom. 8:29). The point is that Arius chose to interpret these texts in a different manner from his opponents in orthodoxy. Both sides on the Arian controversy were able to amass texts that seemed to support their cases. The real question concerned the overall picture disclosed by the New Testament. Indeed, the Arian controversy can be argued to be about how an ensemble of biblical texts is to be integrated, in that each side had no difficulty in identifying individual texts that supported their position.[13] Identifying the overall pattern disclosed by those texts proved to be the decisive issue.

The most fundamental Arian belief was that Jesus Christ was not divine in any meaningful sense of the term. He was "first among the creatures"—that is, preeminent in rank, yet unquestionably a creature rather than divine. Christ, as Logos, was indeed the agent of the creation of the world, as stated in the prologue to John's Gospel. Yet the Logos was itself created by God for this purpose. The Father is thus to be regarded as existing before the Son: "There was a time when he was not." This statement places Father and Son on different levels and is consistent with Arius's rigorous insistence that the Son is a creature. Only the Father is "unbegotten"; the Son, like all other creatures, derives from this one source of being. Nevertheless, as we have noted, Arius is careful to emphasize that the Son is not like every other creature. There is a distinction of rank between the Son and other creatures, including human beings. Arius has some difficulty in identifying the precise nature of this distinction. The Son, he argued, is "a perfect creature, yet not as one among other creatures; a begotten being, yet not as one among other begotten beings."[14] The implication seems to be that the Son outranks other creatures while sharing their essentially created and begotten nature.

Arius thus draws an absolute distinction between God and the created order. There are no intermediate or hybrid species. For Arius, God was totally transcendent and immutable. So how could such a God enter into history and become incarnate? As a creature, the Son was changeable (*treptos*) and capable of moral development (*proteptos*), and subject to pain, fear, grief, and weariness. This is simply inconsistent with the notion of an immutable God. The notion of a changeable God seemed heretical to Arius. Furthermore, the notion that God the Son was divine seemed to compromise the fundamental themes of monotheism and the unity of God—themes that, of course, would reemerge as central in early Islam.

Pursuing this line of argument, Arius emphasizes that the utter transcendence and inaccessibility of God means that God cannot be known by any other creature. The Son is to be regarded as a creature, however elevated above all other creatures. Arius therefore argues that the Son cannot know the Father. "The one who has a beginning is in no position to comprehend or lay hold of the one who has no beginning."[15] The radical distinction between Father and Son is such that the latter cannot know the former unaided. In common with all other creatures, the Son is dependent upon the grace of God to perform whatever function has been ascribed to him.

Arius thus affirmed the humanity of Jesus of Nazareth, declaring that he was supreme among the creatures. Like Ebionitism, Arius declined to accept that Jesus could be said to be divine in any meaningful sense of the term. Yet Ebionitism set out to interpret the significance of Jesus within the framework of existing Jewish models of divine presence within humanity, particularly the notion of a prophet or spirit-filled individual. Arius, in contrast, sought to accommodate Jesus of Nazareth within the frameworks made available by the strict Greek philosophical monotheisms of his age, which precluded any notion of the Incarnation as inconsistent with the changelessness and transcendence of God. Ebionitism and Arianism may appear to say similar things; however, they begin from very different starting points and are guided by significantly different assumptions.

It is often suggested that Arius developed his position on the identity of Jesus of Nazareth on the basis of a preconceived philosophical position that declared that, as a matter of principle, God could not become incarnate. There is some truth in this point, but it is not quite the whole truth. Arius's concerns were partly apologetic, in that he clearly believed that many were being alienated from Christianity on account of its increasing emphasis upon an idea—the Incarnation—that educated Greeks were unable to accept. Arius saw his approach to Christianity, in contrast, as representing a measured and judicious amalgam of philosophical sophistication and responsible biblical exegesis.

So why did this strongly rational approach to the identity of Jesus of Nazareth attract such vigorous criticism? Arius's most indefatigable critic was Athanasius of Alexandria. For Athanasius, Arius had destroyed the internal coherence of the Christian faith, rupturing the close connection between Christian belief and worship.[16] There are two points of particular importance that underlie Athanasius's critique of Arius.

First, Athanasius argues that it is only God who can save. God, and God alone, can break the power of sin and bring humanity to eternal life. The fundamental characteristic of human nature is that it needs to be redeemed. No creature can save another creature. Only the creator can redeem the creation. If Christ is not God, he is part of the problem, not its solution.

Having emphasized that it is God alone who can save, Athanasius then makes the logical move that the Arians found difficult to counter. The New Testament and the Christian liturgical tradition alike regard Jesus Christ as Savior. Yet, as Athanasius emphasized, only God can save. So how are we to make sense of this? The only possible solution, Athanasius argues, is to accept that Jesus is God incarnate.

1. No creature can redeem another creature.

2. According to Arius, Jesus Christ is a creature.

3. Therefore, according to Arius, Jesus Christ cannot redeem humanity.

Arius was firmly committed to the idea that Christ was the savior of humanity;[17] Athanasius's point was not that Arius denied this, but that he rendered the claim incoherent. Salvation, for Athanasius, involves divine intervention. Athanasius thus draws out the meaning of John 1:14 by arguing that the "Word became flesh": in other words, God entered into our human situation in order to change it.

The second point that Athanasius makes is that Christians worship and pray to Jesus Christ. This pattern can be traced back to the New Testament itself, and is of considerable importance in clarifying early Christian understandings of the significance of Jesus of Nazareth.[18] By the fourth century, prayer to and adoration of Christ were standard features of Christian public worship. Athanasius argues that if Jesus Christ were a creature, then Christians would be guilty of worshipping a creature instead of God; in other words, they had lapsed into idolatry. Did not the Old Testament law explicitly prohibit the worship of anyone or anything other than God? Arius was not in disagreement with the practice of worshipping Jesus; he refused, however, to draw the same conclusions as Athanasius.

The point at issue here concerns the relationship between Christian worship and Christian belief. Orthodoxy maintains a view of the identity of Jesus Christ that is completely consistent with the worship patterns of the church. Christians, Athanasius argued, were right to worship and adore Jesus Christ, because by doing so they were recognizing him for what he was—God incarnate. If Christ were not God, it would be totally improper to worship him. If Arius was right, Christian worship would have to be drastically altered, breaking the link with the earliest patterns of Christian prayer and adoration. Arius seemed to be guilty of making the traditional way in which Christians prayed and worshipped incoherent. Though affirming the tradition of worshipping Jesus, Arius had undermined its integrity. If Arius was correct, Christians ought not to adore or pray to Christ in this way. Christ could be honored as "first among the creatures"; he should not, however, be worshipped.

We see here what we have identified as the fundamental characteristic of heresy: the maintenance of the outward appearance of faith coupled with the subversion of its inward identity. To focus only on the two points we have considered, Arius affirmed that Christ was the savior of humanity and that the church should worship him, yet he interpreted his identity in such a manner that neither salvation nor adoration was proper. Such a clear tension between theology and practice could not be sustained for long without causing their rupture.

So how was Arianism declared to be a heresy? At this point, we must return to a point made earlier—the politicization of a theological debate due to the conversion of Constantine, and the new status of Christianity as an imperial religion.[19] Constantine saw this controversy as posing a threat to the unity of the church, and hence to the unity of the empire. The stakes were now vastly greater than with any previous theological dispute. He wanted it resolved—quickly and permanently. It seemed to Constantine that because the church itself possessed multiple centers of authority in rivalry with one another, it would be unable to achieve such a resolution. Constantine therefore determined to resolve the matter in a way that would achieve political expediency and efficiency while at the same time respecting theological integrity. The evidence suggests that Constantine ultimately could have worked with either the position espoused by Athanasius or that espoused by Arius, yet he had a preference for the latter. Constantine was quite clear about his role; it was the church itself that had to decide which was right and bring the dispute to an end. His role was to bring about an unequivocal conclusion.

Constantine's method of conflict resolution was without precedence in postbiblical Christianity.[20] He summoned all the bishops of the church to a council held in Nicaea, in Bithynia (now Iznik, in modern Turkey), in May 325. It is estimated that there were around one thousand bishops in the Eastern church and eight hundred in the Western. According to Eusebius of Caesarea, who was present at the council, only two hundred and fifty bishops attended.[21] The fact that the emperor had summoned the council made it quite clear where ultimate authority lay within imperial Christianity.

This was reinforced by Constantine's decision to model the proceedings of the council on those of the Roman Senate.[22] The structures of the church were subtly being aligned with those of the state.

In the end, the council voted decisively against Arius[23] and authorized an expanded version of existing creeds that would explicitly counter Arian ideas. Some bishops had wanted to retain older, more open-ended creeds; in the end, however, the majority voted for more explicit rejections of Arius's teaching. Much debate developed over possible descriptions of the relation of the Father to the Son. The term *homoiousios,* "of like substance" or "of like being," was seen by many as allowing the proximity and intimacy between Father and Son to be asserted without requiring any further speculation on the precise nature of their relation. However, the rival term *homoousios,* "of the same substance" or "of the same being," eventually gained the upper hand at Nicaea. In his final address, bringing the council to a close, Constantine once more emphasized his aversion to divisive theological controversy; he wanted the church to live in harmony and peace, and contribute to the stability of the empire. Sadly, such tranquillity proved elusive, and the discordances of the Arian controversy rumbled on for some time before any degree of resolution can be said to have been achieved.

Although the Council of Nicaea decisively rejected Arianism, the historical evidence clearly suggests that this was Constantine's preferred option.[24] What reasons might lie behind this preference? One celebrated answer to this question was put forward by the German scholar Erik Peterson (1890–1960) in 1935. In a detailed study of the political implications of monotheism within the Roman Empire, Peterson pointed out that monotheism entails a single legitimate political authority.[25] There is, Peterson argued, a direct analogy between the idea of the total cosmological authority of a single God (a principle often expressed in the term *monarchia*) and the total political authority of a single ruler. Arianism endorsed the notion of the divine *monarchia,* thus lending theological support to the notion of the supreme political and religious authority of Constantine in the Roman Empire.

Yet as Peterson further pointed out, both the orthodox doctrine of the identity of Christ and the doctrine of the Trinity undermined any such monotheistic political theology. Why? Because both insisted that there was no earthly analogy to the divine authority, thus robbing the notion of absolute imperial authority of its theological legitimation. While the accuracy and validity of Peterson's historical analysis have come in for serious criticism in recent years,[26] a number of leading theologians—most notably Jürgen Moltmann— have championed the notion that absolute monotheisms, such as that proposed by Arius, provide a theological foundation for political authoritarianism.[27]

So what would Christianity have looked like if Arius had won? It needs to be made clear that what Arius was proposing was not a minor rearrangement of the theological furniture of the Christian faith, to be compared with adjusting the position or changing the color of a favored chair in the living room. Arius's understanding of the identity of Christ differed so greatly from that proposed by Athanasius and the orthodox that it can only be regarded as constituting a separate religion. Arian Christianity is much closer to Islam than to orthodox Christianity, in relation both to its notion of God and to its understanding of the religious role of its founder. Its concept of absolute divine *monarchia* has important political associations in that it points to an analogy of absolute authority on earth and in heaven.

Most important, Arianism emphasized the inscrutability of God. There was an absolute ontological gulf between God and the world of the creatures. Christ, himself a creature, did not have direct knowledge of God and was thus unable to mediate a direct, reliable, and authoritative revelation of God. God's will might be known, albeit circumspectly; God's face remained averted and unknown. The Arian notion of divine revelation is similar to that found in Islam, raising significant questions about the authority and competency of the revealer to disclose the revealed.

Christian orthodoxy offered a theological framework that authorized Christ to reveal God and provided a secure link between the revealer and the revealed. To put it somewhat abruptly: if Christ is God, then Christ can disclose both what God is like and what God wants. The face and will of God are both made accessible on account of an incarnational vision of God and the Nicene interpretation of the identity of Jesus Christ. For Arius, Christ cannot be held to "be" God in any meaningful sense of the term; furthermore, Christ cannot even be held to "know" God directly. Like all creatures, he knows God indirectly and at second hand, in a manner that may exceed that of other human beings in terms of quantity yet not in quality.

Orthodoxy understood Christ as the mediator between God and humanity, and appreciated that his "dual nature" as truly divine and truly human was a means of ensuring that this bridge was secure. Only God could disclose the face and will of God to humanity; only God could save humanity. The Nicene account of the identity of Jesus Christ safeguarded the actuality of both revelation and salvation. Arianism, however, offered a bridge that failed to extend sufficiently far to reach its divine goal—and by failing to connect with God, it was unable to permit humanity either reliable and authentic knowledge of God or the salvation promised by the gospel. For Arius, Christ had no direct knowledge of God, mediating a secondhand knowledge of God that may have been superior in quality to that of other human beings but was nevertheless equal in kind.

Arius and his supporters made it clear that they believed that Jesus of Nazareth did reveal God, and insisted that it was proper to speak of Christianity as a religion of salvation. Yet the conceptual framework that they proposed for understanding both the nature of God and the identity of Christ ultimately made these ideas incoherent and unstable. Arianism subverted some core themes of the Christian proclamation, offering aspirations where orthodoxy offered actualities, a shadow in place of a reality. The Christian vision of the risen Christ, glimpsed from time to time in all its fullness, radiance, and glory, proves remarkably difficult to express in the right words and with the right ideas. And the words and ideas used by Arius were finally judged to have failed in this respect. Instead, a new vocabulary and a new set of ideas were demanded to do justice to the reality of Christ. Dorothy L. Sayers (1893–1957) made this point with great force, and her words remain relevant to any discussion of this point:

> The central dogma of the Incarnation is that by which relevance stands or falls. If Christ was only man, then He is entirely irrelevant to any thought about God; if He is only God, then He is entirely irrelevant to any experience of human life. It is, in the strictest sense, necessary to the salvation of relevance that a man should believe rightly the Incarnation of Our Lord Jesus Christ.[28]

Donatism: The Nature of the Church

The second major heresy that we shall consider in this chapter is known as *Donatism,* and concerns some aspects of the church and sacraments.[29] As we noted earlier, under the Roman emperor Diocletian (284–313), the Christian church was subject to various degrees of harassment and persecution. Although the historical evidence is not totally secure, there are reasons for suggesting that a "culture of martyrdom" developed within the African church in response to this wave of persecution, with its members deliberately courting both persecution and execution at the hands of the Roman authorities.[30]

This caused some controversy within the African church. Mensurius, bishop of Carthage, and his archdeacon Caecilianus took a robust stand against what they regarded as a fanatical craving for martyrdom. Others, however, saw this as tantamount to encouraging collaboration with the Roman authorities who persecuted them.

Feelings ran high. An issue of especial importance concerned Christian leaders who had surrendered their sacred texts to the authorities. Under an edict of February 303, Christian leaders were ordered to hand over their books to be burned. Those Christian leaders who handed over their books to be destroyed in this way came to be known as *traditores*—"those who handed over [their books]."[31] Tensions ran high between *traditores* and those who idealized martyrdom.[32] Mensurius himself was accused of being a *traditor* by his critics, although he himself maintained he had merely handed over some heretical works he happened to have at hand and never surrendered any sacred texts.

With the accession of Constantine, the persecution came to an end. But a sensitive issue arose in its aftermath: how were those who had lapsed or otherwise compromised themselves during the persecution to be treated? The problem was especially acute in the case of Christian leaders who had lapsed under pressure. Some took a hard line, demanding their expulsion; Mensurius, however, had taken a generous and lenient line toward those who had lapsed during his lifetime. Because the bishop of Carthage was widely accepted as the senior bishop in Africa, his views on the matter had a significant impact on how the matter was viewed.

Mensurius died in 311. So who would succeed him? Hard-liners, headed by a wealthy and influential widow named Lucilla, and the bishops of Numidia wanted him replaced with one sympathetic to the martyr cult, who would take a hard line toward those who had lapsed. The Numidians represented an ancient Berber kingdom, occupied by the Romans, with nationalistic aspirations. In the eyes of the Numidian bishops, Mensurius had been too sympathetic to the Roman colonists. It was time, in their view, for a Numidian to become bishop of Carthage and give a firm moral lead to the church.

The more moderate faction, aware of the situation, decided to move quickly and elected Caecilianus as bishop before the Numidian delegation could arrive. The consecration of Caecilianus was carried out by three bishops, including Felix, bishop of Aptunga—a *traditor*. Many local Christians were outraged that such a person should have been allowed to be involved in this consecration and declared that they could not accept the authority of Caecilianus as a result. The Numidian bishops refused to recognize his consecration and demanded a fresh election, arguing that the new bishop's authority was compromised on account of the fact that the bishop who had consecrated him had lapsed under the pressure of persecution. The hierarchy of the Catholic Church was thus tainted as a result of this development. The church ought to be pure and should not be permitted to include such people. The Numidian bishops demanded that Caecilianus appear before them to defend his election and consecration. When he failed to do so, the rigorists deposed and excommunicated him and appointed Majorinus in his place. Majorinus died in 313 and was replaced by Donatus the Great, who commanded substantial local support. In the end, Constantine found himself dragged into the controversy and declared in favor of Caecilianus. The North African church broke into two parties, the larger of which followed Donatus.

The controversy was fueled by the ambivalences and tensions within the theology of a leading figure of the African church in the third century—the martyred bishop Cyprian of Carthage. In his *Unity of the Catholic Church* (251), Cyprian had insisted upon two fundamental principles.[33] First, schism is totally and absolutely unjustified. The unity of the church cannot be broken, no matter what the pretext or occasion. To step outside the bounds of the church is to forfeit any possibility of salvation. For Cyprian, "there is no salvation outside the church."[34]

Second, it follows from this that lapsed or schismatic bishops should be deprived by the church of any right to administer the sacraments or act as a minister of the Christian church. By choosing to stand outside the sphere of the church, they have lost their spiritual gifts and authority. They should therefore not be permitted to ordain anyone. Furthermore, anyone whom they have baptized, ordained, or consecrated must be regarded as in need of rebaptism, reordination, or reconsecration.

Yet the situation following the easing of the Diocletian persecution raised a serious problem. Just what should happen if a bishop lapses under persecution and subsequently repents? Cyprian's theory turned out to be somewhat ambiguous on this point, being open to two quite different lines of interpretation. First, that by lapsing, the bishop has committed the sin of apostasy (literally, "falling away"). He has therefore placed himself outside the bounds of the church and can no longer be regarded as administering the sacraments validly. Second, that by his repentance, the bishop has been restored to grace and is able to continue administering the sacraments validly. The Donatists adopted the first position; the Catholics (as their opponents came to be universally known), the second.

The Donatists believed that the entire sacramental system of the Catholic Church had become corrupted on account of the lapse of its leaders. How could the sacraments be validly administered by people who were tainted in this way? It was therefore necessary to replace these people with more acceptable leaders, who had remained firm in their faith under persecution. It was also necessary to rebaptize and reordain all those who had been baptized and ordained by those who had lapsed.

It will be obvious that a legitimate theological debate was rendered much more complex and nuanced by its political associations and overtones in the early fourth century. The Donatists tended to be indigenous Berbers, while the Catholics tended to be Roman colonists. Those who urged generosity and toleration toward *traditores* were thus generally supportive of Roman imperial rule in the region. Given the ethnic complexities of late antique Roman Africa,[35] and the nationalist and anticolonial sentiments that smoldered in the region, it was inevitable that theological agendas found alignment with political tensions. It has often been suggested that heretical movements are linked with suppressed nationalisms.[36] While it would clearly be incorrect to suggest that any given heresy is simply a social or national movement transposed into a theological key, there are excellent reasons for arguing that a theological approach could easily become associated with a social or political agenda.

The issues were still alive nearly a century later, when Augustine was consecrated bishop of Hippo in Roman North Africa in 396.[37] Augustine responded to the Donatist challenge by putting forward a theory of the church that he believed was more firmly grounded in the New Testament than the Donatist teaching. In particular, Augustine emphasized the *sinfulness of Christians.* The church is not meant to be a "pure body," a society of saints, but a "mixed body" (*corpus permixtum*) of saints and sinners.[38] Augustine finds this image in two biblical parables: the parable of the net that catches many fish, and the parable of the wheat and the weeds (or "tares," to use an older word familiar to readers of the King James Bible). It is this latter parable (Matt. 13:24–31) that is of especial importance, and requires further discussion.

The parable tells of a farmer who sowed seed and discovered that the resulting crop included both wheat and weeds. What could be done about it? To attempt to separate the wheat and the weeds while both are still growing would be to court disaster, probably involving damaging the wheat while trying to get rid of the weeds. But at the harvest, all the plants—whether wheat or weeds—are cut down and sorted out, thus avoiding damaging the wheat. The separation of the good and the evil thus takes place at the end of time, not in history. For Augustine, this parable refers to the church in the world. It must expect to find itself including both saints and sinners. To attempt a separation in this world is premature and improper. That separation will take place in God's own time, at the end of history. No human can make that judgment or separation in God's place.

A related biblical passage concerns John the Baptist's prediction that Jesus of Nazareth will bring a judgment that can be compared to a threshing floor (Matt. 3:11–12). Both the wheat and chaff lie on the threshing floor and are to be separated. So how is this to be interpreted? Two very different approaches emerged.[39] For the Donatists, the threshing floor referred to the world at large, containing both wheat and chaff. The process of separation led to the emergence of the church as the community of the pure; the chaff remained in the world. For Augustine, the church itself was the threshing floor, in that its members included both wheat and chaff.

So in what sense can the church meaningfully be designated as "holy"? For Augustine, the holiness in question is not that of its members, but of Christ. The church cannot be a congregation of saints in this world, in that its members are contaminated with original sin. However, the church is sanctified and made holy by Christ—a holiness that will be perfected and finally realized at the Last Judgment. In addition to offering this theological analysis of holiness, Augustine slyly noted that the Donatists failed to live up to their own high standards of morality. They were, he suggested, just as capable as their opponents of moral lapses.

Augustine made a similar point in connection with the theology of the sacraments. For the Donatists, sacraments—such as baptism and the Eucharist or Lord's Supper—were effective only if they were administered by someone of unquestionable moral and doctrinal purity. This attitude can be seen in a letter written in 402 by Petilian, the Donatist bishop of Cirta, to Augustine, which sets out at some length the Donatist insistence that the validity of the sacraments is totally dependent upon the moral worthiness of those who administer them.

Responding to this, Augustine argued that Donatism laid excessive emphasis upon the qualities of the human agent and gave insufficient weight to the grace of Jesus Christ. It is, he argued, impossible for fallen human beings to make distinctions concerning who is pure and impure, worthy and unworthy: This view, which is totally consistent with his understanding of the church as a "mixed body" of saints and sinners, holds that the efficacy of a sacrament rests not upon the merits of the individual administering it but upon the merits of the one who instituted them in the first place—Jesus Christ. The validity of sacraments is thus independent of the merits of those who administer them. There may be a pastoral advantage to the sacraments being administered by someone of unblemished reputation, but there is no theological necessity for this. Christ is the ultimate guarantor of the efficacy of the sacraments; the minister plays only a secondary and subordinate role.

So why did Donatism come to be regarded as a heresy rather than merely as a mistaken opinion? Why not treat it as a simple misunderstanding or overreaction, whose origins can easily be explained in terms of the complex social and political situation faced by the Christian church in Roman North Africa in the fourth century?[40] The best way of understanding the threat posed by Donatism is to look closely at its understanding of the nature of the church, and the benefits that its sacraments offer to believers.

Donatus and his followers insisted that the efficacy of the church and its sacramental system was dependent upon the moral or cultic purity of its representatives. The grace and healing power of the Christian gospel was thus understood to be contingent upon the purity of the church and its ministers. For Augustine, this amounted to making salvation indirectly dependent upon human purity rather than the grace of Christ. Ministers and sacraments were merely the channels, not the cause, of the grace of God. Donatism threatened to make the salvation of humanity dependent upon holy human agents rather than upon the death and resurrection of Jesus Christ. Christ thus plays a secondary role in either the securing or sustaining of salvation, whereas the human agent plays a primary role of crucial importance.

We see here a major theme of Augustine's understanding of the Christian faith: that human nature is fallen, wounded, and frail, standing in need of the healing and restoring grace of God. The church, according to Augustine, is more to be compared to a hospital than to a club of healthy people. It is a place of healing for people who know that they stand in need of forgiveness and renewal. The

Christian life is a process of being healed from sin rather than a life of sinlessness—the cure completed and the patient restored to full health. The church is an infirmary for the sick and for convalescents. It is only in heaven that we will finally be righteous and healthy.

The Donatist approach represents a principled yet ultimately dogmatic refusal to appreciate that all of humanity—including priests and bishops—is in need of the same healing that the gospel provides. The ministers of the Christian church proclaim the same healing that they themselves require. They are to be considered as spiritual convalescents who are able to administer to others the same salves and medicines that have set them on the road to recovery but have yet to heal them fully.

We could say, then, that while the Donatist heresy appears to concern our understanding of the church and sacraments, it is more deeply rooted in a flawed understanding of human nature, which ultimately makes the ministration of grace dependent on human merit rather than divine grace. A similar issue arose during the Pelagian controversy, to which we now turn.

Pelagianism: Human Nature and Divine Grace

We introduced Augustine of Hippo in the previous section; some more needs to be said about him, in that he features prominently in the Pelagian debate, to be considered in this section. Augustine was born in 354 in the town of Thagaste, now known as Souk-Ahras, in Roman North Africa, to a pagan father and Christian mother. Perhaps wearied through by the attempts of his mother, Monica, to convert him to Christianity, Augustine fled to Rome and pursued a career in the Roman imperial administration.

Augustine recounts his spiritual pilgrimage in his *Confessions,* a work that mingles autobiography with theological reflection. Augustine relates how, through a series of apparent happenstances, he found himself brought to a point at which he found himself impelled toward the Christian faith.[41] Augustine's moment of crisis came in August 386, while he was sitting under a fig tree in the garden of his house at Milan, troubled by his apparent inability to master his lower nature. As he ruminated over his weaknesses and failures, he heard some children playing in a neighboring garden, singing "Take up and read! Take up and read!" Augustine rushed indoors, opened his New Testament at random, and read the verses that seemed to leap out at him from the page: "Clothe yourselves with the Lord Jesus Christ, and do not think about how to gratify the desires of your lower nature" (Rom. 13:14). He closed the book and told his friends he had become a Christian.

Yet Augustine was convinced that this conversion was not a matter of his own choosing. As he reflected on the apparent happenstances that led him to faith, he became convinced that he discerned the grace of God preceding him at every point, nudging him toward the critical moment of conversion. Time and time again, Augustine interrupts his account of his career in his *Confessions* to praise God for the way in which his hand has been at work in his life. Augustine frequently expresses his profound sense of being totally dependent upon the mercy of God: "My whole hope is only in your mercy. Give what you command, and command what you will."[42] For Augustine, a sinful and fractured humanity was totally dependent upon a gracious and loving God, just as a wounded and damaged patient was dependent upon the ministrations of a caring and competent physician.

While Augustine mused contentedly upon the graciousness of the God whom he had found so late in life, others were finding his words distinctly uncomfortable, perhaps even unhelpful. One of the less appreciative readers of Augustine's *Confessions* was Pelagius (c. 355–c. 435), a British monk who had embarked on a reforming crusade within the Roman church. Pelagius, we must note, is a figure in church history who evokes strong reactions. The noted patristic scholar Robert Evans comments: "Pelagius is one of the most maligned figures in the history of Christianity. It has been the common sport of the theologian and the historian of theology to set him up as the symbolic bad man and to heap upon him accusations which often tell us more about the perspective of the accuser than about Pelagius."[43] While conceding the danger of prejudicial stereotyping, it remains important that we identify Pelagius's core ideas and understand their origins and motivation as well as the reaction they provoked on the part of others. This is not entirely easy, as Pelagianism is prone to a degree of theological vagueness,[44] the emphasis falling upon the need for moral renewal rather than theological precision.

A further complication concerns the variegated nature of Pelagianism itself, which is best regarded as an amalgam of the ideas of several writers—primarily Pelagius himself, Caelestius, and Rufinus of Syria,[45] but also the later writer Julian of Eclanum. Pelagianism certainly included some ideas and emphases deriving from Pelagius; yet, other ideas linked with the movement owe their origins to others. For example, Pelagianism's views on mortality and the transmission of sin appear to owe more to Caelestius and Rufinus than to Pelagius.[46]

Pelagius set out to reform the church, emphasizing that all people possess a God-given power to improve themselves.[47] Similar ideas had been advanced around this time by other writers, including Rufinus, who arrived at Rome in 399 as Jerome's representative at a theological debate concerning the ideas of Origen.[48] Also present in Rome at this time was Caelestius, who advocated the following ideas:

1. Adam's sin harmed only himself, not the human race as a whole.

2. Children are born in the same state as Adam before his fall.

3. The Law of Moses is just as good at leading us to heaven as the gospel of Christ.

It was perhaps inevitable that a degree of confluence between the ideas and approaches of these three writers should take place, yielding the composite set of ideas of Pelagianism, which is best regarded as an amalgam of related ideas deriving from different sources. The notion that there was a coherent movement termed Pelagianism, linked specifically with the writer Pelagius, seems largely due to Augustine. Yet there is growing evidence that this may have been a rhetorical construction on Augustine's part, in which a composite and complex series of beliefs and attitudes, only some of which are due to Pelagius, were represented as if they were a coherent movement focusing on Pelagius himself.

A more cautious interpretation of the historical evidence suggests not only that Pelagius did not hold some of the theological positions that are traditionally attributed to him, but also that Pelagius was rather more concerned with encouraging exemplary Christian moral behavior than indulging in theological speculation. Pelagius is better seen as a reforming activist and pragmatist rather than a theologian. The elaboration of a theological system that arguably encouraged and undergirded such behavior was due more to Caelestius and Rufinus.[49] The outcome of this is a degree of difficulty in distinguishing Pelagius's personal theological views from those that emerged from the informal network that is usually termed "Pelagianism." The assumption that "Pelagianism" refers to the views of Pelagius turns out to be rather less secure than earlier generations had appreciated.

The origins of the Pelagian controversy are traditionally held to date from 405,[50] when Pelagius read Augustine's words "Give what you command, and command what you will." These words, which we considered earlier (see p. 160), caused him considerable offense. They seemed to strike at the heart of his reforming program, denying the human right and obligation to seek perfection. And so the Pelagian controversy began, even though the ideas and attitudes that lay behind Pelagianism had emerged beforehand. This was a complex debate, touching on a number of issues.[51] However, for our purposes, it will be helpful to focus on two of its major themes: the dynamics of the human situation, and the nature of divine grace. In each case, Pelagianism developed an essentially coherent vision of the Christian life that differed significantly from that proposed by Augustine.

We begin by considering the issue of human nature. Pelagianism insisted that human beings are completely free in all their actions, holding that some such belief was the essential prerequisite for moral action and spiritual renewal. The behavior of human beings is not influenced significantly by hidden forces, nor is it restricted by powers that ultimately lie beyond their control.[52] We are the masters of our own destiny. If we are told to stop sinning, we can stop sinning. Sin is something that we can and must resist. In many ways, Pelagianism developed views similar to those expressed in the last stanza of William Ernest Henley's poem "Invictus" (1875), a great favorite in the Victorian age:

> *It matters not how strait the gate,*
> *How charged with punishment the scroll.*
> *I am the master of my fate:*
> *I am the captain of my soul!*

For Pelagianism, God has given us the Ten Commandments and the example of Jesus Christ, and believers should live according to them. The significance of Christ is to be located primarily in his teaching and example.

So, can human beings actually live up to these elevated standards? According to Pelagianism, any imperfection in human nature that might stop us from acting morally could reflect badly on God. After all, God made us in the first place. To suggest that something is fundamentally wrong with human nature means that God did not create humanity particularly well. Pelagius himself set out this idea in a letter to Demetrias, a Roman woman of high social standing:

[Instead of regarding God's commands as a privilege,] we cry out at God and say, "This is too hard! This is too difficult! We cannot do it! We are only human, and hindered by the weakness of the flesh!" What blind madness! What blatant presumption! By doing this, we accuse the God of knowledge of a twofold ignorance—ignorance of his own creation and of his own commands. It would be as if, forgetting the weakness of humanity—God's own creation—God had laid upon us commands which we were unable to bear. . . . No one knows the extent of our strength better than the God who gave us that strength. . . . God has not willed to command anything impossible, for God is righteous; and will not condemn anyone for what they could not help.[53]

It is clear that Pelagius had many supporters at Rome, such as Demetrias, who saw his reforms as little more than sanctified common sense.[54] What exactly was the problem with demanding moral improvement from people? The idea was developed further by Julian of Eclanum (c. 386–c. 455), who set out what was virtually a gospel of self-improvement adapted to the norms of Roman culture.[55] The result was that Pelagianism resonated strongly with many in Rome at this time, offering a sophisticated vision of self-improvement with a strong spiritual core.

The consonance between Pelagianism and Roman cultural norms also emphasized that Augustine was an outsider to Roman society. A perception appears to have developed that Augustine of Hippo represented a rather provincial African approach to theology that was inferior to the more urbane and cosmopolitan theology of Rome itself. The insight that Augustine was one of Christendom's greatest thinkers may be evident to modern readers; however, this was not a judgment that was shared by his contemporaries at Rome, some of whom appear to have seen his theology as provincial—even parochial—and lacking cultural credibility. Some went further and hinted that Augustine's theology was tainted with Manichean fatal-ism; others, that it failed to take into account the sophisticated theological riches of the Eastern church, which were then gaining increasing attention and influence in Rome.[56]

For Augustine, Pelagian views on human nature, far from being culturally sophisticated, were theologically naive and bore little relation to either the New Testament teaching or human experience. Augustine's fundamental belief is that human nature, although created without any problems, is contaminated by sin as a result of the fall.[57] There is a fatal, even tragic flaw in human nature, one that is not itself the outcome of divine creation. Augustine develops the image of the "fall" to designate a fundamental defection of humanity from the trajectory mapped out for it by God at creation. The Genesis creation accounts make it abundantly clear that God created us well. Yet as a result of this "fall," Augustine insists, human nature is characterized by a bias toward sin and away from God. Fallen human beings thus have an inbuilt tendency to sin.

Augustine thus affirms natural human freedom, in that we do not do things out of any necessity but as a matter of freedom. Yet at the same time, he insists that we recognize our freedom's limitations. Human free will has been weakened and incapacitated—but not eliminated or destroyed—through sin. In order for that free will to be restored and healed, it requires the operation of divine grace. In order to explain this point, Augustine deploys the analogy of a pair of scales with two balance pans. One balance pan represents good, and the other evil. If the pans were properly balanced, Augustine points out, the arguments in favor of doing good or doing evil could be weighed and a proper conclusion drawn. The parallel with human free will is obvious: we weigh up the arguments in favor of doing good and evil, and act accordingly. But what, asks Augustine, if the balance pans are loaded? What happens if someone puts several heavy weights in the balance pan on the side of evil? The scales will still work, but they are seriously biased toward making an evil decision.

Augustine argues that human free will is now biased toward evil. The balance of free will really exists, and really can make decisions—just as the loaded scales still work. But instead of giving a balanced judgment, a serious bias exists toward evil. Using this and related analogies, Augustine argues that human free will really exists in sinners but is compromised by sin. Augustine declares that we have no control over our sinfulness. It is something that contaminates our lives from birth and dominates our lives thereafter. Augustine understands humanity to be born with a sinful disposition as part of human nature, with an inherent bias toward acts of sinning. In other words, sin causes sins: the state of sinfulness causes individual acts of sin.

Augustine develops this point using a series of analogies—original sin as a "disease," as a "power," and as "guilt." Sin is like a hereditary disease that is passed down from one generation to another. It weakens humanity, and it cannot be cured by human agency. Christ is understood as the divine physician, by whose "wounds we are healed" (Isa. 53:5), and salvation is understood in essentially sanative or medical terms. We are healed by the grace of God so that our minds may recognize God and our wills may respond to the divine offer of grace. Or again, sin is like a power that holds us captive and from whose grip we are unable to break free by ourselves. Human free will is captivated by the power of sin and may be liberated only by grace. Christ is thus seen as the liberator, the source of the grace that breaks the power of sin. Or thirdly, sin is a type of guilt or moral impurity that is passed down from one generation to another. Christ thus comes to bring forgiveness and pardon.

For Pelagianism, however, sin was to be understood in a very different light. The idea of a human disposition toward sin has no place in Pelagianism, which affirmed that it was always possible for humans to discharge their obligations toward God and their neighbors. Failure to do so could not be excused on any grounds. Pelagianism thus seems at times to amount to a rather rigid form of moral authoritarianism—an insistence that humanity is under obligation to be sinless, and an absolute rejection of any excuse for failure. Humanity is born sinless and sins only through deliberate actions. Pelagius insisted that many Old Testament figures actually remained sinless. For Pelagius, only those who were morally upright could be allowed to enter the church—note the important parallels with Donatism here—whereas Augustine, with his concept of fallen human nature, was happy to regard the church as a hospital where fallen humanity could recover and grow gradually in holiness through grace.

Augustine's view of human nature is that it is frail, weak, and lost, and needs divine assistance and care if it is to be restored and renewed. Grace, according to Augustine, is God's generous and quite unmerited attention to humanity, by which this process of healing may begin. Human nature requires transformation through the grace of God, so generously given:

> Human nature was originally created blameless and without any fault; but the human nature by which each one of us is now born of Adam requires a physician, because it is not healthy. All the good things, which it has by its conception, life, senses, and mind, it has from God, its creator and maker. But the weakness which darkens and disables these good natural qualities, as a result of which that nature needs enlightenment and healing, did not come from the blameless maker but from original sin.[58]

Pelagianism interpreted the term "grace" in a very different way. In the first place, grace is to be understood as referring to the natural human faculties. For Pelagius, these are not corrupted or incapacitated or compromised in any way.[59] They have been given to humanity by God, and they are meant to be used. When Pelagius asserted that humanity could, through grace, choose to be sinless, what he meant was that the natural human faculties of reason and

will should enable humanity to choose to avoid sin. As Augustine
was quick to point out, this is not what the New Testament understands by the term. Furthermore, why did Christians pray to God
unless it was to acknowledge dependence upon him?[60]

Secondly, we must consider the nature of divine grace. Pelagianism understood grace to be primarily external guidance or enlightenment provided for humanity by God. When God demands that
we must be perfect, he does not leave us in the dark about what
he wants us to do. Grace refers to God's guidance concerning
what he wants us to do and be. Pelagius gave several examples of
such guidance—for example, the Ten Commandments and the
moral example of Jesus Christ. Grace informs us as to what our
moral duties are (otherwise, we would not know what they were);
it does not, however, assist us in performing them. We are enabled
to avoid sin through the teaching and example of Christ. God does
not just demand that human beings should be perfect; God provides certain specific guidance as to what form of perfection is
required—such as keeping the Ten Commandments and becoming like Christ. As one modern scholar has summarized the Pelagian approach:

> God "helps" by revealing in Scripture the wisdom pertinent to
> human nature and its obligations to God. Revelation illumines
> the mind, stirs the will, thus lifting the veil of ignorance and
> the moral paralysis inflicted by the prolonged habits of the
> sinful heart. We can summarize by saying that grace means to
> Pelagius the following: (1) the original endowment of free will
> by which one may live sinlessly, (2) the moral Law of Moses,
> (3) the forgiveness of sins won by Christ's redemptive death
> and mediated through baptism, (4) the example of Christ, and
> (5) the teaching of Christ, as a new law and as wisdom con-
> cerning human nature and salvation. Pelagius has no doctrine
> of grace other than this.[61]

Augustine argued that Pelagianism was obliged "to locate the grace of God in the law and in teaching." The New Testament, according to Augustine, envisaged grace as divine assistance to humanity rather than just moral guidance. For Pelagius, grace was something external and passive, something outside us. Augustine understood grace as the real and redeeming presence of God in Christ within us, transforming us—something that was internal and active.

For Augustine, humanity was created good by God and proceeded to defect from him. God, in an act of grace, then came to rescue fallen humanity from its predicament. God assists us by healing us, enlightening us, strengthening us, and continually working within us in order to restore us. For Pelagius, humanity merely needed to be shown what to do and could then be left to achieve it unaided; for Augustine, humanity needed to be shown what to do and then gently aided at every point if this objective was even to be approached, let alone fulfilled.

The differences between Augustine and Pelagius concern the human situation on the one hand and the nature of divine salvation on the other. For Augustine, humanity is damaged, wounded, and seriously ill. There is no point in demanding that humanity improve itself when the essence of its condition is that it is trapped in its predicament. Augustine took the view that Pelagius was in denial about the human situation. Pelagius's naive approach, though unquestionably well intentioned, could be compared to ordering a blind man to see things properly. Spiritual healing, not moral direction, is required.

Augustine's understanding of the situation can be seen, for example, in his commentary on Christ's command to the paralytic at the Pool of Bethesda: "Arise, take up your bed, and walk" (John 5:6–9). Augustine interprets the text as "Arise! Take up your bed, and walk."[62] An affirmation of the actuality of healing ("Arise!") is thus followed by two commands that would have been impossible prior to the curing of the paralytic but that now publicly demonstrate the reality of his healing and transformation. But if the paralytic had not been healed, he could not have picked up his bed and walked. Pelagius commands the paralyzed to take up their beds and walk, yet offers no means by which these commands can enter within the bounds of human possibility. It is comparable to ordering a blind person to see. The Pelagian gospel demands perfection and offers guidance as to what form it should take. Yet, Augustine insists, it fails to address either the reality of the human predicament or the inner transformative potential of divine grace. For that reason, Augustine holds that Pelagianism is really no gospel at all. Pelagianism is essentially a theologically naive moralism.

Yet Pelagianism continues to be a deep influence on Western culture, even if its name means little to most. It articulates one of the most natural of human thoughts—that we are capable of taking control of ourselves and transforming ourselves into what we would have ourselves be.[63] There is a clear link, which often passed unnoticed,[64] between the Pelagian view of humanity and the Donatist view of the church. Both rest on the belief that we can become what we believe we ought to be. There is no place for failure or weakness, and still less for other human traits that point to our frailty. Both set out demands for an idealized humanity—and hence idealized Christian believers—that simply cannot be achieved in practice. Pelagianism held that we can be perfect, Donatism that true believers would never crack under persecution. The New Testament, however, seems to suggest a more realistic view of human nature: "The spirit is willing, but the flesh is weak." How does the behavior of Peter in denying Jesus in the courtyard of the High Priest (Mark 14:27–31, 66–72) fit into a Pelagian view of human nature or a Donatist view of the capacity of Christian leaders? It is no accident that Augustine chose to fight both Donatism and Pelagianism, rightly discerning that they were the two sides of the same theological coin.

∙ ∙ ∙

In this chapter, we have explored some of the themes of three major heresies of the later patristic era. Not one of them can conceivably be considered as the outcome of malice, egotism, or some kind of personal theological depravity. Arianism, Donatism, and Pelagianism all rest on serious attempts to engage major points of religious and spiritual importance. All reflect the noble motives of those concerned to defend the Christian faith as they understood it. Nor can they be dismissed simply as perverse misrepresentations of the Bible or the Christian tradition. All three grounded themselves in the Bible—though admittedly focusing on a "canon within a canon," a group of texts that suited their needs and agendas better than others.

Each group made points of importance, often in response to weaknesses or inadequacies within prevailing patterns of Christian orthodoxy. Yet these are indications of the need for possible correction of orthodoxy at points, not its rejection. As John Henry Newman pointed out in his *Essay on the Development of Doctrine* (1846), debate and criticism are catalysts that lead to the crystallization of orthodoxy around its core themes.

The problem lay not with the motivations of an Arius, Donatus, or Pelagius, but rather with the outcomes of their voyages of theological exploration. While undertaken with the best of intentions, those voyages had, the church concluded, turned out to be dead ends, impoverished and distorted versions of the Christian faith that could not be endorsed by the community of faith as a whole.

Yet such theological exploration was not limited to the patristic era; it continues throughout Christian history until today, as theologians and church leaders continue to quest for the most authentic means of expressing the gospel, especially in the light of local and global cultural changes. Some of these new approaches will turn out to be fruitful and persuasive and have long-term value for the churches; others will prove to be dead ends. The issues explored in these two chapters must never be seen as part of the early church's history that now has no relevance to today. Far from it: the journey continues.

This means that we need to give careful consideration to the intellectual and cultural motivations for heresy. These pressures, evident in the patristic era, remain embedded in the contemporary church. We shall consider these in more detail in the following chapter.

part four

The Enduring Impact of Heresy

eight

Cultural and Intellectual Motivations for Heresy

How are the origins of heresy to be understood? What are the motivating concerns that led to its emergence? Early Christian writers offered a variety of explanations for the origins of heresy: heretics were driven by personal ambitions, ecclesiastical jealousies, a naive enthusiasm for philosophical speculation, or an inflated sense of their own theological genius. Yet despite the fulminations of some early Christian heresiologists such as Tertullian, there are no real grounds for supposing that heresy was the outcome of malevolent and arrogant apostates plotting to destroy Christianity by reckless, eccentric biblical interpretation and driven by a paganizing agenda.

This older stereotype is found in most nineteenth-century accounts of heresy written by stalwart supporters of orthodoxy. For John Henry Newman (1801–90), heresy was a phenomenon whose origins lay outside of the church. Arianism, for example, was an ungodly byproduct of its environment, combining the worst elements of pagan culture, particularly Judaism and syncretistic philosophy.[1] For H. M. Gwatkin (1844–1916), Arianism was "an illogical compromise" between Christianity and paganism, tipping the balance in favor of paganism. It was "a mass of presumptuous theorizing" that was "utterly illogical and unspiritual."[2] Subsequent scholarship has raised troubling difficulties for such assertions, especially in relation to the motivation of those considered heretics. While it is notoriously difficult to psychologize the dead, the idea that the essential "person description" of a heretic includes obstinacy and arrogance, supplemented by some degree of mental incompetence and institutional disloyalty, seems to bear little relation to what is known of early heretics.

The historical evidence, though not unequivocally clear on this matter, suggests that we should think of heresies as the outcomes of journeys of exploration that were originally intended to enable Christianity to relate better to contemporary culture. Heresy arose through a desire to preserve, not to destroy, the gospel. In this chapter, I propose to set to one side the idea that the movements that came to be identified as heresies owed their origins primarily to perversion or malevolence, and to explore the more disturbing notion that heresies might originate instead from natural, well-intentioned, and essentially benign motivations.

And if this analysis even approaches the truth, it has an important corollary—namely, that heresy cannot be thought of as a past problem that has now been resolved and tamed. The journey of theological and spiritual exploration continues. Every new avenue that is opened up for investigation is potentially a wrong turn and dead end as much as a navigable channel for faith. To explore why this remains a contemporary rather than a historical issue, we need to consider something of the new discipline of the "cognitive science of religion," which has important insights to offer concerning how at least some types of heresy arise.

Heresy and the Cognitive Science of Religion

In recent years, a new way of approaching the origins of heresy has been made possible through the development of the cognitive science of religion.[3] This approach aims to clarify how religious beliefs are shaped and developed, avoiding the reductionist approaches that have led to sensationalist, easily discredited claims to "explain away" religious beliefs.[4] The cognitive science of religion aims to explore the basic cognitive structure of beliefs that might be termed "religious." Its fundamental assumption is that human conceptual structures are not contingencies shaped by culture or history but reflect deeper patternings within the human mind. Human conceptual structures, which can be investigated experimentally, thus both inform and constrain cultural expression.

So how do these studies have any bearing on the origins of heresy? One of the most interesting outcomes of the cognitive science of religion concerns the "naturalness" of certain beliefs.[5] Certain "nonreflective" habits have a significant impact on the way in which ideas are developed and evaluated. A critical question is often, Which of several options has the greater natural appeal? An understanding of what is "natural" is, of course, derived from a variety of sources, including personal observation and cultural influences.

In the case of Christianity, heresy often—but not invariably—results from what we might call the "naturalization" of Christian belief—that is, the assimilation of orthodoxy to more "natural" ways of thinking. For example, detailed historical analysis of the origins and development of the "two natures" doctrine in Christology and the doctrine of the Trinity allow us to identify the intellectual arguments that led to the emergence of these apparently deeply counterintuitive ideas.[6] Yet no matter how good these arguments may be, these ideas—that of Jesus Christ being both divine and human, and that of one God being three persons—remain counterintuitive, causing difficulty for those accustomed to more "natural" ways of thinking. The cognitive science of religion offers us a framework for allowing us to see why some assimilate these "unnatural" ideas to more "natural" counterparts. It is much more "natural" to think of Jesus Christ as simply a human being, or of God as simply one source of ultimate authority.[7]

So what "natural" ways of thinking can we identify, ways that may have had a significant role in catalyzing the emergence of heresy? One obvious possibility is a long cultural familiarity with certain ideas, giving the impression that they are "natural" when in fact they have merely been culturally dominant over an extended period of time. An excellent example of this is provided by the various forms of Platonism that were present in the eastern Roman Empire of the early Christian age, and especially in the cosmopolitan city of Alexandria. This led to a cluster of metaphysical commitments being seen as self-evidently true or "natural," opening the door to the metaphysical assimilation of Christian doctrines to what were seen by some as more "natural" ways of thinking.

Yet this process of assimilation was not necessarily seen as detrimental by most early Christian writers. When subject to careful controls and limits, it could establish an important bridge between Christianity and other groups. Christianity could adapt itself tactically to these more "natural" ways of thinking without losing its distinct identity. A good example of this process can be found in Justin Martyr's use of the categories and vocabulary of Middle Platonism during the second century. By correlating the Christian faith with the categories of Platonism, Justin appears to have enabled Christianity to gain a not unsympathetic hearing in the Hellenistic world of the Mediterranean during the second century. Perhaps most notably, Justin noted how the Platonic notion of the Logos offered important apologetic possibilities. The fundamental Christian theme of Christ as mediator between humanity and God could be developed and explained to a Platonic audience through a judicious use of this notion.[8]

Justin's approach illustrates both the potential and the risks of such a procedure. By judicious translation of some leading themes of the Christian faith into the intellectual vernacular of the region, Justin made them far more accessible to its educated elite than would otherwise have been the case. Furthermore, the intellectual rigor of such forms of Platonism was a stimulus to the development of a comparable precision within theology. Yet there was a downside. Justin risked collapsing distinctively Christian notions into their Platonic equivalents. An approach designed to allow the expansion of Christian influence within the Platonic community might backfire, leading to an increase of Platonic influence within the Christian community. The correlation of the Christian gospel with contemporary culture is thus a two-way street.

The point can be seen from Augustine of Hippo's classic analysis of the relation of faith and secular philosophy.[9] In exploring this issue, Augustine uses the narrative of the exodus of Israel from Egypt to make sense of the church's attitude toward the intellectual and cultural riches of classic culture. Israel left behind the "idols and burdens" of Egypt while taking with her a "wealth of gold and silver and clothes." Israel discarded what she regarded as theologically dangerous or oppressive while appropriating what was excellent and valuable. And so, Augustine argues, should the church approach the riches of contemporary culture—appropriating what is good and useful, and disregarding what is dangerous and oppressive.

Augustine's analogy is impressive and generally helpful. Yet it raises a question that is fundamental to any attempt to make sense of the phenomenon of heresy. How is the Christian community to reach a decision concerning which doctrinal approaches or formulations are positive and appropriate, and which are negative and inappropriate? What happens if something is initially believed to be good and useful, yet ultimately turns out to be dangerous and oppressive? Early Christian writers were deeply concerned about the possibility of irreversible intellectual contamination and degeneration: might some ideas, once appropriated within the church, turn out to be like yeast or mold, permanently infecting or damaging their host? Augustine himself believed that there was a distinctively Christian language, what he called the "church's way of speaking [*ecclesiastica loquendi consuetude*]."[10] What happens if this is lost, or corrupted, through the importation of other ways of speaking?

It will be argued in this chapter that the desire to communicate the Christian faith effectively to other groups on the one hand, and to incorporate into Christianity the "best" of alternative or supplementary wisdoms on the other, represents one of the most fundamental causes of heresy. This most emphatically does not imply that there is anything wrong with either wanting to communicate the faith or enabling it to make the best use of contemporary cultural riches. There is nothing wrong with the method; the problems begin when some of its outcomes prove to be dangerous. What happens if the new ideas turn out to be Trojan horses, allowing intellectual forces outside the gates of the church to take it over?

In what follows, we shall explore a number of pressures that appear to be implicated in the genesis of heresy. The five most significant pressures appear to be the following:

1. *Cultural norms.* A perception that Christianity is significantly out of touch with contemporary cultural values often leads to pressure for certain intellectual adjustments to be made.

2. *Rational norms.* The belief that certain Christian ideas are contrary to "right reason" often leads to their elimination or modification in order to make them conform to prevailing criteria of rationality.

3. *Social identity.* All social groups need to establish their identity, and this often involves religious notions. Heresy often arises as a means of religious self-identification of marginalized social groupings.

4. *Religious accommodation.* The coexistence of Christianity with rival religious groupings often leads to pressure to modify certain aspects of the Christian faith in order to facilitate coexistence, or to develop a credible apologetic.

5. *Ethical concerns.* Heresy often arises from the perception that religious orthodoxy is excessively morally permissive or anarchic on the one hand, or restrictive or oppressive on the other.

In this chapter, we shall consider each of these five issues, noting how they bear on the classic heresies of the patristic age as well as more recent debates.

Heresy and Contemporary Social Norms

Christianity has existed in a wide variety of social contexts, each of which is characterized by certain cultural norms. Some of these resonate with Christian values; others are in tension with them. Christian apologists often focus on the former, using the resonance between the Christian faith and certain cultural beliefs and values as bridges for the communication and commendation of faith. But what of the areas of tension?

Many Christian theologians have been content to live with this tension. Others, however, have believed that these tensions constitute a significant barrier to faith. Certain aspects of the Christian faith, they argue, are an apologetic liability. Why not jettison them? Or assimilate them to contemporary cultural norms? This process of assimilation to cultural norms often leads to forms of heresy. We shall illustrate this by considering an aspect of the Pelagian controversy before moving on to make some broader points.

A central theme of the New Testament is that Christians are saved not by works but by grace (Eph. 2:5, 8–9). The notions of "salvation by grace" and "justification by faith" are firmly woven into the fabric of the New Testament, especially the Pauline epistles.[11] Yet these ideas were in tension with some fundamental values of the imperial Roman culture of the late fourth century. As Christianity was by now the official religion of the Roman Empire, any tensions between Roman cultural norms and Christianity were a matter of some significance. Many Roman Christians—including Pelagius (c. 355–c. 435) and Julian of Eclanum (c. 386–c. 455)—argued that certain ways of understanding the Christian faith (most notably, that of Augustine of Hippo) needed modification if they were to be culturally acceptable. How could such provincial theological ideas prove useful in the metropolis?

A central issue concerned this question: what does it mean to say that God is "righteous [*justus*]"? Classic Roman thinking on this matter had been shaped by Marcus Tullius Cicero (106–43 B.C.), who had laid down that the essence of "righteousness" or "justice"—the two English words that are widely used to translate the single Latin term *justitia*—is to give someone their due.[12] Applied to God, this means that God deals with people according to their entitlements, rewarding the good and punishing the evil.

This is certainly how the idea of divine justice was interpreted by Julian of Eclanum, perhaps the most culturally sophisticated of the Pelagian writers, noted for his thoroughgoing assimilation of the Christian gospel to the social and civil norms of Roman society.[13] For Julian, it was self-evident that the idea of the "righteousness of God" was to be assimilated to prevailing cultural norms. God gave each their due. Justification was thus about God rewarding the righteous and punishing the wicked.

Yet this idea of divine justice sat very uneasily with the Old Testament notion of divine righteousness. While emphasizing the importance of social justice in maintaining virtue and discouraging vice, the Old Testament links the idea of the "justice of God" with salvation. An appeal to God's righteousness is fundamentally a plea for salvation and deliverance, as is evident from the following classic passage from Psalm 31:

> In you, O Lord, do I take refuge,
> Let me never be put to shame.
> *In your righteousness* deliver me and rescue me.[14]

In his exegetical and systematic writings, Augustine of Hippo emphasized that secular notions of justice were not suitable for describing God's dealings with humanity. The "justice of God" was quite distinct from human justice. For Augustine, any assimilation of the "righteousness of God" to the Ciceronian idea of "giving to each their due" was called into question by many biblical passages that indicated that this cultural notion of righteousness could not be used without significant adaptation. In countering Julian, Augustine appealed to the parable of the laborers in the vineyard (Matt. 20:1–16) to demonstrate that the idea of the "justice of God" primarily refers to God's fidelity to the gospel promises of grace, irrespective of the merits of those to whom the promise was made. Each laborer, in a Ciceronian definition of justice, was entitled to different rewards, given that each worked for different periods. Yet each had been promised the same reward, often in excess of what strict justice demanded. Divine justice was about God's faithfulness to his generous and gracious promises.

A central theme in the debate between Augustine and Julian of Eclanum therefore concerned precisely what the idea of the "righteousness of God" actually entailed.[15] Julian defined divine justice in terms of God rendering to each individual their due, without fraud or grace, so that God would be expected to justify those who merited his grace on the basis of their moral achievements. This approach yielded a doctrine of the justification of the *godly*, whereas Augustine held the essence of the gospel to be the justification of the *ungodly*.

Julian's concern was unquestionably apologetic. His goal was to explain the Christian faith in ways that would resonate with prevailing notions of justice and entitlement within late classical antiquity. The idea that undeserving people should receive divine approbation was culturally distasteful and would, in Julian's view, simply alienate many persons of distinction.

This single case study illustrates the more general point, highlighting the difficulties that arise when a central Christian theme or value is perceived to exist in tension with cultural norms. Other examples illustrating the same problem could easily be given.

Heresy and Accommodation to Secular Reason

In the previous section, we noted how tensions between Christianity and cultural norms have been the occasion of the origins of heresy. A related tension concerns prevailing notions of reason. Each social context has its own idea of what counts as rational. Commenting on the success of C. S. Lewis (1898–1963) as an apologist, the Oxford theologian and New Testament scholar Austin Farrer (1904–68) pointed out how the rationality of faith was important for its cultural acceptance.

> For though argument does not create conviction, the lack of it destroys belief. What seems to be proved may not be embraced; but what no one shows the ability to defend is quickly abandoned. Rational argument does not create belief, but it maintains a climate in which belief may flourish.[16]

Lewis's success, Farrer argued, reflected his ability to offer "a positive exhibition of the force of Christian ideas, morally, imaginatively, and rationally."

Farrer's wise comments point to a significant danger for Christian theology: that some of its core themes appear indefensible in the light of contemporary ideas about what is "rational." Patristic writers were acutely aware of this issue, in that certain core themes of the Christian faith did indeed seem "irrational" in the light of the norms of classic Greek philosophy.[17] A good example is that of the Incarnation, which was widely ridiculed by pagan writers as incoherent. The origins of Arianism are often attributed to a concern that Christianity was rendering itself as intellectually risible in a culture dominated by Greek philosophy.

Similar concerns were expressed about the doctrine of the Trinity during the patristic age. However, the most significant critiques of the Trinity emerged during the sixteenth century, when the radical wing of the Reformation began to press for the abandonment of certain traditional teachings, partly because they seemed to be irrational, and partly because they were held not to be well grounded in the Bible. Radical groups, angry with what they regarded as compromises on the part of Martin Luther and Huldrych Zwingli, demanded more sweeping changes.[18] Traditional doctrines that Luther and Zwingli had regarded as entirely orthodox and not in need of revision were now openly questioned. Many radicals argued that the doctrine of the Trinity was not explicitly stated in the Bible. Far from being an authentic Christian doctrine, it reflected the later speculations and elaborations of misguided theologians.

Anti-Trinitarianism, already evident in the late 1520s, became a hallmark of the radical Reformation in the 1550s,[19] causing widespread concern in both Protestant and Catholic circles. It was given significant intellectual momentum in the writings of Fausto Paolo Sozzini (1539–1604), often known by the Latin form of his name, Faustus Socinus. The movement, which came to be known as "Socinianism," began to pose a challenge to both Protestant and Catholic orthodoxy in the late sixteenth century. Although Socinus's writings ranged widely, challenging many aspects of traditional Christian beliefs, he is especially associated with anti-Trinitarianism. Abandoning the doctrines of the Incarnation and Trinity, which he rightly discerned to be interconnected, he argued for a more generalized religious belief in Jesus of Nazareth as a divinely inspired person with exceptional abilities to keep the commands of God.[20]

The motivation for this critique of the doctrine of the Trinity was partly biblical but predominantly rational. To put it simply: the doctrine seemed scandalously irrational, and thus threatened to cause reputational damage to Christianity. As rationalism began to gain cultural influence throughout much of western Europe in the seventeenth and eighteenth centuries, there was growing pressure for Christianity to abandon what was seen as Trinitarian irrationality and return to a more reasonable notion of God, such as that advocated by Deism.[21] The resurgence of the doctrine of the Trinity in the twentieth century, mainly resulting from the work of Karl

Barth (1886–1968) and Karl Rahner (1904–84), can be seen partly as the outcome of the erosion of the rationalism that predominated in the early Enlightenment as its weaknesses and difficulties became increasingly obvious.

At this point, we should also note the fact that many prominent scientists often have heterodox religious beliefs. This applies as much to Islam and Judaism as to Christianity.[22] For example, Isaac Newton's attempt to apply scientific methods to his Christian faith led him to reject the doctrine of the Trinity, although he was careful not to draw attention to this fact during his lifetime.[23] We see here the same tension between orthodox religious belief and the methods of a particular community. While some scientists maintained perfectly orthodox religious beliefs, others found that the concept of "reasonableness" that prevailed in their community led them to draw quite different conclusions. In his well-documented study of Arianism in the early modern period, Maurice Wiles notes the particular prevalence of this heresy among many early modern scientists.[24]

The way in which prevailing cultural notions of rationality can lead to distorted or inauthentic notions of God raises some difficult questions for Christian apologists. For example, the traditional discipline of "natural theology" aims to argue for the existence of God by an appeal to human reason or the ordering of nature. The American philosopher William Alston defines natural theology as "the enterprise of providing support for religious beliefs by starting from premises that neither are nor presuppose any religious beliefs."[25] Yet historically, the application of natural theology tends to lead to a deistic God that bears little relation to the fully orbed Trinitarian God of the Christian tradition.[26] There remains a significant gap between notions of God that may be inferred from the natural realm or deduced from reason on the one hand, and the Christian vision of God on the other.

Heresy and the Shaping of Social Identity

The importance of religion in communal self-definition has often been noted.[27] If communities are to survive over time, centers need to be defined and boundaries policed. Religion often provides a marker of communal identity—not necessarily the only marker, but often one of the most prominent. More specifically, religious beliefs often serve as a means of creating a sense of social identity, shaping the outlook of a community and justifying its original and continued existence in the face of rival communities with comparable claims. It assists in defining both the limits of, and the conditions for entering, such a community. Effective social cohesion requires the fixing of boundaries and the fostering of a sense of community identity.[28] A distinct religious commitment is one of a number of options for marking the identity of a community. So, in a situation dominated by Christianity—for example, western Europe during the Middle Ages—might some communities adopt heretical religious views as markers of their identity? Might the perceived need for a distinct identity lead communities into adopting heterodox beliefs?[29]

The evidence is far from secure, and it is best to suggest that this represents an interesting possibility that may cast at least some light on the origins and appeal of heresy. To explore this point, we may consider Donatism in more detail. We have already considered the historical emergence of this heresy and noted some aspects of its theology (pp. 152–59). The observation that Roman settlers in North Africa tended to adopt the Catholic position whereas native Berber Christians tended toward Donatism is certainly suggestive of some link between communal identity and theology, whether orthodox or heterodox.

Supporters of this view argue that Donatism was particularly associated with the rural population of areas that were less populated by Roman colonists, and with the poorer classes in the towns.[30] Numidia, for example, was the least Romanized province in North Africa; it was here that Donatism was at its strongest. Again, there is a considerable degree of overlap between the areas of North Africa in which the Donatists were dominant and those areas in which the Berber language is still spoken today. In contrast, Catholic Christianity was the religion of the Romanized upper classes.[31]

Yet there are difficulties with this position. For example, it is relatively easily demonstrated that many Donatist leaders were actually rather wealthy and socially influential. Augustine of Hippo complained about wealthy Donatist landowners purchasing land and forcing the rebaptism of their acquired workers.[32] More significantly, recent studies have emphasized the importance of *religious* rather than social or economic factors in causing and sustaining Donatism.[33] The view that Donatism was essentially a socioeconomic movement with an accidental or superficial association with religious ideas does not sit easily with what is known of the movement. The evidence seems to fit better a more traditional approach that holds that Donatism was, at heart, an essentially loose religious movement that came to have an especial appeal to socially alienated groups but was not itself constituted by such concerns.

A similar conclusion seems to be required for other dissident movements linked with heterodoxy—for example, Catharism and Hussitism. Yet while such movements appear to have had an essentially religious basis, it must be conceded that political and social issues may have helped to consolidate their sense of identity, or to cause the movements to be viewed with particular alarm in certain quarters. Yet these religious ideas do not appear to have emerged as accidental markers of identity of already existing movements, often with socioeconomic agendas. Rather, they seem to have been embedded within the movement's identity, generally being a major factor in having brought it into existence in the first place.

Religious Contextualization and Heresy

From its earliest period, Christianity found itself immersed in a complex religious situation. On the one hand, it had emerged from Judaism as a distinct belief system, affirming continuity with its past (Marcion's view on this matter failing to prevail); on the other, it was at the same time being forced to engage with other world-views, secular and religious, as it expanded into new geographical regions. Its strongly evangelistic impulse impelled Christianity to build bridges to such communities—for example, by restating some core Christian ideas in terms already familiar to them. The manner in which Christian apologists engaged Platonist audiences in Alexandria is widely regarded as a classic example of such a strategy.

It is, however, a profoundly risky strategy. What might initially have been envisaged as a tactical reworking of some basic Christian ideas seems to have had the propensity to end up as a longer-term reconceptualization of Christianity itself. There is no doubt that this was a serious concern within the early Christian community, moving Tertullian to declare a virtual embargo on serious dialogue between Christianity and philosophy on account of the associated risk of contamination.

Exploration of how Christianity related to other religious groups was a major stimulus to theological reflection in the early Christian period and is associated with two landmark heresies. Ebionitism may be regarded as Christian assimilation to Judaism, and Marcionism as a Christian rejection of Christianity's Jewish heritage. These two heresies define the extremities of a spectrum of possibilities, with orthodoxy navigating a via media.

Yet Judaism may rightly be observed to be a special case in that it defined the religious matrix from which Christianity emerged. What of other religious movements within the late classical period? One group that some early Christian writers believed to be significant was the loose, multifaceted movement often referred to as Gnosticism. As we have already seen, the origins of this movement remain obscure, and it is likely that further investigation will reveal multiple origins of a complex entity, reflecting an essentially diverse movement with considerable variation. Our current state of knowledge of Gnosticism is simply not good enough to allow us to answer some of the most fundamental questions concerning its origins and development with any confidence.

That being said, there is no doubt that several influential early Christian writers encountered Gnosticism, especially in Egypt, and came to regard it as a movement that demanded engagement. Valentinus, for example, seems to have encountered Gnosticism at Alexandria. On migrating to Rome—note the ease of travel that proved so important in transferring ideas around the Mediterranean coastline—Valentinus sought to advance this engagement, clearly believing that it was in the church's interest to do so.

But what form did this engagement take? The evidence is insufficient to allow us to decide whether Valentinus was of the view that Christianity could restate its fundamental ideas in essentially Gnostic terms to advance the evangelization of that movement, or whether he regarded Gnostic ideas as being so robust that Christianity would benefit from incorporating them into its own way of thinking and making any appropriate conceptual adjustments. Whatever his intentions, the outcome of Valentinus's strategy was seen to be the distortion of Christianity and the contamination of certain of its core ideas—such as the identity of the God of the Old and New Covenants.

Ethical Discontent and the Origins of Heresy

The Christian faith offers a moral vision that allows the world of social reality to be seen in a certain way, leading to corresponding modes of action.[34] Christian ethics and political action require a vision that will render action intelligible. Yet many found themselves dissatisfied with the moral vision offered by the forms of Christianity that history permitted them to know, and sought alternatives. This sense of moral discontent often led to heretical conclusions.

Popular accounts of heresy often suggest that orthodox Christianity was ethically restrictive and authoritarian, leading enlightened individuals to seek more libertarian ways of life and thought. It seems to have become axiomatic in recent years that heresy is morally and intellectually liberating, to the extent that orthodoxy is stifling. This tells us a lot about the cultural mood of postmodernity, and the agendas of some of those who find heresy to be attractive.

Yet it needs to be pointed out that history completely forbids us from drawing such a simplistic conclusion, however attractive it may be to those alienated from religious orthodoxy, for whatever reasons. As we shall see, certain heresies did indeed regard Christian orthodoxy as somewhat forbidding and repressive; other heresies, however, regarded orthodoxy as dangerously lax and permissive, and sought to impose moral rigor on the Christian community. It is indefensible to suggest that moral or intellectual libertarianism is an essential characteristic of heresy. There is clearly considerable variation among heresies, some having no quarrel with prevailing orthodox ethical outlooks, others seeing them as heavy-handed and puritanical, and still others seeing them as lax and degenerate.

An obvious example of a heresy that regarded Christian orthodoxy as morally careless and slipshod is Pelagianism. The origins of this movement, as we noted earlier (pp. 159–70), lay in Pelagius's shock at the moral degeneracy that he found in the Roman church on his arrival from Britain. It was a common enough reaction: Benedict of Nursia (480–547) felt the same way about the Roman church on his arrival in the city a century later. Nor was Pelagius's asceticism particularly original. What really mattered was the emphasis he placed upon asceticism, and the theological conclusions he drew from it.

Pelagius and his circle developed a theology that authorized an emphasis upon a Christian quest for moral perfection, arguing that the best solution to the lack of moral vision within the Roman church was to make certain adjustments to the prevailing theological consensus. Humanity, Pelagius and his circle argued, had an intrinsic God-given capacity for perfection, which it needed to actualize through moral attentiveness. In all fairness to Pelagius, there are no grounds for suggesting that he set out to intentionally subvert Christianity. His rigid moralism was more of a reaction to the ethical and spiritual laxity he saw all around him. Initially, Pelagius probably saw himself as doing nothing more than attempting to give some sorely needed words of exhortation. Yet his analysis of what theological presuppositions were necessary to undergird his moral exhortations led him, in Augustine's view, to develop some thoroughly unchristian views.[35] Even allowing for some degree of interpenetration between the theological agendas of Pelagius himself and other moral activists at Rome (most notably, Caelestius and Rufinus of Syria), it is difficult to avoid the conclusion that the moral emphasis of Pelagianism stimulated the formulation of some theological principles intended to serve this end, yet that were in tension with the New Testament's views on sin, grace, and human nature.

As we noted earlier, both Pelagius and Benedict of Nursia were distressed by the moral laxity of the Roman church. It is instructive to compare their quite different responses. Where Pelagius and his circle altered the theological framework governing and informing Christian morality, Benedict created a new environment grounded in an orthodox conception of human nature yet adapted to the fostering of morality. If humanity had difficulty in coping with the moral complexities of life in a fallen world, the situation could be remedied, at least to some extent, by transferring these complexities to a context in which these weaknesses were recognized and addressed. For Benedict, the answer thus lay in a monastic community with a rule of life that was aspirational in its goals yet realistic in its assumptions.

Pelagianism is one of a group of heresies that regarded orthodox Christianity as morally deficient. Another example is Montanism, which attracted a theologian of the status of Tertullian. It emerged during the third century and emphasized the holiness of God and its implications for human behavior.[36] While most theological attention has concerned Montanism's views on prophecy and the role of the Holy Spirit (which seem to anticipate some aspects of modern Pentecostalism), its moral rigor also merits attention. Tertullian's decision to convert to Montanism appears to have been motivated at least in part by its stringent and strident moralism.

Interestingly, Pelagianism provoked certain extreme reactions that were in themselves regarded as heresies. Some reacted against Pelagian asceticism with such force that they ended up being considered heretical on account of their antiascetical views. An excellent example of this phenomenon is to be found in Jovinian (d. c. 405), who was initially a strident advocate of monastic asceticism.[37] He was excommunicated as a heretic at a synod convened by Ambrose of Milan in 390 for a variety of theological reasons, although it is possible that the real concern was that Jovinian had become something of a scandal on account of his love for the good life. While some aspects of the situation remain unclear, it seems that Jovinian was seen as having "flipped" from one extreme to the other, abandoning self-denial and embracing self-indulgence. For Ambrose, there had to be a middle way between these extreme moral positions.

Yet other heretical movements adopted much more libertarian approaches to morality. The classic example of this is a network of individuals during the later Middle Ages who are often grouped together as representing the "Heresy of the Free Spirit."[38] This loosely connected movement, which is generally thought to have flourished in the fourteenth century, is often held to be characterized by its hostility toward ecclesiastical authoritarianism, and by its subversion of traditional morality. It is often difficult to determine the reliability of some accounts of its beliefs and activities, as these are thought to be open to exaggeration by those concerned to discredit them. As Norman Cohn pointed out fifty years ago, what emerges from contemporary accounts of this heresy is "an entirely convincing picture of an eroticism which, far from springing from a carefree sensuality, possessed above all a symbolic value as a sign of spiritual emancipation."[39]

The brief historical overview presented in this section makes it clear that moral discontent with orthodoxy is not of the essence of heresy. It can be one of its features, but it is not necessarily of central importance. Yet the notion that heresy is *intrinsically* liberating cannot be sustained. This represents a retrojection onto history of the ideals and aspirations of those alienated from conventional religion on account of the alleged "authoritarianism" of forms of orthodoxy. This notion of heresy is partly imagined and invented, and bears relatively little resemblance to the historical realities of heresy.

The material we have explored in this chapter points to a number of pressures that, though not heretical in themselves, can lead to heresy as outcomes. The common theme here is that of the adaptation of orthodoxy to a specific cultural environment, which may—but does not *necessarily*—lead to heresy. This observation fits in well with the fivefold analysis of heresy offered by the British patristic scholar H. E. W. Turner, who suggests that heresy can be conceived as the outcome of five related yet distinct processes: dilution; truncation; distortion; archaism; and evacuation.[40] As we noted earlier, the fourth of these can be seen as representing a refusal to concede that Christian theology must develop—not merely reiterate—the ideas of the New Testament (pp. 66–67). Yet it will be clear that Turner's four remaining categories point to the possibility of cultural and intellectual assimilation of the Christian faith, either by incorporating alien ideas or by abandoning Christian ideas, in response to cultural pressures.

It is clearly necessary and appropriate for Christianity to engage with its cultural environment. Church history indicates that this process of engagement has been an integral part of the long process of Christian expansion and consolidation through the ages. To suggest that this process might lead into heretical byways is not to invalidate the process, but simply to mandate theological vigilance in its execution.

Yet there remains one issue that needs closer attention. To what extent are heresy and orthodoxy the outcomes of power struggles? Given the importance of this issue in some recent speculation about the origins and nature of heresy, it clearly deserves closer analysis.

nine

Orthodoxy, Heresy, and Power

Heresy is the orthodoxy of history's losers. This view, expressed and given a somewhat inadequate historical justification in the writings of Walter Bauer (pp. 73–77), points to the potential importance of power in determining what is orthodox. For Bauer and his more recent followers, heresy is just an orthodoxy that had the bad luck to get mixed up with the wrong people. The other side won and enforced their ideas as the regnant orthodoxy. Theological victory rested with those who had the power to enforce their viewpoints.

This development is of considerable importance, not least because it helps account for the growing cultural interest in—not to mention sympathy for—heresies. In this reading of things, heresy is the orthodoxy of the plucky underdog, the voice of suppressed and downtrodden cultural groups. Scholarship can reverse the judgments of history, which is invariably written by its winners, and restore the ideas and values of those who were culturally vanquished to their proper place. The rehabilitation of heresy can thus be seen as a profoundly moral action. It is, it must be conceded, very difficult to defend this reading of history. To its critics, it appears to represent an attempt to read certain cultural judgments or biases into history rather than attempt a critical historical analysis of the emergence and character of "heresy."

From a Christian perspective, however, heresy has a very different sense.[1] The term has come to refer to a set of beliefs that maintain the outward form of the gospel yet ultimately subvert its essence. Heresy renders the Christian faith incoherent and unstable, and thus undermines its longer-term prospects for survival in a fiercely competitive world of ideas. To use a familiar Darwinian image: if it is the fittest who are to survive, then the fittest form of Christianity must be identified and promoted—namely, Christian orthodoxy. In this volume, I have explored this Christian approach to heresy, trying to identify what was potentially so subversive or destructive about the classic movements within the early church that were ultimately declared to be heretical.

Yet the scholarly study of heresy has undergone significant change in recent years. Heresy is no longer seen as a specifically Christian notion but as a broader social phenomenon, ultimately reflecting questions of power and influence. Heresy is a concept found in other world religions (though sometimes under other names) as well as Christianity,[2] ultimately reflecting the fact that these are social movements linked with questions of power and influence.

These factors are taken into account in this study, which can be thought of as offering a "critical realist" account of heresy.[3] Critical realism has gained increasing influence recently in the social sciences, and is characterized particularly by its exploration of the interaction of ideas with their social contexts. Critical realism recognizes that ideas emerge within, and are modulated by, their social context and often play critical social roles—for example, in defining the boundaries of communities. In the present chapter, we shall explore some of the sociological issues that relate to the origins and development of heresy, focusing especially on the complex interplay between heresy, orthodoxy, and power.

Sociological Approaches to Heresy

The origins of an essential social account of heresy can be traced back to early Marxism. Karl Marx (1818–83) set out an account of the origins of ideologies (the "production of ideas, of conceptions, of consciousness," a notion that might now be translated as "world-views") that held that they were fundamentally expressions of social and economic factors. Ideology acts as the superstructure of a civilization or culture, in that it defines the conventions and beliefs that make up the dominant ideas of a society. The "ruling ideas" of a given historical epoch are thus those of the ruling class:

> The ideas of the ruling class are in every epoch the ruling ideas, i.e., the class which is the ruling *material* force of society is also its ruling intellectual force. . . . The ruling ideas are nothing more than the ideal expression of the dominant material relationships, the dominant material relationships grasped as ideas; hence of the relationships which make the one class the ruling one, therefore, the ideas of their dominance.[4]

This approach leads to heresy being seen as the ideology of a defeated or oppressed group, whereas orthodoxy is the ideology of the ruling class. Although this approach to heresy has obvious applications to the institution of the church, it is not limited to them. Heresy has, in effect, thus been conceived in social or institutional—rather than *theological*—terms. Friedrich Engels (1820–95) made this connection in his important *Peasant War in Germany* (1850). Engels's objective in writing this book was primarily to offer consolation to those discouraged by the failure of attempted revolutionary activity in 1848–49, drawing a parallel with the earlier failure of the German Peasants' Revolt of 1525.[5] Yet the work also set out the idea that heresies are manifestations of class conflict. The theological differences between Martin Luther and the radical leader Thomas Müntzer were actually grounded in social and political issues.

In eras that were dominated by the conceptualities and language of the Christian church, alternative social movements had little option other than to use religious language as a means of expressing their identity. Yet the heart of such movements, in this reading, is not religious—despite outward appearances of religious concerns—but political, social, or economic. Recent studies of the sociology of heresy have emphasized this point. For example, George Zito observes that heresy is not primarily "a religious phenomenon, but an institutional phenomenon." It initially developed within religious contexts "only because of the religious institution's central position in governing the discourses of a particular historical moment."[6]

Given that heresy and orthodoxy need to distinguish themselves, intellectual divergence between them is inevitable. Yet in this sociological understanding of heresy, this sort of divergence is ultimately of limited significance. The real point at issue lies underneath the ideas and is not directly expressed in or by those ideas. The orthodox and heretical are to be distinguished socially, institutionally, or economically. Heretical *ideas* are the superstructure erected on a sociological foundation and are not themselves of primary importance.

This important development leads directly into one of the most characteristic features of contemporary writing on heresy. Where earlier generations of heresiologists lauded orthodoxy and castigated heresy, most recent writing in the field appears simply to have inverted this judgment. If the distinction between heresy and orthodoxy rests on power and dominance, sympathy now seems to lie decidedly with the heretic. The issue is not that of "right" and "wrong"; rather, it is who has the power to compel assent to their way of seeing things. Today's orthodoxy can thus easily transmute into tomorrow's heresy. All that is required is a radical change in the social relationship of the parties involved.

To what extent, then, has the church's discussion of heresy been shaped by interests and relationships of power? We begin by considering the patristic era, interacting particularly with the six classic heresies that we considered in chapters 6 and 7.

Power, Heresy, and the Patristic Age

To begin with, we need to reiterate a point made earlier: the Christian church in the first and second centuries possessed no political power of any significance, and appears to have had no means at its disposal to enforce orthodoxy. There is no persuasive evidence to suggest that early heresies of the second century—such as Valentinism and Marcionism—were subjected to any form of coercion from Roman church leaders in order to force them to conform to Roman theological norms. Marcion and Valentinus, irritated at failing to secure acceptance within the church, founded their own communities. They were not forcibly expelled against their wishes.

The importance of power interests in defining early Christianity has often been noted. For example, the sociologist Max Weber (1864–1920) proposed that the process of the formation of any canon of texts was ultimately a struggle for power. Thus Weber argued that "most, though not all, canonical sacred collections became officially closed against secular or religiously undesirable additions as a consequence of a struggle between various competing groups and prophecies for control of the community."[7] Not surprisingly, Weber sees the process of closure of the Christian and Hebrew biblical canons in terms of power struggles between rival groups, the outcome determining which would dominate the shape of any institution governed by such texts.[8] Heresy could therefore be interpreted as arising from the decision to recognize an alternative canon of Scripture, its distinctive ideas arising primarily from using different sources than those used by orthodoxy rather than from placing different interpretations upon the same sources as those used by orthodoxy.[9]

Yet it is questionable whether such an analysis based on power can be applied credibly to the period of "proto-orthodoxy." Walter Bauer, whose approach reflects Weber's ideas, seems to have retrojected the later political power and status of the Roman church into the second century. Yet this anachronism cannot be defended.

It was not until the conversion of Constantine in the early fourth century that Christianity can be said to have had any real political clout in Rome. In the second century it was an illegal religion on the margins of society, without access to political or social influence, let alone any way of enforcing its viewpoints.

This is not to say that the church was not concerned about threats to Christian authenticity, or was failing to pay attention to how the most authentic expressions or performances of faith might be identified and sustained. For example, the writings of Origen can be considered as an attempt to identify "orthodoxy" as the most consistent rendering of Scripture, not least in terms of the patterns of divine action that it disclosed.[10] It is clear that informal networks of bishops and theologians were in the process of clarifying the nature of orthodoxy, often through personal correspondence.[11] Yet this process was fundamentally concerned with the crystallization of perceptions within the church, not the imposition of some predetermined outcome.

Yet all this changed with the accession of Constantine and the gradual transformation of the social and political status of Christianity from a fringe religious movement to the established religion of the Roman Empire. Divisions within imperial Christianity now had the potential to cause division and potential instability within the empire. Constantine appeared to have little interest in the theological issues underlying such debates. His responses suggest a pragmatic determination to sort out the issues expeditiously yet civilly.

Constantine was dragged into the Donatist controversy at an early stage, partly on account of its implications for Roman colonial policy in North Africa. His involvement initially took the form of strong suggestions that the respective parties sort things out between them, followed by the imposition of a mechanism for conflict resolution. After the failure of this, Constantine himself adjudicated the issue, settling in favor of the Catholic party. Yet it is clear that his involvement in the affair was reluctant, his fundamental instinct being to allow the church to sort out its own disputes.

A similar issue arose in the Arian controversy, where Constantine again reluctantly found himself drawn into a theological dispute for which he regarded himself as ill equipped. Once more, Constantine's concern was to reestablish unity within the church, and again he proposed a mechanism for the resolution of the conflict. The Council of Nicaea (325), modeled on classic Roman senatorial precedents, was not intended to impose Constantine's views on Christology; indeed, there are indications that his preference may have been for an Arian Christology.[12] His primary objective in becoming involved in these disputes appears to have been the establishment of concord and agreement within the church.

Yet while Constantine appears to have been content to allow the church to sort out its own theological debates, he had no hesitation in using the force of the state to impose uniformity once this decision had been reached. Constantine moved to enforce Nicene orthodoxy, exiling those who refused to accept it—including Arius himself, the deacon Euzoios, and the Libyan bishops Theonas of Marmarica and Secundus of Ptolemaïs. He also ordered all copies of the *Thalia,* the book in which Arius had expressed his teachings, to be burned.

The state may not have defined orthodoxy; it was, however, certainly prepared to enforce it. Once this point is recognized, it has important implications for the Bauer thesis—namely, that the enforcement of orthodoxy, found repugnant by many of Bauer's disciples, would have applied equally had movements now designated as heretical been declared to be orthodox. If the driving force for suppression of diversity is imperial unity, whatever view is designated as "orthodoxy" will be enforced. This has clear implications for the curious recent perception that heresy is intrinsically libertarian and orthodoxy repressive. The social function of these movements does not appear to be determined by the ideas themselves, but by their espousal and endorsement by the state.

If Donatism had won Constantine's approval rather than the Catholic position, it would have been enforced as a matter of imperial policy, for the good of the social cohesion of the empire. Similarly, if Nicaea had endorsed Arianism, that would also have been enforced in the same way, and for the same reason. Imperial stability demanded ecclesiastical uniformity and conformity. It is a theme that recurs throughout the history of church-state relations—witness, for example, Elizabeth I's "Act of Uniformity" (1559), designed to stabilize the religious and political situation in England in a period of national and international tension.[13]

That this is no whimsical speculation is indicated by developments that took place after Constantine's death in 337. His son, Constantius, reopened the Nicene debates with a view to reversing the original judgment on Arianism. Advised by the Arian Eusebius of Nicomedia, Constantius inverted Nicene orthodoxy, declaring Athanasius of Alexandria to be heterodox and Arius orthodox. Constantius proceeded to use in defense of Arianism the same imperial power that Constantine had used to enforce the Athanasian position. Athanasius was exiled, as were other supporters of the theology hammered out at Nicaea.[14] The situation was reversed in 381, when the Council of Constantinople reaffirmed and consolidated the basic ideas of the Council of Nicaea.[15]

Constantius's declaration of the orthodoxy of Arianism and the heterodoxy of the "two natures" doctrine might appear to confirm the view that orthodoxy is simply a religious ideology favored by those in positions of power. A shift in power thus led to a corresponding shift in orthodoxy: Arianism, having been declared heretical in 325, was the regnant orthodoxy twenty years later. However, a closer examination of the events between the councils of Nicaea (325) and Constantinople (381) suggests that they actually *undermine* the idea that heresy and orthodoxy are essentially a matter of power politics.

The political decision that Arianism was orthodox and its rivals heretical provoked detailed intellectual examination of the credentials of the theological options available to the church. Writers such as Basil of Caesarea and Gregory of Nazianzus offered a theological analysis that led to a significant tension emerging between the intellectual merits of a theology and its political expediency. Arianism might have been imposed upon the church by an act of imperial authority; it was, however, becoming clear that it was not the best intellectual option.[16] In the end, political influence proved inadequate to sustain a deficient vision of the Christian faith. While Arianism would continue to exercise influence in peripheral regions of the church for some time, its centers of influence had been won over again to the Nicene vision of the faith.

Power, Heresy, and the Middle Ages

The gradual collapse of the Roman Empire led to a series of realignments in both the Eastern and Western churches.[17] In the West, the church gradually emerged as the guarantor of the established social order. This development reflects a number of factors, including the weakness of alternative authority structures. As the only agency to possess any significant credibility or influence throughout the Middle Ages, the church played a decisive role in the settling of international disputes.[18] Under Innocent III (pope from 1198 to 1216), the medieval papacy reached a hitherto unprecedented level of political authority in western Europe.[19] This was given theological justification in 1198, when Innocent III laid down the basic principle of the subordination of the state to the church. Just as God established "greater" and "lesser" lights in the heavens to rule the day and night—a reference to the sun and moon—so God had ordained that the power of the pope exceeded that of any monarch. It was part of the order of things, lying beyond challenge. The church's authority was often recognized with great reluctance; there was, however, no other institution in western Europe with anything remotely approaching its influence.

It is important to appreciate that the medieval church stood at the heart of the social, spiritual, and intellectual life of western Europe throughout the Middle Ages. An individual's hope of salvation rested on their being part of the community of saints, whose visible expression was the institution of the church. The church could not be bypassed or marginalized in any account of redemption: there was, as Cyprian of Carthage had so cogently argued in the third century, no salvation outside the church.[20] It was a point tangibly expressed and reinforced in the architecture of churches.

An excellent illustration of this point can be see in the French Benedictine priory church of St.-Marcel-lès-Sauze, which was founded in 985 and extensively developed during the twelfth century.[21] An inscription over the main door to the church reads as follows: "You who are passing through, you who are coming to weep for your sins, pass through me, since I am the gate of life." Those who were searching for the consolation of heaven or the forgiveness of sins could not secure these benefits without the intervention and interposition of the institution of the church and its authorized ministers.[22] Salvation had been institutionalized.

With these developments, heresy came to have a new significance. As heretical movements were formally deemed to be "outside the church," they were regarded as formally incapable of leading to salvation. Yet perhaps more significantly for the theme of this chapter, they were also seen as challenging the authority of the church by offering an alternative belief system, master narrative, or reading of Scripture. Heretical movements, although based on certain essentially religious ideas, ultimately represented alternative visions of both church and society, posing a significant threat to the monopoly that the church was in the process of establishing.

Heresy began to emerge as a significant problem in the eleventh century, having had a remarkably low profile in the previous three centuries.[23] Some have suggested that the year 1000 was seen as possessing mystical significance, triggering a wave of heretical speculation during the "millennial generation" (1000–1033).[24] The study of heresy in western Europe during the Middle Ages raises some important questions of definition.[25] Some of the movements that were declared to be heretical seem to represent renewal or modification of older heresies. An excellent example of this is provided by the Cathars, a religious sect that appeared in the Languedoc region of France in the eleventh century and flourished in southern France during the following two centuries.[26] This sect adopted views that are recognizably Gnostic, perhaps originating from eastern Europe—such as the notion that matter is intrinsically evil, and a dialectic between an inferior creating divinity and a superior redeeming divinity.

Others, however, seem to fall into a more political category—movements that posed a threat to the authority of the church. This challenge might take the form of an alternative vision of society or of the privileged place of the church in the interpretation of Scripture. An example of such a movement is Waldensianism, a reform movement that emerged in southern France about the year 1170 as a result of the activity of a wealthy Lyonnais merchant by the name of Valdés.[27] Valdés embarked on a reforming ministry that was based upon a literal reading of the Bible, particularly injunctions to poverty, and biblically based preaching in the vernacular. This ethos contrasted sharply with the somewhat loose morality of the clergy at that time and attracted considerable support in southern France and Lombardy. Although this was little more than a grassroots movement seeking reform, it was regarded as a significant threat to the power and status of the church.

The politicization of the notion of heresy is perhaps best seen in the church's reaction to John Wycliffe (c. 1320–81), an English theologian who is often credited with inspiring the first English translation of the Bible. The defining issue for Wycliffe was who has the right to read and interpret a text—all believers, or a spiritual elite? As Kantik Ghosh pointed out, Wycliffe treats Scripture above all as an "ideologically empowering concept."[28]

There is a fundamental issue of power here. By insisting that the Bible should be translated into English, Wycliffe was expanding the circle of those who had access to this text and those who believed they had the right to interpret it. Those who resisted Wycliffe's demands for the democratization of biblical interpretation offered a traditionalist theological defense of their elitist conception of the right to interpret the Bible.[29] Nevertheless, the motivation of issues of power and the consolidation of the status quo can hardly be overlooked. The effect of the Wycliffite "heresy" was to weaken the church's grip on the control of how the Bible was to be interpreted.

There is a pattern here that needs to be noted. Although the Middle Ages did indeed see the revival, often with local transmutations, of older heresies, many movements were branded as heretical for political reasons. The establishment of the Inquisition can be seen as marking a confirmation of the increasing political and institutional significance of heresies deemed to pose a threat to papal authority.[30] This represents a significant move away from patristic attempts to encapsulate the essence of heresy, which focused on the threat it posed to the Christian faith as a whole—not to Christian individuals or institutions. The use of the term "heresy" to denote a threat to the church is to be seen as inquisitorial rather than theological. As Herbert Grundmann pointed out in 1935, many of the religious movements of the Middle Ages that were branded heretical were really nothing of the sort. There was a serious case to be made for abandoning the use of the word "heresy" to designate many of them.[31]

The importance of this point can be seen by considering the Catholic Church's response to the emergence of Protestantism, to which we now turn.

A New Heresy? Protestantism

An upsurge of radical religious reflection began in earnest in western Europe during the 1510s. Reforming movements had sprung up throughout Europe, demanding the renewal and reform of the church from within.[32] When Martin Luther raised some fundamental questions about the sale of indulgences, partly intended to raise funds for the rebuilding of St. Peter's Basilica in Rome, things began to spiral out of control. Luther's famous "Ninety-Five Theses," nailed on the castle door at Wittenberg in October 1517, eventually caused Leo X to issue the papal bull *Exsurge Domine* ("Arise, O Lord"), which condemned Luther as a heretic in 1520. The theological basis of this condemnation was seriously flawed. But theology was not the real issue here. The genuine concern was the challenge to papal influence and authority now posed by Luther.

Luther had no intention of recanting his ideas. Indeed, in the year of his condemnation as a heretic he published three popular works in quick succession, setting out his vision for the reformation of the church. His *Appeal to the Christian Nobility of the German Nation,* widely regarded as the most important of these works, set out the case for reform of the church, and argued that German nobles had every right to demand change. *The Babylonian Captivity of the Church* criticized the church's teaching on sacraments. *The Freedom of a Christian* explained Luther's views on justification in easily accessible terms. While all three posed a threat to papal authority, the most serious such challenge lay in the *Appeal.*

Luther's core argument in this work is that the church has shielded itself from criticism and demands for reform by erecting defensive walls around itself. In the first place, a fundamental distinction is drawn between the "temporal" and "spiritual" orders— in other words, between the laity and the clergy. The government of the church is declared to be a matter for the clergy, not the laity, who are seen as subordinate in matters of faith. Second, the right to interpret the Bible is denied to the laity and ultimately rests with the pope. Third, only a pope can convene a reforming council. Like the walls of Jericho, Luther declares, these must be brought to the ground. The metaphorical trumpet blasts that Luther directs against these walls encapsulate some of the fundamental themes of the Reformation, themes that set a pattern that would gradually become normative for much of Protestantism.

Luther began his critique of the church by setting out one of the greatest themes of the Reformation—the democratization of faith.

Luther uses the German term *Gemeinde* ("community") to refer to
the church, anxious to emphasize that it is fundamentally a gather-
ing of believers, not a divinely ordained institution with sacred
powers and authority vested exclusively in its clergy. All believers,
men and women, by virtue of their baptism, are priests. Luther
noted an important corollary of this doctrine: the clergy should be
free to marry, like all other Christians. This right to clerical marriage rapidly became a defining characteristic of Protestantism.

Luther grounded his doctrine of the "priesthood of all believers"
in the New Testament's concept of the church as a corporate "royal
priesthood."[33] There was no basis, Luther argued, for asserting that
the clergy were superior to the laity, as if they were some kind of
spiritual elite, or that their ordination conferred upon them some
special "indelible character." The clergy are merely laity who have
been recognized by other laity within the community of the church
as having special gifts and are authorized by their colleagues to exercise a pastoral or teaching ministry among them. The authority to
make such decisions thus rests with all Christians, not with an auto-
cratic elite or putative spiritual aristocracy.

Luther developed this point with a civil analogy, as accessible
today as it was five hundred years ago. The clergy are "office hold-
ers" who are elected by the laity as their representatives, teachers,
and leaders. There is no fundamental difference between clergy
and laity in terms of their status; the difference lies entirely in the
former being elected to the "office" of a priest. All believers already
have this status, on account of their baptism. This election to office
is reversible; those who are thus chosen can be deselected if the occasion demands it.

On the basis of this doctrine of the universal priesthood of believers, Luther insisted that every Christian has the right to interpret
the Bible and to raise concerns about any aspect of the church's
teaching or practice that appears to be inconsistent with the Bible.
There is no question of any "spiritual" authority, distinct from or
superior to ordinary Christians, who can impose certain readings of

the Bible upon the church. The right to read and interpret the Bible is the birthright of all Christians. At this stage, Luther clearly believes that the Bible is sufficiently clear for ordinary Christians to be able to read and understand it. Following through on his democratizing agenda, Luther insists that all believers have the right to read the Bible in a language they can understand, and to interpret its meaning for themselves. The church is thus held to be accountable to its members for its interpretation of its sacred text, and is open to challenge at every point.

The significance of Luther's point can hardly be overlooked. By insisting that it had a divinely ordained monopoly on biblical interpretation, the medieval church had declared itself to be above criticism on biblical grounds. No external critic had the authority to interpret Scripture, and thus to apply it to criticize the church's doctrines or practices. Luther's response was to empower the laity as interpreters of the Bible, and to hold the church accountable *to its people* for what it taught. And if they were not satisfied with the outcome, they, as laity, had the right to demand that a reforming council should be convened to address their concerns.

This final point was perhaps the most dangerous of all, as Luther seemed to have an important historical precedent on his side. Tongue placed firmly in his cheek, Luther reminded his readers that it was the Roman emperor Constantine who was responsible for summoning the Council of Nicaea (325), one of the most important councils of Christian history. If a lay ruler could summon such a council back then, why should not the German princes do the same twelve hundred years later?

Luther and other Protestants were roundly denounced as heretics by the church. For many Catholic apologists, Lutheranism was simply the reappearance of earlier heresies. In condemning as heretical or heterodox Luther's early theological theses in the sixteenth century, the University of Paris attempted to establish the essential continuity between earlier heresies and the ideas now being expounded by Luther.[34] Luther's ideas were thus not to be regarded as original, but were essentially the republication of older heresies. Thus Luther was a Hussite in his theology of contrition, a Wycliffite in his doctrine of confession, and a Manichaean in his theology of grace and free will. According to the University of Paris, the Reformation represented little more than the reappearance of older heresies that were already known and condemned.

Yet the unbiased reader of Luther is more impressed by his continuity with the patristic tradition than his departure from it. In terms of the great classic heresies of Christianity, Luther is to be judged as broadly orthodox at every point, save possibly in relation to his doctrine of the church. Given the political situation of the 1520s, Luther believed that it was necessary to break away from the church, ideally only temporarily, in order to retain the purity of the Christian faith. Luther was convinced that the church of his day had compromised its doctrine of grace, in effect upholding the Pelagian view that salvation was something earned or merited (a judgment that most scholars now dispute). For Luther, the historical circumstances of the time forced him to choose between holding an orthodox doctrine of the church, on the one hand, and of grace, on the other. According to the great nineteenth-century American Protestant theologian B. B. Warfield, "The Reformation, inwardly considered, was just the ultimate triumph of Augustine's doctrine of grace over Augustine's doctrine of the church."[35] This aligns Luther with Donatism at this specific point rather than with the views of Augustine of Hippo. Yet in other respects, Luther's doctrine of the church is thoroughly anti-Donatist.

Furthermore, both Luther and the mainstream Reformation as a whole regarded alignment with the classic forms of Christianity of the patristic era as essential to their self-understanding. Where some more radical Protestant movements abandoned traditional practices such as infant baptism and beliefs such as the doctrine of the Trinity, Luther and Calvin both insisted that their reforming programs were a direct extension of the classic patristic approach.

Protestantism would endorse Athanasius's and Augustine's judgments on what was orthodox and what was heretical.[36]

So was Luther really a heretic? And what of Protestantism as a whole? The passing of time has seen a marked mellowing of Catholic attitudes toward Luther and the churches of the Reformation. The Second Vatican Council (1962–65), for example, affirmed that the Holy Spirit was active in non-Catholic Christian communities. All who have been baptized and justified by faith can justly be said to be "members of Christ's body" and have a right to be called "Christian" and "brothers" by the Catholic church.

Yet our concern here is not with ecumenical relations between Protestantism and Catholicism, which have improved substantially in the last fifty years, but with the question of whether the concept of heresy was used with a different agenda after the patristic era. During the classic era, the concept has a robustly theological significance, denoting a manner of articulating or conceptualizing the Christian faith that ultimately renders it incoherent or indefensible. Yet in the Middle Ages, the term comes increasingly to mean a social or religious movement that is seen as a threat by or to the pope. In my judgment, Herbert Grundmann is correct to argue that it is inappropriate to use the term "heresy" in this way, in that it comes to be defined by the historical contingencies of the ecclesiastical politics of the age rather than the core ideas of the movements in question.

Protestantism and the Problem of Heresy

As we noted earlier, Protestantism was rapidly branded as a heresy by the Catholic Church. Protestants responded with indignation, retorting that they had recovered orthodoxy from its medieval distortions. What was Protestantism if not the recovery of the orthodox faith of the early church?[37] Yet Catholics had little difficulty in arguing that, while Protestantism might be perfectly capable of recovering earlier biblical interpretations, it lacked the means to determine whether what it had retrieved was orthodox or hetero-dox. And lacking any such capacity to discriminate such interpreta-tions, Protestants were obligated to repeat the judgments of the Catholic church on these matters. In their turn, Protestants argued that, since they were committed to restoring the authentic teaching of the early church, this naturally extended to the church's views on orthodoxy and heresy.

The Protestant approach to heresy worked well, providing it was restricted to the reaffirmation of the church's condemnation of ex-isting heresies or their revival in new forms. A good example of this revival of older heresies in modern forms can be seen in the rise of anti-Trinitarianism in Italian Protestant circles, which rapidly gained a following in northern Europe.[38] For Juan de Valdés and others, the doctrine of the Trinity was simply not to be found in the Bible, nor could it be defended on its basis. Protestants who were faithful to the Bible were therefore not only under no obligation to accept this doctrine; they had a responsibility to challenge it as a distortion of biblical truth. Forced out of Italy by the Inquisition, many settled in the independent republic of the Grisons in south-eastern Switzerland, where their influence upon Reformed Protes-tantism began to grow.

In this case, Protestantism was able to deal with such heterodox trends by an appeal to the consensus of faith of the church as set out in the councils of Ephesus and Chalcedon. Christianity as a whole had declared such teachings to be heretical; Protestantism thus en-dorsed this pattern of traditional teaching and, in doing so, rejected anti-Trinitarianism as heretical. These ideas arose within Protes-tantism yet were relatively easily discredited as new forms of older heresies. Yet what of new religious teachings, arising specifically within Protestantism, that had no real precedents in earlier Chris-tian history? Could these be described as heretical if they were found unacceptable?

An excellent example of this question lies in the Arminian con-troversy, which arose over the teachings of Jakob Arminius (1560–

1609) on predestination.[39] This major controversy within Calvinism arose over the doctrine of predestination and led to a fundamental bifurcation between Calvinism and Arminianism. Calvinist orthodoxy in the seventeenth century held that an individual's eternal destiny was entirely a matter of divine sovereignty. Arminianism held that human beings were, if only to a limited extent, implicated in their own election, having the capacity to resist God's calling. Each accused the other of being heretical. Yet in reality, each could equally claim to represent coherent interpretations of the Bible, interpretations that happened to differ substantially in terms of both their basic ideas and their implications for the Christian life.

The difficulty for Protestantism was that it was found to possess no higher authority that can declare one or the other to be in the right. If Scripture is the supreme rule of faith, no interpretative authority can be placed above Scripture. In the end, the only practical means of deciding the question was a vote within the Protestant constituency in question—as, for example, at the Synod of Dort (1618–19), which established the boundaries of Calvinist orthodoxy. Orthodoxy thus ran the risk of being defined as the theology with the most votes within a given constituency, and heterodoxy as the minority voice.

The problem here is that "heresy" is ultimately a teaching judged unacceptable by the entire church; the term is not properly applicable to either Calvinism or Arminianism, which represent divisions within one constituency of Protestantism—namely, the Reformed church. One can certainly speak of heresy arising within Protestantism—for example, the revival of Arianism in seventeenth- and eighteenth-century Anglicanism.[40] Yet in that case, ideas that the entire church regarded as heretical made their reappearance. The nature of Protestantism is such that it is very difficult to use the term "heresy" to refer to divergent schools of thought within that movement, and limited to that movement, *unless* they reproduce ideas that the church as a whole had already agreed to be unorthodox. We find here a set of competing Protestant orthodoxies, each with its own grounding in the Bible, its own understanding of the internal dynamics of faith, and its own parameters of adjudication as to what is acceptable and what is not. It is difficult to avoid the conclusion that the term "heresy" is simply not appropriate in this situation. A heresy is a teaching that the whole Christian church, not a party within that church, regards as unacceptable.

Yet there are significant voices within Protestantism that called for—and continue to call for—a reconsideration of the relation between orthodoxy and power, especially in the light of the right of individuals to interpret the Bible as they see fit. The great English Puritan theologian and poet John Milton (1608–74), for example, argued that freedom of religious conscience was of central importance to any attempt to define orthodoxy. The very idea of the imposition of orthodoxy ran counter to Milton's deepest theological and cultural instincts.[41] Orthodoxy designates an interpretation of Scripture that seems right to the individual Protestant conscience. We see here a reaction against authoritarianism, framed in terms of an appeal to the theological judgment and exegetical integrity of the individual. For what is the church if not a collection of individuals, all attempting to make sense of the same Scripture as seems best to them? For Milton, a "heretical" opinion is any religious opinion that rests upon external authority instead of individual conscience:

> Seeing therefore that no man, no synod, no session of men . . . can judge definitively the sense of scripture to another man's conscience . . . it follows plainly, that he who holds in religion that belief or those opinions which to his conscience and utmost understanding appear . . . in the scripture, though to others he seems erroneous, can no more be justly censur'd for a heretic than his censurers; who do but the same thing themselves while they censure him for so doing.[42]

Milton's analysis thus highlights the difficulties in which Protestantism has found itself when trying to deal with the notion of heresy. Protestantism places the interpretation of Scripture at the heart of its theology and recognizes no authority above Scripture.[43] This being the case, it is obliged to recognize that multiple interpretations of Scripture will ensue, with no authorized means of determining which is "orthodox" and which "heretical." This difficulty can be alleviated, but not resolved, by appealing to the judgment of antiquity concerning which views were heretical and which orthodox. Yet ultimately Protestantism would wish to keep such questions open, at least theoretically maintaining the possibility that such patristic judgments might require revision in the light of ongoing biblical interpretation. Protestantism thus finds itself entangled in some theological difficulties when dealing with the connected notions of "heresy" and "orthodoxy." We shall return to consider this point again later in this chapter.

Postmodernism, Heresy, and the Suspicion of Power

In this chapter, we have explored some aspects of the relationship between heresy, orthodoxy, and power. While there can be little doubt that the concept of heresy is linked with issues of power, this does not mean that heresy is defined by those with power or that there is no intellectual essence or characteristic of heresy. The classical heresies of the Christian faith, all of which arise from the journeys of theological exploration of the patristic era, may well have political and social implications. They are not, however, ultimately political or social constructs but are better understood as theological dead ends.

There is a further point that must be explored a little further in closing this chapter. We have already noted that contemporary Western culture finds heresy attractive. The values of postmodern culture are such that they offer implicit reasons for preferring heresy over orthodoxy—such as the pervasive belief that heresy is less moralistic and authoritarian than orthodoxy, that heresy is more intellectually exciting than its stolid orthodox rival, or that orthodoxy has suppressed the truth about heresy in an attempt to cover up its own intellectual or historical shortcomings. All of these perceptions are difficult to defend historically; yet they resonate with the cultural mood. The history of Western culture suggests that such perceptions rapidly become realities.

Yet history indicates that many heresies—such as Montanism—were much more authoritarian and morally rigorous than orthodoxy. Far from being "innovative" or "radical," many heresies were actually rather conservative, attempting to hold on to traditional ideas that were being undermined by the more radical ideas developed by early Christianity. The ideas of Gnosticism, for example, seem rather dull and plodding compared with the transformative Christian notion of the Incarnation. And the recent surge in historical interest in the early Christian world, including the origins of heresy, has provided little in the way of ammunition for the conspiracy theorists. Dan Brown's *Da Vinci Code* (2003) is of interest more for its selective manipulation of history than for any credible critique, historical or intellectual, of Christian orthodoxy. The novel's success partly reflects its resonance with the cultural mood.

Yet two aspects of the somewhat fuzzy postmodern attitude toward heresy merit closer attention. The new cultural fascination with heresy in the West is partly due to two of postmodernity's distinctive beliefs: first, that regnant orthodoxies are simply the outcome of power; and second, that any attempt to achieve "closure" of debates is improper. We shall explore these briefly, and note their significance.

First, we need to note the deep suspicion of orthodoxy that lurks within postmodernity. Orthodoxy, in a postmodern reading of things, is not about the merited triumph of ideas that were clearly superior to their rivals. It is about the imposition of such ideas by those in power as a way of both expressing and buttressing their social positions. Orthodoxy is thus a controlling ideology, designed to enhance and defend the vested interests of the establishment. To use Michel Foucault's famous image, orthodoxy was the "panopticon," the "all-seeing place," from which everything could be controlled and manipulated, in order to preserve the status quo.[44]

Foucault's critique of any privileged viewpoint merits close consideration, not least because it correctly notes how concepts of "truth" are easily subverted in the interests of power. Readers familiar with the history of the Soviet Union will recall the title of the organ of the Communist Party: *Pravda*—the Russian word for "truth." Foucault's point has force when dealing with the use of the notion of heresy in the Middle Ages in that the idea was often used to disempower, and provide an intellectual justification for the elimination of, individuals or groups who were deemed to pose a threat to the papacy. For this reason, among others, I am inclined to limit the use of the term "heresy" to the classic period, ending with the formulations of the Council of Chalcedon in 451.

In the classic period, the evidence points strongly to the consensual emergence of the idea of heresy. The term was occasionally used by some patristic writers in an attempt to denigrate their rivals and opponents, especially when matters of ecclesiastical politics were involved. Yet these personal accusations of heresy were subject to evaluation and reception by the church as a whole.[45] The concept of heresy was a matter for the church, not for powerful individuals or interest groups. It is thus significant to note that the exercise of ecclesiastical power by emperors in the fourth century tended to favor Arianism rather than orthodoxy, suggesting that, if anything, heretical positions were privileged by this use of power.

Secondly, some regard the notion of "orthodoxy" with suspicion on account of its sense of closure. Are these not questions that ought to remain open? Is not orthodoxy a *provisional* notion, one that needs to be kept under constant review? This is certainly the view of the postmodern writer Hilary Lawson, whose critique of the idea of closure merits consideration here. For Lawson, "closure can be understood as the imposition of fixity on openness." It represents an improper "closing of that which is open."[46] All journeys of intellectual exploration are ongoing and do not arrive at a fixed or permanent destination. Lawson thus argues for a permanent state of openness concerning reality. We do not arrive at a destination in our intellectual voyaging, but only at a "temporary resting point."[47]

Lawson's demand for a permanent suspension of judgment, a keeping open of all intellectual options, has value in emphasizing the importance of constant theological vigilance. Yet it is questionable whether it has any merit beyond affirming the importance of avoiding complacency and regularly reexamining intellectual options. Lawson's position is that reality is wide-open and that human observers falsely and improperly "close" it through their theories, which inevitably limit and distort our grasp of things. The only way of avoiding this distortion, according to Lawson, is to avoid closure itself.

There is merit in this point, although not perhaps as Lawson states it. As one who is very happy to identify himself as a representative of classic Protestantism, I am committed to the notion of the constant interrogation and review of existing formulas of faith, constantly wishing to ensure that the church uses only the best and most authentic means of expressing the fundamental themes of its faith. This means that orthodoxy is understood to be a viewpoint that is sufficiently robust and coherent that such a process of interrogation can lead only to its confirmation and vindication. Orthodoxy does not demand to be dogmatically imposed, but rather calls out to be recognized on account of its intrinsic virtues.

In any case, it would be misleading to speak, for example, of the Council of Chalcedon as having secured total closure of the question of the identity of Jesus of Nazareth. The council's pronouncements are better seen as identifying some ground rules for thinking about the person of Christ, marking off some options as inadequate while legitimating a range of possibilities as orthodox. If the range of possible interpretations of Christ's identity and significance is a field, Chalcedon simply placed a hedge around the good pastures. As the noted theologian Karl Rahner pointed out, the Council of Chalcedon actually marked a new beginning to Christian reflection on the identity of Christ rather than the ending of any such process.[48]

Yet underlying these points is something that is often over-looked—namely, that Christian orthodoxy is as much an ongoing process as a fixed set of outcomes. As a classic Protestant, for example, I would hold that I have every reason to suppose that a certain set of beliefs constitute "orthodoxy"; yet at the same time, I am committed to their constant interrogation in case they should prove to be in some way inadequate or inauthentic. Orthodoxy is thus, in a certain sense, *unfinished,* in that it represents the mind of the church as to the best manner of formulation of its living faith at any given time. Conflicts and tensions past and present may help the crystallization of fresh insights and the development of new ways of expressing traditional ideas, or they may bring about the realization that a certain way of speaking and thinking, once thought to be adequate, must now be regarded as problematic.

The history of early Christian thought makes clear the dangers of theological complacency. Ideas that were once regarded as orthodox turned out, on closer examination—often over extended periods of time—to be inadequate. Indeed, it is possible to argue that Arius was actually a theological traditionalist who failed to appreciate that his "tidying up" of the Christian tradition actually impoverished it and severely impaired its conceptual and linguistic capacity to accommodate the realities of faith.[49] Paradoxically, those who woodenly define orthodoxy as the verbal repetition of theological formulas of the past risk fossilizing the Christian faith, trapping it in one of its specific historic forms without giving it the conceptual and verbal spaciousness to remain true to the mystery it attempts to express and convey.[50]

In this chapter, we have considered the interplay of orthodoxy and heresy on the one hand and political power on the other. While there is unquestionably an interactive dynamic between them, it will be clear that it is not possible to maintain the idea that Christian orthodoxy simply represents the establishment's preferred outcome during the patristic era, when many Christian doctrines crystallized into their present forms. Yet when Christianity morphed from being a religious movement outside the establishment to becoming a major political player, culminating in the emergence of Christendom, the idea of heresy inevitably developed new associations. The politicization of orthodoxy inevitably entails a corresponding politicization of its antithesis—heresy.

The social outcome of this was perhaps inevitable. Where a dominant politicized orthodoxy was experienced as privileged, repressive, or uncaring, heretical movements offered individuals an alternative religious vision and structure. They had the capacity to become effective movements of social protest on account of their political context, which created space for this social function. Given this context, it is not difficult to understand how heresy came to be tinged with aspirations of libertarianism in early modern Europe. Indeed, the postmodern fascination with heresy is grounded largely in this lingering cultural memory. The social realities may have changed, but their memory and associations live on.

ten

Heresy and the Islamic View of Christianity

The analysis presented in this book has tended to focus on the past rather than the present. Yet an understanding of the past can nevertheless be helpful in making sense of the present and engaging some contemporary questions. One highly important example may be noted, even though its full discussion lies beyond the scope of this work. One of the most significant and difficult relationships in the contemporary world is the uneasy and suspicious dynamic between Christianity and Islam. Both are expanding, and in the course of their mutual expansion they have the potential to encounter each other as potential rivals and combatants.

Yet a respectful dialogue between Christianity and Islam has much to offer, partly in reducing tension between the two faiths, and partly because their differences help illuminate their distinct identities. A classic example concerns how the two faiths deal with the question of divine revelation. As Richard Martin and Mark Woodward put it, "How can the transcendent and eternal divine exist in historical, human context? For Christians, the problem centered on a person, Jesus Christ. For Muslims, it centered on a book, the Qur'an."[1] While there are forms of Christianity that come close to Islam's emphasis on the supreme authority of a text—most notably, certain forms of Protestantism[2]—Christianity has traditionally accorded to Christ the position that Islam accords to the Qur'an. The scholar of religion Wilfred Cantwell Smith writes:

> Muslims and Christians have been alienated partly by the fact that both have misunderstood each other's faith by trying to fit it into their own patterns. The most usual error is to suppose (on both sides) that the roles of Jesus Christ in Christianity and of Muhammad in Islam are comparable. . . . If one is drawing parallels in terms of the structure of the two religions, what corresponds in the Christian scheme to the Qur'an is not the Bible but the person of Christ—it is Christ who is for Christians the revelation of (from) God.[3]

So how does our exploration and characterization of Christian heresy relate to the depiction of Jesus within Islam, and especially within the Qur'an? What if the Qur'an's criticisms or representations of Christianity's understanding of the person and place of Jesus reflect familiarity with its heretical, rather than its orthodox, forms?

One of the more troubling questions that hover over the surface of attempts to ease this difficult relationship is that of Islam's representation of core Christian ideas such as the doctrine of the Trinity and the divinity of Christ. Most Christians find that the Qur'anic representation of these concepts bears little relation to their orthodox statements. Muslims whose knowledge of Christian beliefs rests solely upon the Qur'an often find themselves distressed by the manifest tension between what they have been led to suppose that Christians believe about Jesus and what they actually discover in conversation with Christians. Is there a way in which this situation can be resolved with integrity on both sides?

The ideas set out in this volume lay the groundwork for a solution that is both historically and theologically plausible. The problematic Qur'anic representation of Christianity can be argued to reflect knowledge, whether direct or indirect, of *heretical* versions of Christianity that are known to have been present in this region. As we have insisted throughout this work, heresies must be considered to arise within the church, and hence can be regarded as "Christian," even though in a weak sense of the term. Nevertheless, they cannot be regarded as *authentically* Christian. The Qur'an thus critiques ideas that lie on the fringe of the Christian faith—and that virtually all Christians would also agree to be defective.

We shall illustrate this by considering two points at which the presentation of Christian ideas in the Qur'an raises concerns: the doctrine of the Trinity, and the doctrine of the divinity of Christ.

The Qur'anic representation of the doctrine of the Trinity has caused some bewilderment to Christians. Even allowing for a modest degree of textual ambiguity, the Qur'an appears to represent Christians as worshipping a trinity of three distinct persons— God, Jesus, and Mary.[4] Although a number of scholarly Islamic writers have been careful to present what Christians actually believe,[5] this curious tritheistic representation of Christianity remains perplexingly influential within popular Islam. This view simply cannot be sustained by any comparison with orthodox Christianity. So how are we to account for its origins? Why does the Qur'an attribute such a view to Christians when it is so clearly alien to mainline Christian orthodoxy?

The Qur'anic view of the Trinity appears to show at least some degree of familiarity with a heretical school within Christianity that was known to have been influential in the region of Arabia at that time. The heresy in question is that of the Collyridian sect, which flourished in the area that would now be called the Middle East.[6] One of its most distinctive characteristics is treating Mary as a goddess, offering her worship and honor comparable to what might be expected for God himself.[7] It is significant that the geographical regions within which Collyridianism appears to have flourished in the fifth century coincided with those once associated with the worship of female divinities such as Demeter and Rhea. The movement is one of the eighty "heresies" identified by Epiphanius of Salamis

(c. 310–403) in his *Panarion*. The fact that it is ranked seventy-eighth on Epiphanius's list of eighty heterodox sects suggests that he did not regard it as being particularly important; nevertheless, it appears to have been influential in the region that would later become the crucible within which Islam emerged. Do the Qur'anic comments on the Trinity reflect familiarity with this local Arabian heresy?

The same issue emerges as significant in considering the Qur'anic view of Jesus of Nazareth. The geographical and cultural location of early Islam had a significant impact on its understanding and evaluation of Christianity. Chalcedonian orthodoxy seems to have been slow to find its way into the Arabian Peninsula, let alone to command general acceptance in that remote region. Heretical views of the identity of Jesus of Nazareth appear to have had a significant impact in this region. In the absence of an alternative, heretical Christologies appear to have had a significant influence, especially at the popular level.

The Qur'an represents Christians as understanding and worshipping Jesus as a physically divine figure, which is tantamount to paganism, idolatry, or polytheism. This criticism can be defended only with some difficulty in the face of orthodox Christian thought,[8] especially given that the relationship between God the Father and God the Son is not understood physically.[9] However, the Qur'anic depiction of Jesus of Nazareth makes sense when seen in the context of the intrinsic Docetism of many Gnostic Christologies, which are known to have been influential in this region of Arabia around this time.[10] The suggestion that the Qur'an's critique of Christology has been evoked by local Christologies influenced by Sethian Gnosticism does not detract from the validity of the criticisms it offers. It is simply to note that a local inauthentic version of the Christian faith is being criticized, not its definitive orthodox form.

For example, let us consider again a passage we considered earlier (see p. 116), taken from a significant work of Sethian Gnosticism, the Second Treatise of the Great Seth. This work, believed to date from the fourth century, is an important witness to Gnostic understandings of Jesus of Nazareth prevalent in Egypt and Arabia. This work refuses to accept that Jesus was crucified, offering an alternative account of the events of Good Friday that is written in the first person.

> I did not succumb to them as they had planned. But I was not afflicted at all. Those who were there punished me. And I did not die in reality but in appearance. . . . For my death, which they think happened, [happened] to them in their error and blindness, since they nailed their man unto their death. For their Ennoias did not see me, for they were deaf and blind. But in doing these things, they condemn themselves. Yes, they saw me; they punished me. It was another, their father, who drank the gall and the vinegar; it was not I. They struck me with the reed; it was another, Simon, who bore the cross on his shoulder. It was another upon Whom they placed the crown of thorns.[11]

It will be obvious that this teaching bears a remarkable similarity to Islamic teachings about Jesus of Nazareth, which reflect a similar disinclination to accept that Jesus suffered and died upon the cross. The central passage in the Qur'an chastises the children of Israel for killing God's prophets, for vilifying Mary, and for claiming to have killed the Christ.

> They say: "We have surely killed the Christ, Jesus son of Mary, the messenger of God." They did not kill him, nor did they crucify him; rather, it was made only to appear so to them. . . . They did not kill him. . . . Rather, God took him up to himself, for God is mighty and wise.[12]

Although there are some grammatical questions about how this passage is to be translated, most Qur'anic exegetes have regarded

this as amounting to an explicit denial of the death and crucifixion
of Christ at the hands of his enemies. Many Islamic commentators
have taken a similar line, arguing that the New Testament includes
material that detracts from the divinity or honor of Jesus. For example, the eleventh-century writer Ibn al-Juwayni (1028–85)
argued that the Gospel writers ought to have omitted references to
events such as the scourging of Jesus and the crowning with thorns,
which humiliate Jesus.[13] Similarly, Abu Hamid al-Ghazali (1058–
1111) took exception to the description of Christ's passion in the
Gospel of Matthew, in particular words attributed to Christ such as
"Let this cup pass away from me" and "Father, why have you abandoned me?" These, he argues, point to Jesus as a human being
rather than a divine figure.

Some scholars, such as Mahmoud Mustafa Ayoub (b. 1938), have
suggested that the Qur'anic view of Jesus, although superficially
Docetic, is actually merely substitutionist.[14] This, however, is to limit
Docetism to only one of its specific historical forms. Ayoub seems
unaware of the complexity of Docetism, in particular the tendency of
some of its forms to deny the death by crucifixion of Jesus of Nazareth as demeaning or humiliating, thereby compromising his divinity. In this view, as we have seen, Jesus is held not to have died on the
cross, being replaced by a substitute such as Simon of Cyrene.

So what are the Qur'an's sources on this matter? It seems increasingly clear that the Qur'anic representation of the fundamental
ideas of Christianity has been shaped by an encounter with the
forms of Christianity that were prevalent in the Arabian Peninsula.
These, it seems, may have been predominantly heretical rather than
orthodox. The issue is not so much the Qur'anic view of Jesus itself,
but its sources. Where did Muhammad derive these views? The
presence of these ideas in the Nag Hammadi collection of texts is
suggestive, given their geographical vicinity to the Arabian Peninsula. Islam's problematic characterization of Christianity gives
every appearance of having been shaped by sources influenced by
Sethian Gnosticism rather than Chalcedonian orthodoxy.

This way of looking at things, if correct, opens the way to a significant degree of theological rapprochement between Christianity and Islam. Since Christian heresies are forms of Christianity, no matter how defective, deformed, or distorted, the recognition that the Qur'an knows of, and criticizes, heretical forms of Christianity allows Muslims to affirm that what is being criticized is indeed a form of Christianity, and Christians to respond by pointing out that they are not *authentic* or *representative* forms of Christianity. Indeed, Christians would concur in criticizing such beliefs as they are presented in the Qur'an. Muhammad may well have been correct in identifying unacceptable Christian views about Jesus and God— but the inadequacy of these views would be accepted by Christians, and their representative character called into question.

Further exploration of this point will be important to Christian-Muslim relations. If the Qur'an shows familiarity primarily with heretical views on the Trinity and Christology, which could be extrapolated to generalizations about Christianity itself, there is no doubt that the often tense relationship between these faiths could be improved by more detailed investigation of these issues.

conclusion

The Future of Heresy

"Morality, like art, means drawing a line somewhere" (Oscar Wilde). This book has explored the idea of heresy within the Christian tradition, trying to understand at least something of its nature and origins—about how theological lines had to be drawn, and came to be drawn, between the realms of orthodoxy and heresy. It does not set out to offer any new insights into individual heresies, but tries to distill and collate a significant body of academic research into the phenomenon of heresy, using certain heresies as case studies to illustrate points of importance. And while this exploration is undoubtedly of academic interest, its real significance lies in its implications for the life of the church. In bringing this book to a close, we therefore turn away from the great scholarly questions of the nature and origins of heresy, to consider, however briefly, its contemporary significance for Christian communities.

Some have suggested that heresy is essentially an outmoded idea, with little or no relevance to modern church life.[1] Even a casual reading of recent writings on the early church indicates that there has been a persistent intensifying of skeptical presumptions concerning the contemporary legitimacy and utility of the notion of heresy. It is widely held that it reflects the concerns and agendas of long-bygone eras in the history of the church, and can safely be discarded. However, the analysis offered in this work indicates that this is simply not correct, primarily for two reasons.

First, the pursuit of orthodoxy is essentially the quest for Christian authenticity. The relentless attempt to find the best formulations of Christian truth claims reflects the insight that Christianity is capable of stating and understanding its ideas inadequately and inauthentically. In a fiercely competitive religious and cultural context, Christianity's future existence and prosperity will depend upon its presenting itself in its most authentic forms.[2] To put it somewhat bluntly and pragmatically, defective and damaging forms of the Christian faith—in other words, heresies—will limit its survival prospects. The quest for orthodoxy is above all a search for authenticity.

Secondly, heresies, like history, have a habit of repeating themselves. The historian may treat Gnosticism as a complex intellectual and cultural movement of late classical antiquity, raising some interesting questions for academic historians yet perhaps not for anyone else. However, those who are concerned about the relationship of Christianity and modern culture see a somewhat different picture. Gnosticism lives on today, not necessarily knowing its real name or even its history.[3] Yet its spoor is unmistakable. Its echo is heard today in those who interpret Christianity as a religion of self-discovery, not redemption. Religion is the quest for true inner identity, the "real me," the inner spark of divine life, or the gold in the mud. The challenge faced by the churches is whether they can counter such cultural stereotypes rather than inadvertently reinforcing them.

The new interest in heresy so characteristic of the late twentieth and early twenty-first centuries goes far beyond the renewal of scholarly interest in a neglected or misunderstood phenomenon of the past. Indeed, some have suggested that modern scholarship in this area is not simply "enamored" of ancient heresies but practices "historical advocacy" at the expense of "even-handed" history.[4] There is no doubt, for example, that many recent scholars have advocated Gnosticism as a congenial alternative to what they regard as the failings and vices of traditional Christianity. Elaine Pagels, for example, clearly regards Gnosticism (or at least certain forms of it) as more egalitarian than Christian orthodoxy. As we have seen, this is a highly problematic reading of the situation. Yet while such stereotypes can be challenged by historical scholarship, the underlying perception persists. Indeed, for many the perception has become the reality. It needs to be challenged and corrected.

The lure of the religious forbidden can be accounted for, at least to some extent, on social psychological grounds.[5] However, its appeal is not due simply to the psychology of proscribed forms of social cognition; it reflects a disturbing perception within Western culture that Christian orthodoxy is dull and damaging, which encourages the rise of the counterperception that heresy is intellectually exciting and spiritually liberating. This perception can be discerned within the so-called Victorian crisis of faith[6] and remains a potent threat to the popular appeal of orthodoxy to this day. As one English commentator on the "Death of God" debate of the 1960s pointed out: "While most of the philosophy and theology contained in the 'Death of God' literature seems to be very second-rate or worse, it is very necessary to reflect on how absolutely deadly must have been the experience which the writers of this literature must have had, both in the worshipping and in the theological lives of their churches."[7] Was it so surprising that people concluded that God was dead when the supposed communities of his habitation were so dreary and uninteresting?

Yet the real challenge faced by the churches cannot be neutralized by the demonstration that theological orthodoxy is both necessary and appropriate for the well-being of Christian communities.[8] Can orthodoxy once more be sprinkled with stardust? If Christianity is to regain the imaginative ascendancy, it must rediscover what G. K. Chesterton (1874–1936) termed "the romance of orthodoxy."[9] It is not sufficient to show that orthodoxy represents the most intellectually and spiritually authentic form of the Christian faith or that it has been tried and tested against its intellectual alternatives. The problem lies deeper, at the level of the imagination and feelings. If Christ is indeed the "Lord of the Imagination,"[10] the distinction between orthodoxy and heresy ought to have significant imaginative implications. The real challenge is for the churches to demonstrate that orthodoxy is imaginatively compelling, emotionally engaging, aesthetically enhancing, and personally liberating. We await this development with eager anticipation.

Notes

INTRODUCTION

1. Geoffrey Chaucer, *Canterbury Tales,* Wife of Bath's Prologue, l. 525.
2. Patrick Henry, "Why Is Contemporary Scholarship So Enamored of Ancient Heresies?" in *Proceedings of the 8th International Conference on Patristic Studies,* ed. E. A. Livingstone (Oxford: Pergamon Press, 1980), 123–26.
3. Peter Gay, *Modernism: The Lure of Heresy from Baudelaire to Beckett and Beyond* (New York: W. W. Norton, 2008).
4. Will Herberg, *Faith Enacted as History: Essays in Biblical Theology* (Philadelphia: Westminster Press, 1976), 170–71.
5. The term "new atheism" is used to refer to a group of writings that appeared in 2004–7, especially Sam Harris, *The End of Faith: Religion, Terror, and the Future of Reason* (New York: W.W. Norton & Co., 2004); Daniel C. Dennett, *Breaking the Spell: Religion as a Natural Phenomenon* (New York: Viking, 2006); Richard Dawkins, *The God Delusion* (Boston: Houghton Mifflin Co., 2006); and Christopher Hitchens, *God Is Not Great: How Religion Poisons Everything* (New York: Twelve, 2007).
6. For the original German edition, see Walter Bauer, *Rechtgläubigkeit und Ketzerei im ältesten Christentum* (Tübingen: Mohr, 1934). For the more influential (and much later) English translation, see Walter Bauer, *Orthodoxy and Heresy in Earliest Christianity* (Philadelphia: Fortress Press, 1971).
7. See Bart D. Ehrman, *Lost Christianities: The Battles for Scripture and the Faiths We Never Knew* (New York: Oxford Univ. Press, 2003), 163–80.
8. Dan Brown, *The Da Vinci Code: A Novel* (New York: Doubleday, 2003). The significant subtitle was dropped from later editions.
9. Michael Baigent, Richard Leigh, and Henry Lincoln, *Holy Blood, Holy Grail* (New York: Delacorte Press, 1982).

10. In 2006 Leigh and Baigent (but not Lincoln) unsuccessfully sued Brown in the High Court in London, arguing that he had breached their copyright at this point and others. The issue concerned who had invented these ideas and thus held their intellectual property rights.

11. Brown, *Da Vinci Code,* 233.

12. See, e.g., Bart D. Ehrman, *Truth and Fiction in the Da Vinci Code: A Historian Reveals What We Really Know About Jesus, Mary Magdalene, and Constantine* (Oxford: Oxford Univ. Press, 2004), 23–24: "The view that Teabing lays out is wrong on all key points: Christians before Nicaea already did accept Jesus as divine; the Gospels of the New Testament portray him as human as much as they portray him as divine; the Gospels that did *not* get included in the New Testament portray him as divine as much, or more so, than they portray him as human." Ehrman's comments are all the more significant, given his hostility toward traditional Christian accounts of orthodoxy and heresy.

13. Brown, *Da Vinci Code,* 234.

14. See Robert A. Segal, ed., *The Allure of Gnosticism: The Gnostic Experience in Jungian Psychology and Contemporary Culture* (Chicago: Open Court, 1995).

15. For this development, see Andrew Roach, *The Devil's World: Heresy and Society, 1100–1300* (London: Longman, 2005).

16. Peter L. Berger, *The Heretical Imperative: Contemporary Possibilities of Religious Affirmation* (Garden City, NY: Anchor Press, 1979), 30–31.

17. See the analysis in Don Cupitt, *After God: The Future of Religion* (London: Weidenfeld and Nicolson, 1997).

18. For an introduction to the field of reception theory, see Wolfgang Iser, *The Act of Reading: A Theory of Aesthetic Response* (Baltimore: Johns Hopkins Univ. Press, 1978); and Robert C. Holub, *Crossing Borders: Reception Theory, Poststructuralism, Deconstruction* (Madison: Univ. of Wisconsin Press, 1992).

19. Garrett Green, *Theology, Hermeneutics and Imagination: The Case of Interpretation at the End of Modernity* (Cambridge: Cambridge Univ. Press, 2000), 20.

20. For representative works in this debate, see April D. De Conick, *The Thirteenth Apostle: What the Gospel of Judas Really Says* (London: Continuum, 2007); Bart D. Ehrman, *The Lost Gospel of Judas Iscariot: A New Look at Betrayer and Betrayed* (Oxford: Oxford Univ. Press, 2006); Elaine H. Pagels and Karen L. King, *Reading Judas: The Gospel of Judas and the Shaping of Christianity* (New York: Viking, 2007); and N. T. Wright, *Judas and the Gospel of Jesus: Have We Missed the Truth About Christianity?* (Grand Rapids, MI: Baker Books, 2006).

21. *Mail on Sunday* (London), March 12, 2006. For a full discussion of the media hype and exaggeration of the importance of this document, see Simon J. Gathercole, *The Gospel of Judas: Rewriting Early Christianity* (Oxford: Oxford Univ. Press, 2007), 132–49.

22. For this aspect of Gnosticism, see Birger A. Pearson, *Gnosticism, Judaism, and Egyptian Christianity* (Minneapolis: Fortress Press, 1990).

23. The Gospel of Judas is representative of the specific form of Gnosticism known as Sethianism. See further John D. Turner, *Sethian Gnosticism and the Platonic Tradition* (Louvain: Peeters, 2001).

24. Wright, *Judas,* passim.

25. For reflection on this point, see G. K. Chesterton, *Orthodoxy* (New York: John Lane, 1908), 131–32.

26. For an accessible attempt to engage with this question, see Ben Quash and Michael Ward, eds., *Heresies and How to Avoid Them: Why It Matters What Christians Believe* (London: SPCK, 2007).

27. H. E. W. Turner, *The Pattern of Christian Truth: A Study in the Relations Between Orthodoxy and Heresy in the Early Church* (London: Mowbray, 1954). Turner notes that there is a "fringe or penumbra between orthodoxy and heresy" (79); for a more detailed exploration of this image with reference to the doctrinal developments of the second century, see 81–94.

28. John B. Henderson, *The Construction of Orthodoxy and Heresy: Neo-Confucian, Islamic, Jewish, and Early Christian Patterns* (Albany, NY: State Univ. of New York Press, 1998).

CHAPTER 1: FAITH, CREEDS, AND THE CHRISTIAN GOSPEL

1. William James, "The Will to Believe," in *The Will to Believe and Other Essays in Popular Philosophy* (New York: Longmans, Green, and Co., 1897), 1–31.

2. See esp. Roy Baumeister, *Meanings of Life* (New York: Guilford Press, 1991).

3. Alister E. McGrath, *The Open Secret: A New Vision for Natural Theology* (Oxford: Blackwell, 2008), 113–216.

4. Michael Polanyi, "Science and Reality," *British Journal for the Philosophy of Science* 18 (1967): 177–96, esp. 190–91.

5. There is a huge literature, including works such as Alister C. Hardy, *The Spiritual Nature of Man: A Study of Contemporary Religious Experience* (Oxford: Clarendon Press, 1980); Nicholas Lash, *Easter in Ordinary: Reflections on Human Experience and the Knowledge of God* (Charlottesville: Univ. Press of Virginia, 1988); and Jean Borella, *Le sens du surnaturel* (Geneva: Éditions Ad Solem, 1996).

6. Stanley Hauerwas, "The Demands of a Truthful Story: Ethics and the Pastoral Task," *Chicago Studies* 21 (1982): 59–71; quote at 65–66. Similar points were made earlier in Iris Murdoch, "Vision and Choice in Morality," in *Christian Ethics and Contemporary Philosophy,* ed. Ian T. Ramsey (London: SCM Press, 1966), 195–218.

7. Stanley Hauerwas, *The Peaceable Kingdom: A Primer in Christian Ethics* (Notre Dame, IN: Univ. of Notre Dame Press, 1983), 101–2.

8. C. S. Lewis, "Is Theology Poetry?" in *C. S. Lewis Essay Collection: Faith, Christianity and the Church,* ed. Lesley Walmsley (London: Collins, 2000), 1–21.

9. See here Mark McIntosh, "Faith, Reason and the Mind of Christ," in *Reason and the Reasons of Faith,* ed. Paul J. Griffiths and Reinhart Hütter (New York: T&T Clark, 2005), 119–42.

10. McGrath, *Open Secret,* 171–216.

11. A theme explored in Stanton J. Linden, *Darke Hierogliphicks: Alchemy in English Literature from Chaucer to the Restoration* (Lexington: Univ. Press of Kentucky, 1996), 156–92.

12. Clarence H. Miller, "Christ as the Philosopher's Stone in George Herbert's 'The Elixir,'" *Notes and Queries* 45 (1998): 39–41.

13. N. R. Hanson, *Patterns of Discovery: An Inquiry into the Conceptual Foundations of Science* (Cambridge: Cambridge Univ. Press, 1961). Hanson thus argues that Tycho Brahe (who believed in a geocentric solar system) and Johannes Kepler (a supporter of the heliocentric model of the solar system) "see" very different things when observing a sunrise: Tycho sees the moving sun cross a stationary horizon, while Kepler sees a moving horizon dipping down to expose a stationary sun. For a detailed analysis, see Matthias Adam, *Theoriebeladenheit und Objektivität: Zur Rolle von Beobachtungen in den Naturwissenschafte* (Frankfurt am Main: Ontos Verlag, 2002).

14. An excellent recent example may be found in Rowan Williams, *Tokens of Trust: An Introduction to Christian Belief* (Louisville, KY: Westminster John Knox Press, 2007).

15. For the historical development of the creeds, see J. N. D. Kelly, *Early Christian Creeds*, 3rd ed. (New York: Longman, 1981).

16. James L. Bailey and Lyle D. Vander Broek, *Literary Forms in the New Testament: A Handbook* (Louisville, KY: Westminster/John Knox Press, 1992), 83–84.

17. There is a huge literature on this topic. See, e.g., Colin E. Gunton, *The Actuality of Atonement: A Study of Metaphor, Rationality, and the Christian Tradition* (Grand Rapids, MI: Eerdmans, 1989).

18. Samuel Taylor Coleridge, *Complete Works*, 7 vols. (New York: Harper & Brothers, 1884), 5:172.

19. Hava Tirosh-Samuelson, "Theology of Nature in Sixteenth-Century Italian Jewish Philosophy," *Science in Context* 10 (1997): 529–70.

20. Gerhard May, *Creatio Ex Nihilo: The Doctrine of "Creation Out of Nothing" in Early Christian Thought* (Edinburgh: T. & T. Clark, 1995).

21. There is a very large literature on this subject. See esp. Paul Fiddes, *The Creative Suffering of God* (Oxford: Clarendon Press, 1988); Terence E. Fretheim, *The Suffering of God: An Old Testament Perspective* (Philadelphia: Fortress Press, 1984); and Paul Gavrilyuk, *The Suffering of the Impassible God: The Dialectics of Patristic Thought* (Oxford: Oxford Univ. Press, 2004).

22. See esp. Lewis Ayres, *Nicaea and Its Legacy: An Approach to Fourth-Century Trinitarian Theology* (Oxford: Oxford Univ. Press, 2004).

23. Charles Gore, *The Incarnation of the Son of God* (London: John Murray, 1922), 80–112.

24. Gore, *Incarnation*, 96, 101.

25. Gore, *Incarnation*, 21.

26. See the points made in Rowan Williams, "Defining Heresy," in *The Origins of Christendom in the West*, ed. Alan Kreider (Edinburgh: T. & T. Clark, 2001), 313–35.

27. Rowan Williams, "Does It Make Sense to Speak of Pre-Nicene Orthodoxy?" in *The Making of Orthodoxy,* ed. Rowan Williams (Cambridge: Cambridge Univ. Press, 1989) , 1–23; quote at 2.

28. Robert M. Grant, *Heresy and Criticism: The Search for Authenticity in Early Christian Literature* (Louisville, KY: Westminster/John Knox Press, 1993), 1–13, 89–113.

29. Luke Timothy Johnson, *The Creed: What Christians Believe and Why It Matters* (New York: Doubleday, 2003).

30. See further Alister E. McGrath, *The Genesis of Doctrine* (Oxford: Blackwell, 1990), 1–13.

31. Owen Ware, "Rudolf Otto's Ideal of the Holy: A Reappraisal," *Heythrop Journal* 48 (2007): 48–60. Recent work on the psychology of awe has emphasized the importance of this conceptual vastness in creating this response: Dacher Keltner and Jonathan Haidt, "Approaching Awe, a Moral, Spiritual and Aesthetic Emotion," *Cognition and Emotion* 17 (2003): 297–314.

32. Augustine of Hippo *Sermo* 117.3.5: "Si enim comprehendis, non est Deus."

33. Andrew Louth, *Origins of the Christian Mystical Tradition: From Plato to Denys* (Oxford: Oxford Univ. Press, 2007), 205.

34. Gore, *Incarnation,* 105–6.

35. For accounts of this process, see Maurice F. Wiles, *The Making of Christian Doctrine* (Cambridge: Cambridge Univ. Press, 1967); and Alister E. McGrath, *The Genesis of Doctrine* (Oxford: Blackwell, 1990, 1–13).

36. Jerome *Commentarius in epistulam ad Galatas* 5.

37. See the classic analysis and commentary in Mary Douglas, *Purity and Danger: An Analysis of Concepts of Pollution and Taboo* (London: Routledge, 2003).

38. Dominic Abrahams, Michael A. Hogg, and José M. Marques, "A Social Psychological Framework for Understanding Social Inclusion and Exclusion," in *The Social Psychology of Inclusion and Exclusion,* ed. Dominic Abrahams, Michael A. Hogg, and José M. Marques (New York: Psychology Press, 2005), 1–23.

CHAPTER 2: THE ORIGINS OF THE IDEA OF HERESY

1. As noted in Fergus Miller, "Repentent Heretics in Fifth Century Lydia: Identity and Literacy," *Scripta Classica Israelica* 23 (2004): 113–30.

2. Dietrich von Hildebrand, *Trojan Horse in the City of God: The Catholic Crisis Explained* (Manchester, NH: Sophia Institute Press, 1993). Hildebrand regards secularism as having gained a beachhead in the Catholic Church around the time of the Second Vatican Council (1962–65), leading to an erosion of its values and beliefs.

3. See Thomas Aquinas *Summa Theologiae* 2a2ae q. 11 a. 1: "[H]eresy is a species of unbelief, belonging to those who profess the Christian faith, but corrupt its dogmas."

4. Syofiardi Bachyul Jb, "Two Former Al-Qiyadah Activists Get Three Years for Blasphemy," *Jakarta Post,* May 3, 2008.

5. A similar debate erupted in Egypt recently over the views of Nasr Hamid Abu Zayd. See Charles Hirschkind, "Heresy or Hermeneutics: The Case of Nasr Hamid Abu Zayd," *Stanford Humanities Review* 5 (1996): 35–50.

6. For a penetrating analysis of this point, see Lester Kurtz, "The Politics of Heresy," *American Journal of Sociology* 88 (1983): 1085–1115.

7. Pierre Bourdieu, "Genesis and Structure of the Religious Field," *Comparative Social Research* 13 (1991): 1–43.

8. See the points made in John B. Henderson, *The Construction of Orthodoxy and Heresy: Neo-Confucian, Islamic, Jewish, and Early Christian Patterns* (Albany: State Univ. of New York Press, 1998).

9. See Abigail Lustig, Robert J. Richards, and Michael Ruse, eds., *Darwinian Heresies* (Cambridge: Cambridge Univ. Press, 2004), 1–13.

10. Egbert G. Leigh, "Neutral Theory: A Historical Perspective," *Evolutionary Biology* 20 (2007): 2075–91.

11. For the basis of this suggestion, see Mary Midgley, *Evolution as a Religion: Strange Hopes and Stranger Fears,* 2nd ed. (London: Routledge, 2002).

12. See Paul Root Wolpe, "The Dynamics of Heresy in a Profession," *Social Science and Medicine* 39 (1994): 1133–48; and R. Kenneth Jones, "Schism and Heresy in the Development of Orthodox Medicine: The Threat to Medical Hegemony," *Social Science and Medicine* 58 (2004): 703–12.

13. Brian Martin, "Dissent and Heresy in Medicine: Models, Methods, and Strategies," *Social Science and Medicine* 58 (2004): 713–25.

14. Michelle Zerba, "Medea Hypokrites," *Arethusa* 35 (2002): 315–37.

15. David T. Runia, "Philo of Alexandria and the Greek *Hairesis*-Model," *Vigiliae Christianae* 53 (1999): 117–47. The plural of *hairesis* is *haireses*.

16. Josephus *Antiquitates Judaicae* 13.171.

17. See Andrew D. Clarke, *Secular and Christian Leadership in Corinth: A Socio-Historical and Exegetical Study of 1 Corinthians 1–6* (Leiden: Brill, 1993). While I am sympathetic to the points made by Craig Blomberg, they amount to a demonstration of the New Testament's concerns about the negative impact of false teaching rather than the more specific (and later) idea of heresy: Craig L. Blomberg, "The New Testament Definition of Heresy (or When Do Jesus and the Apostles Really Get Mad?)," *Journal of the Evangelical Theological Society* 45 (2002): 59–72.

18. See Tyndale's translation of 1 Corinthians 11:19; Galatians 5:20; and 2 Peter 2:1. Tyndale translated the Greek term *haeresis* as "heresy" at Acts 24:14.

19. The older English word "privily" (Tyndale: "prevely") means "privately" or "secretly." For discussions of these classic English translations of the Bible and their impact upon the shaping of the English language, see David Daniell, *William Tyndale: A Biography* (New Haven, CT: Yale Univ. Press, 1994), 83–150; and Alister E. McGrath, *In the Beginning: The Story of the King James Bible* (New York: Doubleday, 2001).

20. Richard Norris, "Heresy and Orthodoxy in the Late Second Century," *Union Seminary Quarterly Review* 52 (1998): 43–59.

21. Henry Chadwick, *East and West: The Making of a Rift in the Church: From Apostolic Times Until the Council of Florence* (Oxford: Oxford Univ. Press, 2003), 2.

22. As noted in Caroline Humfress, "Citizens and Heretics: Late Roman Lawyers on Christian Heresy," in *Heresy and Identity in Late Antiquity,* ed. Eduard Iricinschi and Holger M. Zellentin (Tübingen: Mohr Siebeck, 2008), 128–42, esp. 142.

23. Michel Desjardins, "Bauer and Beyond: On Recent Scholarly Discussions of *Hairesis* in the Early Church Era," *Second Century* 8 (1991): 65–82.

CHAPTER 3: DIVERSITY

1. For an excellent collection of essays on this theme, see Stephen T. Davis, Daniel Kendall, and Gerald O'Collins, eds., *The Incarnation: An Interdisciplinary Symposium on the Incarnation of the Son of God* (Oxford: Oxford Univ. Press, 2004).

2. See Frank J. Matera, *New Testament Christology* (Louisville, KY: Westminster John Knox Press, 1999); Andrew Chester, *Messiah and Exaltation: Jewish Messianic and Visionary Traditions and New Testament Christology* (Tübingen: Mohr Siebeck, 2007); and Ronald R. Cox, *By the Same Word: Creation and Salvation in Hellenistic Judaism and Early Christianity* (Berlin: De Gruyter, 2007).

3. Raymond E. Brown, *The Churches the Apostles Left Behind* (New York: Paulist Press, 1984).

4. Jerome Murphy-O'Connor, *Paul: A Critical Life* (Oxford: Oxford Univ. Press, 1996), 85–89. There is also much useful material, especially relating to the Roman context, in John Dominic Crossan and Jonathan L. Reed, *In Search of Paul: How Jesus's Apostle Opposed Rome's Empire with God's Kingdom* (San Francisco: HarperSanFrancisco, 2004).

5. For the situation in Palestine, see James S. McLaren, "Jews and the Imperial Cult: From Augustus to Domitian," *Journal for the Study of the New Testament* 27 (2005): 257–78.

6. Larry Hurtado, *At the Origins of Christian Worship: The Context and Character of Earliest Christian Devotion* (Grand Rapids, MI: Eerdmans, 2000).

7. Bruce M. Metzger, *The Canon of the New Testament: Its Origin, Development, and Significance* (Oxford: Clarendon Press, 1987).

8. For a detailed analysis, see Raymond F. Collins, *The Many Faces of the Church: A Study in New Testament Ecclesiology* (New York: Crossroad, 2004).

9. H. E. W. Turner, *The Pattern of Christian Truth: A Study in the Relations Between Orthodoxy and Heresy in the Early Church* (London: Mowbray, 1954), 239–378.

10. See the studies of Harry Y. Gamble, *Books and Readers in the Early Church: A History of Early Christian Texts* (New Haven, CT: Yale Univ. Press, 1995); Kim Hains-Eitzen, *Guardians of Letters: Literacy, Power, and the Transmitters of Early Christian Literature* (New York: Oxford Univ. Press, 2000); and Larry W. Hurtado, *The Earliest Christian Artifacts: Manuscripts and Christian Origins* (Grand Rapids, MI: Eerdmans, 2006).

11. Note especially the comments of Porphyry: Robert L. Wilken, *The Christians as the Romans Saw Them,* 2nd ed. (New Haven, CT: Yale Univ. Press, 2003), 126–63.

12. As Gamble suggests, "We must assume . . . that the large majority of Christians in the early centuries of the church were illiterate, not because they were unique but because they were in this respect typical." Gamble, *Books and Readers,* 5–6.

13. Pieter J. J. Botha, "Greco-Roman Literacy as Setting for New Testament Writings," *Neotestamentica* 26 (1992): 192–215.

14. Rebecca Lyman, "*Lex orandi:* Heresy, Orthodoxy, and Popular Religion," in *The Making and Remaking of Christian Doctrine,* ed. Sarah Coakley and David Pailin (Oxford: Clarendon Press, 1993), 131–41.

15. As noted in Alain Le Boulluec, *La notion d'hérésie dans la littérature grecque, IIe–IIIe siècles,* 2 vols. (Paris: Études Augustiniennes, 1985), 1:226–29.

16. Jerome *Epistola* 107.

17. Alain Le Boulluec, "L'écriture comme norme hérésiologique dans les controverses des IIe et IIIe siècles (domaine grec)," *Jahrbuch für Antike und Christentum* 23 (1996): 66–75.

18. David Brakke, "Canon Formation and Social Conflict in Fourth-Century Egypt: Athanasius of Alexandria's Thirty-Ninth Festal Letter," *Harvard Theological Review* 87 (1994): 395–420. As Brakke correctly notes, Athanasius's concerns were not limited to lists of books alone, but reflected more fundamental conflicts between competing visions and paradigms of Christian authority and ecclesial organization.

19. Bruce M. Metzger, *The Canon of the New Testament: Its Origin, Development, and Significance* (Oxford: Clarendon Press, 1997).

20. A point often made with reference to Priscillian of Avila (d. 385): Virginia Burrus, *The Making of a Heretic: Gender, Authority, and the Priscillianist Controversy* (Berkeley: Univ. of California Press, 1995), 19–21. For a more detailed account of this issue, see Andrew S. Jacobs, "The Disorder of Books: Priscillian's Canonical Defense of Apocrypha," *Harvard Theological Review* 93 (2000): 135–59.

21. For a familiar critique of the idea of early Christian "orthodoxy," see James D. G. Dunn, *Unity and Diversity in the New Testament: An Inquiry into the Character of Earliest Christianity,* 2nd ed. (London: SCM Press, 1990), 1–7.

22. Stephen Neill, *Jesus Through Many Eyes: Introduction to the Theology of the New Testament* (Philadelphia: Fortress Press, 1976).

23. See, e.g., the points made in Ernst Käsemann's classic essay on New Testament concepts of the church: Ernst Käsemann, "Unity and Multiplicity in the New Testament Doctrine of the Church," in *New Testament Questions of Today* (Philadelphia: Fortress Press, 1969), 252–59.

24. Arland J. Hultgren, *The Rise of Normative Christianity* (Minneapolis: Fortress Press, 1994), 86.

25. Dunn, *Unity and Diversity,* 11–32.

26. Dunn, *Unity and Diversity,* 2.

27. Richard B. Hays, *The Moral Vision of the New Testament: Community, Cross, New Creation, a Contemporary Introduction to New Testament Ethics* (San Francisco: HarperSanFrancisco, 1996), 193–205.

28. For the issues, see Alister E. McGrath, *Christianity's Dangerous Idea: The Protestant Revolution* (San Francisco: HarperOne, 2007), 199–241.

29. There are obvious historical continuities between Socianism and Arianism. However, the former took on a specific form in the sixteenth century in the writings of Fausto Paolo Sozzini (1539–1604; usually known by the Latin form of his name, Faustus Socinus), setting its understanding of the identity of Jesus of Nazareth within a unitarian view of God.

30. Elaine H. Pagels and Karen L. King, *Reading Judas: The Gospel of Judas and the Shaping of Christianity* (London: Allen Lane, 2007), 31.

31. Thomas G. Guarino, "Tradition and Doctrinal Development: Can Vincent of Lérins Still Teach the Church?" *Theological Studies* 67 (2006): 34–72.

32. For some significant areas of difficulty at this point, see Mark Vessey, "The Forging of Orthodoxy in Latin Christian Literature: A Case Study," *Journal of Early Christian Studies* 4 (1996): 495–513.

33. This observation raises the fascinating question, too complex to be discussed here, of whether biblical criticism might be a resource for challenging and correcting heresy—a view cautiously propounded by Ernst Käsemann (1906–98). For an evaluation of this possibility, see A. K. M. Adam, "Docetism, Käsemann, and Christology: Why Historical Criticism Can't Protect Christological Orthodoxy," *Scottish Journal of Theology* 49 (1996): 391–410.

34. Ben Quash and Michael Ward, *Heresies and How to Avoid Them: Why It Matters What Christians Believe* (London: SPCK, 2007), 2–3.

35. See the analysis in T. E. Pollard, *Johannine Christology and the Early Church* (Cambridge: Cambridge Univ. Press, 2005). A similar issue arises concerning Marcion: see Ugo Bianchi, "Marcion: Theologien biblique ou docteur gnostique?" *Vigiliae Christianae* 21 (1967): 141–49.

36. See the analysis of a series of biblical texts set out in Eugene LaVerdiere, *The Eucharist in the New Testament and in the Early Church* (Collegeville, MN: Liturgical Press, 1996), 29–126.

37. The growing recognition of the essentially variegated character of early Christian worship is a case in point: see esp. Paul F. Bradshaw, *The Search for the Origins of Christian Worship: Sources and Methods for the Study of Early Liturgy,* 2nd ed. (New York: Oxford Univ. Press, 2002). The diversity of early Christian approaches to initiation is particularly significant (144–70).

38. This point is stressed by writers such as Geoffrey Wainwright, *Doxology: The Praise of God in Worship, Doctrine, and Life: A Systematic Theology* (New York: Oxford Univ. Press, 1980).

39. Prosper of Aquitaine *Capitula Coelestini* 8.

40. Paul V. Marshall, "Reconsidering 'Liturgical Theology': Is There a *Lex Orandi* for All Christians?" *Studia Liturgica* 25 (1995): 129–51.

41. On the Uthmanic recension of the Qu'ran, see Anna M. Gade, *Perfection Makes Practice: Learning, Emotion, and the Recited Qur'an in Indonesia* (Honolulu: Univ. of Hawaii Press, 2004), 25–27.

42. See the analysis in A. I. C. Heron, "The Interpretation of I Clement in Walter Bauer's *Rechtglaubigkeit und Ketzerei im ältesten Christentum,*" *Ekklesiastokos Pharos* 55 (1973): 517–45.

43. Turner, *Pattern of Christian Truth,* 9.

44. For the importance of the family image in forging a sense of shared identity across the churches, see Judith Lieu, *Christian Identity in the Jewish and Graeco-Roman World* (Oxford: Oxford Univ. Press, 2006), 164–69.

45. See the discussion in David G. Horrell, "'Becoming Christian': Solidifying Christian Identity and Content," in *Handbook of Early Christianity,* ed. Anthony J. Blasi, Paul-André Turcotte, and Jean Duhaime (Walnut Creek, CA: AltaMira Press, 2002), 309–36.

46. For reflections on the importance of the "other" in forging Roman perceptions of Christian identity, see Lieu, *Christian Identity,* 269–97. Lieu notes how similar processes led to the Roman classification of other ethnic and cultural groups—e.g., Tacitus's role in forging Roman perceptions of "the Germans."

47. The historical case for this is made in the landmark study of Alain Le Boulluec, *La notion d'hérésie dans la littérature grecque, IIe–IIIe siècles,* 2 vols. (Paris: Études Augustiniennes, 1985).

48. On the importance of this genre, see Averil Cameron, "How to Read Heresiology," *Journal of Medieval and Early Modern Studies* 33 (2003): 471–92. Note also her subsequent points: Averil Cameron, "The Violence of Orthodoxy," in *Heresy and Identity in Late Antiquity,* ed. Eduard Iricinschi and Holger M. Zellentin (Tübingen: Mohr Siebeck, 2008), 102–14.

49. G. E. L. Owen, "Philosophical Invective," *Oxford Studies in Ancient Philosophy* 1 (1983): 1–25.

CHAPTER 4: THE EARLY DEVELOPMENT OF HERESY

1. For its development, see Peter Lampe, *From Paul to Valentinus: Christians at Rome in the First Two Centuries* (Minneapolis: Fortress Press, 2003).

2. See Adolf von Harnack, *Marcion: Das Evangelium vom fremden Gott: Eine Monographie zur Geschichte der Grundlegung der katholischen Kirche,* 2nd ed. (Leipzig: Hinrich, 1924), 16*–28*.

3. Epiphanius's *Panarion* is widely believed to have drawn on the *Syntagma,* a lost work of Hippolytus of Rome at this point: see Einar Thomassen, "Orthodoxy and Heresy in Second-Century Rome," *Harvard Theological Review* 97 (2004): 241–56, esp. 242–43.

4. Marcion is also often represented as a dualist, arguing that matter was fundamentally evil. For an assessment of this aspect of his thought, see Michael A. Williams, *Rethinking "Gnosticism": An Argument for Dismantling a Dubious Category* (Princeton, NJ: Princeton Univ. Press, 1996), 23–26.

5. Epiphanius *Panarion* 42.1–2.

6. Tertullian *De praescriptione haereticorum* 30.2.

7. Tertullian *Adversus Valentinianos* 4.1.

8. Tertullian *De praescriptione haereticorum* 1.1.

9. I here draw on the classic study of H. E. W. Turner, *The Pattern of Christian Truth: A Study in the Relations Between Orthodoxy and Heresy in the Early Church* (London: Mowbray, 1954), 3–8.

10. Tertullian *De praescriptione haereticorum* 7.9.

11. Peter Fraenkel, *Testimonia Patrum: The Function of the Patristic Argument in the Theology of Philip Melanchthon* (Geneva: Droz, 1961), 162.

12. Turner, *Pattern of Christian Truth,* 132–41.

13. For a fuller exploration of this important point, see Alister E. McGrath, *The Genesis of Doctrine* (Oxford: Blackwell, 1990), 1–8.

14. This point has been examined thoroughly in the writings of Rowan Williams. See, e.g., Rowan Williams, "Baptism and the Arian Controversy," in *Arianism After Arius: Essays on the Development of the Fourth-Century Trinitarian Conflict,* ed. Michel Barnes and Daniel Williams (Edinburgh: T. & T. Clark, 1993), 149–80; and Rowan Williams, *Arius: Heresy and Tradition,* 2nd ed. (London: SCM Press, 2001), 235–36. For a discussion of this point, see Benjamin Myers, "Disruptive History: Rowan Williams on Heresy and Orthodoxy," in *On Rowan Williams: Critical Essays,* ed. Matheson Russell (Eugene, OR: Cascade Books, 2008), 47–67.

15. See esp. Renate Struman, "De la perpétuité de la foi dans la controverse Bossuet-Julien (1686–1691)," *Revue d'histoire ecclésiastique* 37 (1941): 145–89; and Richard F. Costigan, "Bossuet and the Consensus of the Church," *Theological Studies* 56 (1995): 652–72.

16. For the best analysis, see Hans Geisser, *Glaubenseinheit und Lehrentwicklung bei Johann Adam Möhler* (Göttingen: Vandenhoeck & Ruprecht, 1971).

17. Wilhem Maurer, "Das Prinzip der Organischen in der evangelischen Kirchenge-schichtsschreibung des 19. Jahrhunderts," *Kerygma und Dogma* 8 (1962): 256–92.

18. John Henry Newman, "The Theory of Developments in Religious Doctrine," in *Conscience, Consensus and the Development of Doctrine,* by John Henry Newman, ed. James Gaffney (New York: Doubleday, 1992), 6–30.

19. See Nicholas Lash, *Change in Focus: A Study of Doctrinal Change and Continuity* (London: Sheed & Ward, 1973), 88; Hugo Meynell, "Newman on Revelation and Doctrinal Development," *Journal of Theological Studies* 30 (1979): 138–52.

20. John Henry Newman, *An Essay on the Development of Christian Doctrine* (London: Longmans, Green & Co., 1909), 74.

21. Réginald Garrigou-Lagrange, "L'immutabilité du dogme selon le Concile du Vatican, et le relativisme," *Angelicum* 26 (1949): 309–22.

22. Thomas G. Guarino, "Tradition and Doctrinal Development: Can Vincent of Lérins Still Teach the Church?" *Theological Studies* 67 (2006): 34–72.

23. While Thomas Aquinas does not use the phrase "doctrinal development," one can speak cautiously of "doctrinal development" in a deeper sense within Aquinas's writings, as pointed out in Christopher Kaczor, "Thomas Aquinas on the Development of Doctrine," *Theological Studies* 62 (2001): 283–302.

24. Charles Gore, *The Incarnation of the Son of God* (London: John Murray, 1892), 85–87.

25. See the important contribution of Yves Congar, "La 'réception' comme réalité ecclésiologique," *Revue des sciences philosophiques et théologiques* 56 (1972): 369–403.

26. Tertullian *De praescriptione haereticorum* 7.9. "Quid ergo Athenis et Hierosolymis? quid academiae et ecclesiae? quid haereticis et christianis?"

27. Christine Trevett, *Montanism: Gender, Authority, and the New Prophecy* (Cambridge: Cambridge Univ. Press, 1996), 77–150.

28. See esp. Vera-Elisabeth Hirschmann, *Horrenda Secta: Untersuchungen zum frühchristlichen Montanismus und seinen Verbindungen zur paganen Religion Phrygiens* (Stuttgart: Franz Steiner Verlag, 2005). For an earlier study of this issue, see Wilhelm E. Schepelern, *Der Montanismus und die phrygischen Kulte: Eine Religionsgeschichtliche Untersuchung* (Tübingen: J. C. B. Mohr, 1929).

29. For a forceful statement of this position, see Kurt Aland, "Der Montanismus und die kleinasiatische Theologie," *Zeitschrift für die Neutestamentliche Wissenschaft* 46 (1955): 109–16.

30. Walter Bauer, *Rechtgläubigkeit und Ketzerei im ältesten Christentum* (Tübingen: Mohr, 1934). An English translation was published a generation later: *Orthodoxy and Heresy in Earliest Christianity* (Philadelphia: Fortress Press, 1971).

31. See, e.g., Helmut Koester, "Gnomai Diaphorai: The Origin and Nature of Diversification in the History of Early Christianity," in *Trajectories Through Early Christianity,* ed. James M. Robinson and Helmut Koester (Philadelphia: Fortress Press, 1971), 114–57.

32. The shift in mood can be discerned in the excellent essay of Hans Dieter Betz, "Orthodoxy and Heresy in Primitive Christianity: Some Critical Remarks on Georg Strecker's Republication of Walter Bauer's *Rechtgläubigkeit und Ketzerei im ältesten Christentum,*" *Interpretation* 19 (1965): 299–311.

33. Koester, "Gnomai Diaphorai," 114.

34. For magisterial surveys of the issue, see Robert M. Grant, *Heresy and Criticism: The Search for Authenticity in Early Christian Literature* (Louisville, KY: Westminster/John Knox Press, 1993); and Arland J. Hultgren, *The Rise of Normative Christianity* (Minneapolis: Fortress Press, 1994). For comments on some specific issues, see Daniel J. Harrington, "The Reception of Walter Bauer's *Orthodoxy and Heresy in Earliest Christianity* During the Last Decade," *Harvard Theological Review* 73 (1980): 289–98.

35. Hultgren, *Rise of Normative Christianity,* 10.

36. Martin Elze, "Häresie und Einheit der Kirche im 2. Jahrhundert," *Zeitschrift für Theologie und Kirche* 71 (1974): 389–409.

37. Adelbert Davids, "Irrtum und Häresie: 1 Clem.—Ignatius von Antiochien—Justinus," *Kairos* 15 (1973): 165–87.

38. See esp. Thomas A. Robinson, *The Bauer Thesis Examined: The Geography of Heresy in the Early Christian Church* (Lewiston, NY: Edwin Mellen Press, 1988), 35–91.

39. Robert Wilken, "Diversity and Unity in Early Christianity," *Second Century* 1 (1981): 101–10.

40. James F. McCue, "Orthodoxy and Heresy: Walter Bauer and the Valentinians," *Vigiliae Christianae* 33 (1979): 118–30, esp. 119–21.

41. Birger A. Pearson, "Pre-Valentinian Gnosticism in Alexandria," in *The Future of Early Christianity,* ed. Birger A. Pearson (Minneapolis: Fortress Press, 1991), 455–66. This work was later expanded: Birger A. Pearson, *Gnosticism and Christianity in Roman and Coptic Egypt* (London: T&T Clark, 2004).

42. Robin Lane Fox, *Pagans and Christians in the Mediterranean World from the Second Century A.D. to the Conversion of Constantine* (London: Penguin, 1988), 276. Fox draws particular attention to the critical evidence assembled in the 1977 Schweich Lectures of the British Academy: see Colin H. Roberts, *Manuscript, Society and Belief in Early Christian Egypt* (London: Oxford Univ. Press), 1979.

43. This is the position developed in the classic study of H. E. W. Turner, *The Pattern of Christian Truth: A Study in the Relations Between Orthodoxy and Heresy in the Early Church* (London: Mowbray, 1954), 81–94. Note esp. Turner's reference to a "fringe or penumbra between orthodoxy and heresy" (79).

44. Robinson, *Bauer Thesis Examined,* 36.

45. Hultgren, *Rise of Normative Christianity,* 11.

46. Elaine H. Pagels, *The Gnostic Gospels* (New York: Random House, 1979).

47. For an early criticism of her work in this respect, see Kathleen McVey, "Gnosticism, Feminism, and Elaine Pagels," *Theology Today* 37 (1981): 498–501. Note McVey's view that Pagels offers an "appealing portrayal of the gnostic Christians as a beleaguered minority of creative persons deprived of their rightful historical role by a well-organized but ignorant lot of literalists" (499).

48. A related approach, equally dependent upon Bauer's problematic model of the origins and nature of heresy, can be found in Gerd Lüdemann, *Heretics: The Other Side of Early Christianity* (London: SCM Press, 1996); and Bart D. Ehrman, *Lost Christianities: The Battle for Scripture and the Faiths We Never Knew* (New York: Oxford Univ. Press, 2003). Sadly, Lüdemann's work is marked by such an obvious bias against orthodoxy that it has restricted value as either a historical analysis or a serious contribution to the discussion of the nature and significance of heresy.

49. Antoine Guillaumont et al., eds., *The Gospel According to Thomas* (Leiden: Brill, 2001), 57. I have corrected the translation at one point, rendering the Greek *hina* in its proper sense as "in order that" rather than "that."

50. Kathryn Greene-McCreight, *Feminist Reconstructions of Christian Doctrine: Narrative Analysis and Appraisal* (New York: Oxford Univ. Press, 2000), 90.

51. For reflection on this point, see Rowan Williams, "Does It Make Sense to Speak of Pre-Nicene Orthodoxy?" in *The Making of Orthodoxy,* ed. Rowan Williams (Cambridge: Cambridge Univ. Press, 1989), 1–23.

52. Larry W. Hurtado, *Lord Jesus Christ: Devotion to Jesus in Earliest Christianity* (Grand Rapids, MI: Eerdmans, 2003), 494.

53. Hurtado, *Lord Jesus Christ,* 495.

54. Hultgren, *Rise of Normative Christianity,* 97–101.

CHAPTER 5: IS THERE AN "ESSENCE" OF HERESY?

1. These ideas are developed in writings such as Bart D. Ehrman, *Lost Christianities: The Battles for Scripture and the Faiths We Never Knew* (New York: Oxford Univ. Press, 2003).

2. As emphasized in Fergus Miller, "Repentent Heretics in Fifth Century Lydia: Identity and Literacy," *Scripta Classica Israelica* 23 (2004): 113–30.

3. See the analysis offered in Denise Kimber Buell, *Making Christians: Clement of Alexandria and the Rhetoric of Legitimacy* (Princeton, NJ: Princeton Univ. Press, 1999). There are also some useful comments in Virginia Burrus, *The Making of a Heretic: Gender, Authority, and the Priscillianist Controversy* (Berkeley: Univ. of California Press, 1995); and Judith M. Lieu, "The Forging of Christian Identity," *Mediterranean Archaeology* 11 (1998): 71–82.

4. See the detailed argument of Judith Lieu, *Neither Jew nor Greek? Constructing Early Christianity* (London: T & T Clark, 2002).

5. I borrow this phrase from Daniel Boyarin, *A Radical Jew: Paul and the Politics of Identity* (Berkeley: Univ. of California Press, 1994), 29.

6. Montanism, a second-century Christian movement noted for its asceticism, placed particular emphasis upon the importance of discipline. Its innovations did not concern "matters central to salvation, but rather the day-to-day disciplined living of the Christian life": Christine Trevett, *Montanism: Gender, Authority, and the New Prophecy* (Cambridge: Cambridge Univ. Press, 1996), 215. As Trevett correctly points out, unorthodox theological trends that had not been present earlier began to develop within Montanism in the early third century, chiefly concerning the doctrine of the Trinity (215–17). Concern about heretical tendencies in ascetic movements continued in later centuries: see esp. David G. Hunter, *Marriage, Celibacy and Heresy in Ancient Christianity* (Oxford: Oxford Univ. Press, 2007), 88–129.

7. It is thus important to note that the term "heresy" is correctly used to refer to ideas, not to practices. Heretical ideas may at times give rise to questionable practices; nevertheless, those practices cannot themselves be described as "heretical."

8. For an accessible introduction to this idea, see Pierre Bourdieu and Terry Eagleton, "*Doxa* and Common Life: In Conversation." *New Left Review* 191 (1992): 111–21.

9. See Robert M. Grant, *Heresy and Criticism: The Search for Authenticity in Early Christian Literature* (Louisville, KY: Westminster/John Knox Press, 1993).

10. For some aspects of these developments, see Paul Kereszetes, "From the Great Persecution to the Peace of Galerius," *Vigiliae Christianae* 37 (1983): 379–99; David Woods, "Two Notes on the Great Persecution," *Journal of Theological Studies* 43 (1992): 128–34; and William Tabbernee, "Eusebius' Theology of Persecution as Seen in the Various Editions of His Church History," *Journal of Early Christian Studies* 5 (1997): 319–34. It may, of course, be argued that persecution served to enhance a sense of shared Christian identity, leading to a growing tendency to identify possible threats to this identity: see Daniel Boyarin, "Martyrdom and the Making of Christianity and Judaism," *Journal of Early Christian Studies* 6 (1998): 577–627.

11. The importance of this issue can be seen by considering aspects of Jewish history in Europe, where a loss of distinct cultural and religious identity was a constant threat. An excellent example can be found in the difficulties faced by the Jewish community in Vienna at the beginning of the twentieth century, when it faced constant pressure to assimilate to Viennese culture. See the analysis in Stephen Beller, "Big-City Jews: Jewish Big-City: The Dialectics of Jewish Assimilation in Vienna c. 1900," in *The City in Central Europe: Culture and Society from 1800 to the Present,* ed. Malcolm Gee, Tim Kirk, and Jill Steward (Ashgate: Aldershot, 1999), 145–58.

12. Tertullian *De praescriptione haereticorum* 7.9.

13. Hippolytus *De Christo et Antichristo* 59. The image was also famously used by the nineteenth-century evangelist D. L. Moody (1837–99): "The place for the ship is in the sea; but God help the ship if the sea gets into it."

14. Grant, *Heresy and Criticism,* 49–73; Richard A. Burridge and Graham Gould, *Jesus Now and Then* (Grand Rapids, MI: Eerdmans, 2004), 129–31.

15. James A. Froude, *Thomas Carlyle: A History of His Life in London, 1834–1881,* 2 vols. (London: Longmans, Green, and Co., 1884), 2:462.

16. This has important implications for the impact of secularism on Judaism: see Stephen Sharot, "Judaism and the Secularization Debate," *Sociological Analysis* 52 (1991): 255–75. For the rival view, based on Maimonides (1135–1204), that one can speak legitimately of Jewish dogma, see Yitzchak Blau, "Flexibility with a Firm Foundation: On Maintaining Jewish Dogma," *Torah u-Madda Journal* 12 (2004): 179–91.

17. Ulrich Schmid, *Marcion und sein Apostolos: Rekonstruktion und historische Einordnung der marcionitischen Paulusbriefausgabe* (Berlin: de Gruyter, 1995). This corrects the highly influential earlier study of Adolf von Harnack, *Marcion—das Evangelium vom fremden Gott: Eine Monographie zur Geschichte der Grundlegung der katholischen Kirche* (Leipzig: Hinrichs, 1921).

18. See, e.g., Francis Watson, *Paul, Judaism and the Gentiles: A Sociological Approach* (Cambridge: Cambridge Univ. Press, 1986), 49–87.

19. See Watson, *Paul, Judaism and the Gentiles,* 178. For a more nuanced approach, see N. T. Wright, *The Climax of the Covenant: Christ and the Law in Pauline Theology* (Edinburgh: T&T Clark, 1991).

20. R. A. Markus, "The Problem of Self-Definition: From Sect to Church," in *Jewish and Christian Self-Definition,* ed. E. P. Sanders, 2 vols. (London: SCM Press, 1980–82), 1:1–15.

21. Wayne A. Meeks, "The Stranger from Heaven in Johannine Sectarianism," *Journal of Biblical Literature* 91 (1972): 44–72. See further David L. Balch, *The Social History of the Matthean Community: Cross-Disciplinary Approaches* (Minneapolis: Fortress Press, 1991). For a critique of the notion of such "communities," see Richard Bauckham, ed., *The Gospels for All Christians: Rethinking the Gospel Audiences* (Grand Rapids, MI: Eerdmans, 1998).

22. Wayne A. Meeks, *The First Urban Christians: The Social World of the Apostle Paul* (New Haven, CT: Yale Univ. Press, 1983), 84–107.

23. Important exceptions must, of course, be noted, such as the Egyptian monastic movement: Derwas J. Chitty, *The Desert a City: An Introduction to the Study of Egyptian and Palestinian Monasticism Under the Christian Empire* (Crestwood, NY: St. Vladimir's Seminary Press, 1995).

24. Tertullian *Apologia* 42.

25. Georg Günter Blum, *Tradition und Sukzession: Studien zum Normbegriff des Apostolischen von Paulus bis Irenaeus* (Berlin: Lutherisches Verlagshaus, 1963). On creeds in general, see J. N. D. Kelly, *Early Christian Creeds,* 3rd ed. (New York: Longman, 1981).

26. S. L. Greenslade, "Heresy and Schism in the Later Roman Empire," in *Schism, Heresy and Religious Protest,* ed. Derek Baker (Cambridge: Cambridge Univ. Press, 1972), 1–20.

27. George W. Knight, *The Pastoral Epistles: A Commentary on the Greek Text* (Grand Rapids, MI: Eerdmans, 1992), 11–12. For the significance of the Pauline letters in our understanding of the emergence of both orthodoxy and heresy, see further William E. Arnal, "Doxa, Heresy, and Self-Construction: The Pauline Ekklesiai and the Boundaries of Urban Identities," in *Heresy and Identity in Late Antiquity,* ed. Eduard Iricinschi and Holger M. Zellentin (Tübingen: Mohr Siebeck, 2008), 50–101.

28. Knight, *Pastoral Epistles,* 88–89.

29. For a representative argument that the concept of heresy is encountered in the New Testament and countered by the teaching of orthodoxy, see the influential paper of Craig L. Blomberg, "The New Testament Definition of Heresy (Or When Do Jesus and the Apostles Really Get Mad?)," *Journal of the Evangelical Theological Society* 45 (2002): 59–72.

30. Larry W. Hurtado, *Lord Jesus Christ: Devotion to Jesus in Earliest Christianity* (Grand Rapids, MI: Eerdmans, 2003), 108–18.

31. Herman N. Ridderbos, *Paul: An Outline of His Theology* (Grand Rapids, MI: Eerdmans, 1997), 369–95.

32. Hurtado, *Lord Jesus Christ,* 605–14.

33. A point emphasized by John Zizioulas: see, e.g., Miroslav Volf, *After Our Likeness: The Church as the Image of the Trinity* (Grand Rapids, MI: Eerdmans, 1998), 73–107.

34. See the careful study of William T. Cavenaugh, "The City: Beyond Secular Parodies," in *Radical Orthodoxy: A New Theology,* ed. John Milbank, Catherine Pickstock, and Graham Ward (London: Routledge, 1998), 182–200, esp. 196.

35. The imagery is due to Charles Gore, *The Incarnation of the Son of God,* 2nd ed. (London: John Murray, 1892), 96–97.

36. On which see Klaus M. Beckmann, *Der Begriff der Häresie bei Schleiermacher* (Munich: Kaiser Verlag, 1959), 36–62.

37. F. D. E. Schleiermacher, *The Christian Faith,* 2nd ed. (Edinburgh: T&T Clark, 1928), 52. For comment on this emphasis, especially in relation to the tension it apparently envisages between the role of the church and Christ in redemption, see Paul T. Nimmo, "The Mediation of Redemption in Schleiermacher's *Glaubenslehre*," *International Journal of Systematic Theology* 5 (2003): 187–99.

38. Richard Hooker *Laws of Ecclesiastical Polity* 5.54.10. For Hooker's views on heresy, see Egil Grislis, "The Role of Sin in the Theology of Richard Hooker," *Anglican Theological Review* 84 (2002): 881–96. Note that Schleiermacher differs from Hooker in identifying two "natural heresies" relating to the person of Christ and two relating to his work. Hooker regards all four natural heresies as relating to the person of Christ.

39. Schleiermacher, *Christian Faith*, 98. See further Henning Paulsen, *Zur Literatur und Geschichte des frühen Christentums: Gesammelte Aufsätze* (Tübingen: Mohr Siebeck, 1997), 73–74.

40. It is instructive to compare Schleiermacher's views on these two heresies with those of Karl Barth: for Barth's judgment, see Paul D. Molnar, "Some Dogmatic Implications of Barth's Understanding of Ebionite and Docetic Christology," *International Journal of Systematic Theology* 2 (2000): 151–74.

41. See, e.g., George V. Vito, "Toward a Sociology of Heresy," *Sociological Analysis* 44 (1983): 123–30; and Jacques Berlinerblau, "Toward a Sociology of Heresy, Orthodoxy, and Doxa," *History of Religions* 40 (2001): 327–51.

42. For the general issue, see A. H. M. Jones, "Were Ancient Heresies National or Social Movements in Disguise?" *Journal of Theological Studies* 10 (1959): 280–86; and W. H. C. Frend, "Heresy and Schism as Social and National Movements," in *Schism, Heresy and Protest,* ed. Derek Baker (Cambridge: Cambridge Univ. Press, 1972), 37–49. See also pp. 155–56 of the present study.

43. See the comments in Elizabeth A. Clark, "Elite Networks and Heresy Accusations: Towards a Social Description of the Origenist Controversy," *Semeia* 56 (1991): 81–107.

44. Lewis Ayres, *Nicaea and Its Legacy: An Approach to Fourth-Century Trinitarian Theology* (Oxford: Oxford Univ. Press, 2004), 78–84.

45. Malcolm Lambert, *Medieval Heresy: Popular Movements from the Gregorian Reform to the Reformation* (Oxford: Blackwell, 2002), 4–5.

CHAPTER 6: EARLY CLASSIC HERESIES

1. For excellent recent accounts, see Philip F. Esler, ed., *The Early Christian World,* 2 vols. (London: Routledge, 2000); Henry Chadwick, *The Church in Ancient Society from Galilee to Gregory the Great* (Oxford: Oxford Univ. Press, 2001); and Peter Lampe, *From Paul to Valentinus: Christians at Rome in the First Two Centuries* (Minneapolis: Fortress Press, 2003).

2. See especially the substantial body of material brought together in Charles Kannengiesser, ed., *Handbook of Patristic Exegesis: The Bible in Ancient Christianity,* 2 vols. (Leiden: Brill, 2003). Although outstanding in many ways, this collection is open to criticism at points: Johannes van Oort, "Biblical Interpretation in the Patristic Era: A 'Handbook of Patristic Exegesis' and Some Other Recent Books and Related Projects," *Vigiliae Christianae* 60 (2006): 80–103.

3. See, e.g., James D. Ernest, *The Bible in Athanasius of Alexandria* (Leiden: Brill, 2004); Elizabeth Dively Lauro, *The Soul and Spirit of Scripture Within Origen's Exegesis*

(Leiden: Brill, 2005); Angela Russell Christman, *"What Did Ezekiel See?": Christian Exegesis of Ezekiel's Vision of the Chariot from Irenaeus to Gregory the Great* (Leiden: Brill, 2005); and Robert C. Hill, *Reading the Old Testament in Antioch* (Leiden: Brill, 2005).

4. Alister E. McGrath, *The Genesis of Doctrine* (Oxford: Blackwell, 1990); Kevin J. Vanhoozer, *The Drama of Doctrine: A Canonical-Linguistic Approach to Christian Theology* (Louisville, KY: Westminster John Knox Press, 2005), 115–237.

5. Robert M. Grant, *Heresy and Criticism: The Search for Authenticity in Early Christian Literature* (Louisville, KY: Westminster/John Knox Press, 1993).

6. Malcolm Lambert, *Medieval Heresy: Popular Movements from the Gregorian Reform to the Reformation* (Oxford: Blackwell, 2002): "I have written as a historian, not a theologian. I have taken 'heresy' to mean whatever the papacy explicitly or implicitly condemned during the period" (xi).

7. Herbert Grundmann, *Religiöse Bewegungen im Mittelalter: Untersuchungen über die geschichtlichen Zusammenhänge zwischen der Ketzerei, den Bettelorden und der religiösen Frauenbewegung um 12. und 13. Jahrhundert und über die geschichtlichen Grundlagen der deutschen Mystik* (Berlin: Emil Ebering, 1935). For his later reflections on the theme, see Herbert Grundmann, *Ketzergeschichte des Mittelalters* (Göttingen: Vandenhoeck & Ruprecht, 1963).

8. As pointed out in Othmar Hageneder, "Der Häresiebegriff bei den Juristen des 12. und 13. Jahrhunderts," in *The Concept of Heresy in the Middle Ages,* ed. W. Lourdaux and D. Verhelst (Louvain: Louvain Univ. Press, 1978), 42–103.

9. Robert I. Moore, *The Formation of a Persecuting Society: Power and Deviance in Western Europe, 950–1250* (Oxford: Basil Blackwell, 1990).

10. The term "Ebionite" is thought to derive from the Hebrew word *Ebyonim* ("the poor"), perhaps originally applied to Christians because they came from lower social groups and tended to be poor (Acts 11:28–30, 24:17; 1 Cor. 1:26–29, 16:1–2). It may also possibly be drawn from the preaching of Jesus of Nazareth: "Blessed are the poor" (Luke 6:20). Paul appears to use the term "poor people [*hoi ptochoi*]" to refer specifically to the churches of Jerusalem and Judea (Gal. 2:10). A number of early church heresiologists, unfamiliar with the Hebrew language, incorrectly inferred the existence of an individual named "Ebion of Pella" as the originator of the heresy, apparently on the basis of the assumption that all heresies were named after their founders: see Hans Joachim Schoeps, *Theologie und Geschichte des Judenchristentums* (Tübingen: J. C. B. Mohr, 1949), 8–9.

11. For the best account, see Richard Bauckham, "The Origin of the Ebionites," in *The Image of the Judaeo-Christians in Ancient Jewish and Christian Literature,* ed. Peter J. Tomson and Doris Lambers-Petry (Tübingen: Mohr Siebeck, 2003), 162–81. This supplements and corrects the earlier study of Hans Joachim Schoeps, "Ebionite Christianity," *Journal of Theological Studies* 4 (1953): 219–24 (based on his earlier study *Theologie und Geschichte des Judenchristentums*).

12. For an early exploration of the issue, see Joseph A. Fitzmyer, "The Qumran Scrolls,

the Ebionites, and Their Literature," *Theological Studies* 16 (1955): 335–72.

13. For an excellent recent survey of the issues contested within early Judean Jewish Christianity, see Richard Bauckham, *God Crucified: Monotheism and Christology in the New Testament* (Grand Rapids, MI: Eerdmans, 1998); and Larry W. Hurtado, *Lord Jesus Christ: Devotion to Jesus in Earliest Christianity* (Grand Rapids, MI: Eerdmans, 2003), 155–216.

14. Bauckham, "Origin of the Ebionites," 162–71.

15. Michael Goulder, "A Poor Man's Christology," *New Testament Studies* 45 (1999): 332–48.

16. See the points made in Darrell D. Hannah, *Michael and Christ: Michael Traditions and Angel Christology in Early Christianity* (Tübingen: Mohr Siebeck, 1999), 173–75; and Timo Eskola, *Messiah and the Throne: Jewish Merkabah Mysticism and Early Christian Exaltation Discourse* (Tübingen: Mohr Siebeck, 2001), 307–9.

17. On Mark's account of the significance of Jesus of Nazareth, see the excellent study of Morna D. Hooker, "'Who Can This Be?' The Christology of Mark's Gospel," in *Contours of Christology in the New Testament,* ed. Richard G. Longenecker (Grand Rapids, MI: Eerdmans, 2005), 79–98.

18. Stevan L. Davies, *Jesus the Healer: Possession, Trance, and the Origins of Christianity* (London: Continuum, 1995), 66–77. More generally, see W. D. Davies and E. P. Sanders, "Jesus from the Jewish Point of View," in *The Cambridge History of Judaism: The Early Roman Period,* ed. William Horbury, W. D. Davies, and John Sturdy (Cambridge: Cambridge Univ. Press, 1999), 618–76.

19. For comment, see James R. Edwards, *The Gospel According to Mark* (Grand Rapids, MI: Eerdmans, 2002), 75–79.

20. See, e.g., Donald A. Hagner, "Matthew: Apostate, Reformer, Revolutionary?" *New Testament Studies* 49 (2003): 193–209, esp. 200–201.

21. Karl Barth, *Church Dogmatics,* 14 vols. (Edinburgh: T&T Clark, 1957–75), 1:402–3. See also Paul D. Molnar, "Some Dogmatic Implications of Barth's Understanding of Ebionite and Docetic Christology," *International Journal of Systematic Theology* 2 (2000): 151–74, esp. 156–58.

22. See, e.g., Gerd Lüdemann, *Heretics: The Other Side of Early Christianity* (London: SCM Press, 1996), 52–53.

23. For some aspects of this, see Lüdemann, *Heretics,* 27–60.

24. Oskar Skarsaune, *In the Shadow of the Temple: Jewish Influences on Early Christianity* (Downers Grove, IL: InterVarsity Press, 2002), 147–62; 259–74.

25. This led Lüdemann to suggest that Paul was virtually regarded as a heretic in Jewish Christian circles; see Lüdemann, *Heretics,* 61–103, developing a point originally made by Walter Bauer (60).

26. Lüdemann, *Heretics,* 53–56.

27. Hurtado, *Lord Jesus Christ,* 155–214.

28. Moishe Rosen, *Y'shua: The Jewish Way to Say Jesus* (San Francisco: Purple Pomegranate Productions, 1982).

29. Juliene G. Lipson, *Jews for Jesus: An Anthropological Study* (New York: AMS Press, 1990), 15. See also David A. Rausch, *Messianic Judaism: Its History, Theology, and Polity* (Lewiston, NY: Edwin Mellen Press, 1982).

30. Georg Strecker, *The Johannine Letters: A Commentary on 1, 2, and 3 John* (Minneapolis: Fortress Press, 1996), 69–77; Paul R. Trebilco, *The Early Christians in Ephesus from Paul to Ignatius* (Tübingen: Mohr Siebeck, 2004), 694–96. Note esp. 1 John 4:1–3: "[E]very spirit which acknowledges that Jesus Christ has come in the flesh is from God." This passage suggests that those who denied that Jesus Christ had come in the flesh, but only "appeared" to take flesh, were to be rejected.

31. Irenaeus of Lyons *Adversus haereses* 1.26.1.

32. Ignatius was one of the earliest known Christian writers to argue that the church should observe the "Lord's Day" (Sunday), rather than the traditional Jewish Sabbath, as the day of rest.

33. Ignatius, *Letter to the Trallians,* 9–10; *Letter to the Smyrnaeans,* 2–3.

34. Clement of Alexandria *Stromateis* 3.69.3, quoting from Valentinus's lost letter to Agathapous.

35. As pointed out in Norbert Brox, "'Doketismus'—eine Problemanzeige," *Zeitschrift für Kirchengeschichte* 95 (1984): 301–14.

36. Brox, "Doketismus," 309. See also Michael Slusser, "Docetism: A Historical Definition," *Second Century* 1 (1981): 163–72.

37. Following the excellent analysis in Guy Strousma, "Christ's Laughter: Docetic Origins Reconsidered," *Journal of Early Christian Studies* 12 (2004): 267–88, esp. 268.

38. Ronnie Goldstein and Guy G. Stroumsa, "The Greek and Jewish Origins of Docetism: A New Proposal," *Zeitschrift für Antikes Christentum* 10 (2007): 423–41.

39. Goldstein and Stroumsa, "Origins of Docetism,"430.

40. See esp. Norman Austin, *Helen of Troy and Her Shameless Phantom* (Ithaca, NY: Cornell Univ. Press, 1994), which has had a significant impact on how Goldstein and Strousma developed their thesis.

41. This phrase does not date from the classical era but is found in Christopher Marlowe's drama *Doctor Faustus,* written around the year 1600: "Was this the face that launch'd a thousand ships / And burnt the topless towers of Ilium?"

42. Plato *Phaedrus* 243a–b.

43. Goldstein and Stroumsa, "Origins of Docetism," 429.

44. See the argument in Strousma, "Christ's Laughter." For the interpretation of the sacrifice of Isaac, see Edward Kessler, *Bound by the Bible: Jews, Christians and the Sacrifice of Isaac* (Cambridge: Cambridge Univ. Press, 2004).

45. Irenaeus of Lyons *Adversus haereses* 1.26.4. For comment, see Daniel Wanke, *Das Kreuz Christi bei Irenaeus von Lyon* (Berlin: de Gruyter, 2000), 75–82.

46. Second Treatise of the Great Seth 55:16–35. See further Paul Gavrilyuk, *The Suffering of the Impassible God: The Dialectics of Patristic Thought* (Oxford: Oxford Univ. Press, 2004), 80–83. For further Gnostic texts taking a similar position, see Gavrilyuk, *Suffering of the Impassible God,* 79–90. This "Sethian" school of Gnosticism differs from Valentinism in a number of ways.

47. Peter Lampe, *From Paul to Valentinus: Christians at Rome in the First Two Centuries* (Minneapolis: Fortress Press, 2003), 301–45. Lampe here speaks of the "fractionation" of the Roman church.

48. Antonia Tripolitis, *Religions of the Hellenistic-Roman Age* (Grand Rapids, MI: Eerdmans, 2002), 16–21.

49. For a recent account, see Roger Beck, "Ritual, Myth, Doctrine, and Initiation in the Mysteries of Mithras: New Evidence from a Cult Vessel," *Journal of Roman Studies* 90 (2000): 145–80.

50. See the interesting collection of essays gathered together in Robert A. Segal, ed., *The Allure of Gnosticism: The Gnostic Experience in Jungian Psychology and Contemporary Culture* (Chicago: Open Court, 1995).

51. Hans Jonas, whose influence on the modern interpretation of this movement has been decisive, defines the essence of Gnosticism as "a certain dualism, an estrangement between man and the world": see Hans Jonas, *The Gnostic Religion: The Message of the Alien God and the Beginnings of Christianity,* 3rd ed. (Boston: Beacon Press, 2001), 325. A similar position is taken in Kurt Rudolph, *Gnosis: The Nature and History of Gnosticism* (San Francisco: Harper & Row, 1983).

52. See esp. Michael A. Williams, *Rethinking "Gnosticism": An Argument for Dismantling a Dubious Category* (Princeton, NJ: Princeton Univ. Press, 1996), 43–44. There is also some useful discussion in Birger A. Pearson, *Gnosticism, Judaism, and Egyptian Christianity* (Minneapolis: Fortress Press, 1990).

53. For the argument in detail, see Phillip A. Tite, "Categorical Designations and Methodological Reductionism: Gnosticism as Case Study," *Method and Theory in the Study of Religions* 13 (2001): 269–92.

54. See, e.g., the conclusions of Karen L. King in *What Is Gnosticism?* (Cambridge, MA: Belknap Press, 2003).

55. King, *What Is Gnosticism?*: "Because the core problem is the reification of a rhetorical entity (heresy) into an actual phenomenon in its own right (Gnosticism), the entire question of origin is a non-issue whose seeming urgency arises only because of its rhetorical function in the discourse of orthodoxy and heresy" (190).

56. King, *What Is Gnosticism?,* 224.

57. Following Christoph Markschies, *Valentinus Gnosticus? Untersuchungen zur valentinianischen Gnosis mit einem Kommentar zu den Fragmenten Valentins* (Tübingen: Mohr, 1992), I take the view that Valentinus did not hold some of the doctrines that were characteristic of later Valentinians.

58. Lampe, *From Paul to Valentinus,* 376; 390–93. Note that the term "Valentinianism" is also regularly used in the literature. Both forms are perfectly acceptable.

59. As pointed out in Einar Thomassen, "Orthodoxy and Heresy in Second-Century Rome," *Harvard Theological Review* 97 (2004): 241–56.

60. The most detailed study to date is Einar Thomassen, *The Spiritual Seed: The Church of the 'Valentinians'* (Leiden: Brill, 2008). As noted earlier (n. 58), the term "Valentinianism" is sometimes used in preference to "Valentinism."

61. Irenaeus of Lyons *Adversus haeresis* 1.24.6.

62. Michael Kaler and Marie-Pierre Bussières, "Was Heracleon a Valentinian? A New Look at Old Sources," *Harvard Theological Review* 99 (2006): 275–89.

63. Joel Kalvesmaki, "Italian Versus Eastern Valentinianism?" *Vigiliae Christianae* 62 (2008): 79–89.

64. On which see John D. Turner, *Sethian Gnosticism and the Platonic Tradition* (Louvain: Peeters, 2001).

65. On this, see Birger A. Pearson, "The Figure of Seth in Gnostic Literature," in *The Rediscovery of Gnosticism,* ed. Bentley Layton (Leiden: Brill, 1980), 472–504.

66. This quotation is taken from the Valentinian tract *The Tripartite Tractate;* for comment, see Thomassen, *Spiritual Seed,* 50.

67. Thomassen, *Spiritual Seed,* 28–30.

68. See the analysis in James F. McCue, "Orthodoxy and Heresy: Walter Bauer and the Valentinians," *Vigiliae Christianae* 33 (1979): 118–30.

69. McCue, "Orthodoxy and Heresy," 122–23.

70. For the importance of Irenaeus's biblical interpretation at this point, see Jacques Fantino, *La théologie d'Irénée. Lecture des Écritures en reponse à l'exégèse gnostique: Une approche trinitaire* (Paris: Éditions du Cerf, 1994).

71. See the full discussion at Irenaeus of Lyons, *Adversus haereses* 2.2.1–4.1. Extracts of that discussion are reproduced here. For a fuller discussion of the issues, see the following classic studies: Georg Günter Blum, *Tradition und Sukzession: Studien zum Normbegriff des Apostolischen von Paulus bis Irenaeus* (Berlin: Lutherisches Verlagshaus, 1963); and Norbert Brox, *Offenbarung, Gnosis und gnostischer Mythos bei Irenäus von Lyon: Zur Charakteristik der Systeme* (Salzburg: Pustet Verlag, 1966).

72. See the points made in Adelbert Davids, "Irrtum und Häresie. 1 Clem.—Ignatius von Antiochien—Justinus," *Kairos* 15 (1973): 165–87.

73. Irenaeus of Lyons, *Adversus haeresis* 1.24.6.

74. See Ragner Holte, "*Logos Spermatikos:* Christianity and Ancient Philosophy According to St. Justin's Apologies," *Studia Theologica* 12 (1958): 109–68.

75. See the classic study of Charles Bigg, *The Christian Platonists of Alexandria* (Hildesheim: G. Olms, 1981).

76. For some aspects of these themes, see Markus N. A. Bockmuehl, *Revelation and Mystery in Ancient Judaism and Pauline Christianity* (Tübingen: Mohr, 1990); and John Joseph Collins, "Natural Theology and Biblical Tradition: The Case of Hellenistic Judaism," *Catholic Biblical Quarterly* 60 (1998): 1–15.

77. Note esp. 2 Tim. 3:16–17.

78. See G. W. H. Lampe and K. J. Woollcombe, eds., *Essays on Typology* (London: SCM Press, 1957).

79. Justin Martyr *Dialogue with Trypho* 94. For a study, see Craig D. Allert, *Revelation, Truth, Canon, and Interpretation: Studies in Justin Martyr's Dialogue with Trypho* (Leiden: Brill, 2002).

80. Justin Martyr *Apology* 1.26.

81. This theme is explored more fully in Ekkehard Mühlenberg, "Marcion's Jealous

God," in *Disciplina Nostra: Essays in Memory of Robert F. Evans,* ed. D. Winslow (Cambridge, MA: Philadelphia Patristic Foundation, 1979), 93–113.

82. Irenaeus of Lyons *Adversus haereses* 1.25.1.

83. Tertullian *Adversus Marcionem* 1.6.

84. Robin Lane Fox, *Pagans and Christians in the Mediterranean World from the Second Century A.D. to the Conversion of Constantine* (London: Penguin, 1988), 332.

85. Stephen G. Wilson, "Marcion and the Jews," in *Anti-Judaism in Early Christianity,* vol. 2, *Separation and Polemic,* ed. Stephen G. Wilson (Waterloo, Ontario: Wilfred Laurier Univ. Press, 1986), 45–58; Heikki Räisänen, "Marcion and the Origins of Christian Anti-Judaism," *Temenos* 33 (1997): 121–35.

86. For an alternative perspective here, see Andrew McGowan, "Marcion's Love of Creation," *Journal of Early Christian Studies* 9 (2001): 295–311.

87. Peter M. Head, "The Foreign God and the Sudden Christ: Theology and Christology in Marcion's Gospel Redaction," *Tyndale Bulletin* 44 (1993): 307–21.

88. John J. Clabeaux, *A Lost Edition of the Letters of Paul: A Reassessment of the Text of the Pauline Corpus Attested by Marcion* (Washington, DC: Catholic Biblical Association of America, 1989).

89. Irenaeus of Lyons *Adversus haereses* 1.27.4.

90. Tertullian *De prescriptione hereticorum* 38.7–10.

91. The text of the prologues can be found in Daniel J. Theron, *Evidence of Tradition: Selected Source Material for the Study of the History of the Early Church, Introduction and Canon of the New Testament* (London: Bowes & Bowes, 1957), 79–83. For comment, see Ulrich Schmid, *Marcion und sein Apostolos: Rekonstruktion und historische Einordnung der marcionitischen Paulusbriefausgabe* (Berlin: De Gruyter, 1995).

92. See Robert Morgan and John Barton, *Biblical Interpretation* (Oxford: Oxford Univ. Press, 1988); and Bertrand de Margerie, *An Introduction to the History of Exegesis,* 3 vols. (Petersham, MA: St. Bede's Publications), 1998.

93. Richard Dawkins, *The God Delusion* (Boston: Houghton Mifflin, 2006), 31.

94. For details, see Dawkins, *God Delusion,* 237–50.

95. See Adolf von Harnack, *Marcion: Das Evangelium vom fremden Gott: Eine Monographie zur Geschichte der Grundlegung der katholischen Kirche,* 2nd ed. (Leipzig: Hinrich, 1924). For a critical assessment, see Wolfram Kinzig, *Harnack, Marcion und das Judentum: Nebst einer kommentierten Edition des Briefwechsels Adolf von Harnacks mit Houston Stewart Chamberlain* (Leipzig: Evangelische Verlagsanstalt, 2004).

96. Kinzig, *Harnack, Marcion und das Judentum,* 200.

97. Gerd Lüdemann, "Zur Geschichte des ältesten Christentums in Rom. I. Valentin und Marcion. II. Ptolemäus und Justin," *Zeitschrift für die Neutestamentliche Wissenschaft* 70 (1979): 86–114, esp. 95–96; Lampe, *From Paul to Valentinus,* 392–93; Thomassen, "Orthodoxy and Heresy," 242.

98. Thomassen, "Orthodoxy and Heresy," 245.

99. For reflections on the theological issues raised by Bauer, see G. Clarke Chapman, "Some Theological Reflections on Walter Bauer's *Rechtglaubigkeit und Ketzerei im*

ältesten Christentum: A Review Article," *Journal of Ecumenical Studies* 7 (1970): 564–74; and David J. Hawkin, "A Reflective Look at the Debate on Orthodoxy and Heresy in Earliest Christianity," *Église et théologie* 7 (1976): 367–78.

CHAPTER 7: LATER CLASSIC HERESIES

1. This theme is prominent in most contemporary accounts of religion. See, e.g., Bryan S. Turner, *Religion and Social Theory,* 2nd ed. (London: Sage Publications, 1991): "Religion may be defined as a system of symbols and values which, through their emotional impact, not only bind people together into a sacred community, but introduce a normative and altruistic commitment to collective ends" (xi).

2. Charles King, "The Organization of Roman Religious Beliefs," *Classical Antiquity* 22 (2003): 275–312.

3. William R. Schoedel, "Christian 'Atheism' and the Peace of the Roman Empire," *Church History* 42 (1973): 309–19.

4. Olivia F. Robinson, "Repressionen gegen Christen in der Zeit vor Decius—noch immer ein Rechtsproblem," *Zeitschrift der Savigny-Stiftung für Rechtsgeschichte. Romanistische Abteilung* 125 (1995): 352–69.

5. J. B. Rives, "The Decree of Decius and the Religion of Empire," *Journal of Roman Studies* 89 (1999): 135–54.

6. The text of the decree is reproduced in Lactantius *De mortibus persecutorum* 34–35.

7. For studies, see Ramsay MacMullen, *Christianizing the Roman Empire (A.D. 100–400)* (New Haven, CT: Yale Univ. Press, 1984); and Charles M. Odahl, *Constantine and the Christian Empire* (London: Routledge, 2004).

8. Caroline Humfress, "Citizens and Heretics: Late Roman Lawyers on Christian Heresy," in *Heresy and Identity in Late Antiquity,* ed. Eduard Iricinschi and Holger M. Zellentin (Tübingen: Mohr Siebeck, 2008), 128–42.

9. Mark J. Edwards, "Justin's *Logos* and the Word of God," *Journal of Early Christian Studies* 3 (1995): 261–80.

10. There is a huge literature on this matter. One of the best introductions remains Aloys Grillmeier, *Christ in Christian Tradition,* 2nd ed. (London: Mowbrays, 1975).

11. For standard accounts of Arius's ideas and their background, see R. P. C. Hanson, *The Search for the Christian Doctrine of God: The Arian Controversy, 318–381* (Edinburgh: T. & T. Clark, 1988); Rowan Williams, *Arius: Heresy and Tradition,* 2nd ed. (London: SCM Press, 2001); and Lewis Ayres, *Nicaea and Its Legacy: An Approach to Fourth-Century Trinitarian Theology* (Oxford: Oxford Univ. Press, 2004). For their abiding appeal, particularly for more rationalist approaches to Christianity, see Maurice F. Wiles, *Archetypal Heresy: Arianism Through the Centuries* (Oxford: Clarendon Press, 1996).

12. See Arius's letter to Eusebius, bishop of Nicomedia, written around 321. This letter is reproduced, with slight variations, in Theodoret of Cyrus *Ecclesiastical History* 1.5.1–4; and Epiphanius of Constantia *Pararion* 69.6. See also Christopher Haas, "The Arians of Alexandria," *Vigiliae Christianae* 47 (1993): 234–45.

13. For an excellent analysis of this point, see T. E. Pollard, *Johannine Christology and the Early Church* (Cambridge: Cambridge Univ. Press, 2005).

14. Cited in Alexander of Alexandria *Depositio Arii* 3.

15. Cited in Alexander of Alexandria *Depositio Arii* 3.

16. For an excellent summary of the issues, see Thomas G. Weinandy, *Athanasius: A Theological Introduction* (Aldershot, UK: Ashgate, 2007), 11–100.

17. This is rightly emphasized (though controversially interpreted) in Robert C. Gregg and Dennis Groh, *Early Arianism: A View of Salvation* (Philadelphia: Fortress Press, 1981).

18. See the points made in Larry Hurtado, *At the Origins of Christian Worship: The Context and Character of Earliest Christian Devotion* (Grand Rapids, MI: Eerdmans, 2000).

19. For an excellent study of this dimension of the controversy, see Timothy D. Barnes, *Athanasius and Constantius: Theology and Politics in the Constantinian Empire* (Cambridge, MA: Harvard Univ. Press), 1993. Barnes focuses on developments during the reign of Constantius, Constantine's son, illuminating in particular the later aspects of Athanasius's career. However, many of the factors that Barnes identifies as significant were already present under Constantine himself. For reflections on the politics and social psychology of the conflict, see Richard E. Rubenstein, *When Jesus Became God: The Epic Fight over Christ's Divinity in the Last Days of Rome* (New York: Harcourt Brace & Co., 1999).

20. The New Testament provides a record of the Council of Jerusalem (see Acts 15), generally dated to around the year 50, which brought together early Christian leaders to determine whether Gentiles could be admitted into the church. See Richard Bauckham, "James and the Jerusalem Church," in *The Book of Acts in Its Palestinian Setting,* ed. Bruce Winter (Grand Rapids, MI: Eerdmans, 1995), 415–80.

21. Ambrose of Milan and Hilary of Poitiers reported 318 bishops in attendance, but this may be a symbolic allusion to the 318 servants of Abraham (Gen. 14:14).

22. There were, however, precedents for this in North African Christianity in the third century: Harvey J. Sindima, *Religious and Political Ethics in Africa: A Moral Inquiry* (Westport, CT: Greenwood Press, 1998), 77–79.

23. In the end, only two bishops sided with Arius, despite a slightly greater degree of support earlier in the council.

24. See the discussion in Timothy D. Barnes, *Constantine and Eusebius* (Cambridge, MA: Harvard Univ. Press, 2006).

25. Erik Peterson, *Der Monotheismus als politisches Problem: Ein Beitrag zur Geschichte der politischen Theologie im Imperium Romanum* (Leipzig: Hegner, 1935). For comment, see Christoph Markschies, "Heis Theos—Ein Gott? Der Monotheismus und das antike Christentum," in *Polytheismus und Monotheismus in den Religionen des vorderen Orients,* ed. Manfred Krebernik and Jürgen van Oorschot (Münster: Ugarit Verlag, 2002), 209–34; Alfons Fürst, "Monotheismus und Monarchie: Zum Zusammenhang von Heil und Herrschaft in der Antike," in *Der Monotheismus als theologisches und*

politisches Problem, ed. Stefan Stiegler and Uwe Swarat (Leipzig: Evangelische Verlagsanstalt, 2006), 61–81.

26. See esp. the collection of critical essays in Alfred Schindler, ed., *Monotheismus als politisches Problem? Erik Peterson und die Kritik der politischen Theologie* (Gütersloh: Mohn, 1978).

27. See Jürgen Moltmann, *The Trinity and the Kingdom: The Doctrine of God* (Minneapolis, MN: Fortress Press, 1993).

28. Dorothy L. Sayers, *Creed or Chaos?* (London: Methuen, 1947), 32–35.

29. The best study of the origins and development of this movement is W. H. C. Frend, *The Donatist Church: A Movement of Protest in Roman North Africa* (Oxford: Clarendon Press, 2000). For some writers, Donatism ought to be considered as a sectarian or schismatic movement rather than as a heresy. In this section, I shall take the traditional view that Donatism is best understood retrospectively as a heresy.

30. Maureen A. Tilley, "Sustaining Donatist Self-Identity: From the Church of the Martyrs to the Collecta of the Desert," *Journal of Early Christian Studies* 5 (1997): 21–35.

31. The modern word "traitor" derives from the same root. Other terms relating to this persecution include *sacrificati* (those who made sacrifices to Roman gods), *thurificati* (those who burned incense at pagan altars), and *libellatici* (those who signed documents indicating their religious conformity).

32. Bernhard Kriegbaum, *Kirche der Traditoren oder Kirche der Märtyrer: Die Vorgeschichte des Donatismus* (Innsbruck: Tyrolia-Verlag, 1986), 59–148.

33. See the excellent analysis in Geoffrey D. Dunn, "Heresy and Schism According to Cyprian of Carthage," *Journal of Theological Studies* 55 (2004): 551–74.

34. Cyprian of Carthage *Epistula* 72: "[S]alus extra ecclesiam non est."

35. For an excellent account of these, see A. H. Merrills, "Vandals, Romans and Berbers: Understanding Late Antique Roman Africa," in *Vandals, Romans and Berbers: New Perspectives on Late Antique North Africa,* ed. A. H. Merrills (Aldershot, UK: Ashgate, 2004), 1–28.

36. For a useful survey of the issues, see W. H. C. Frend, "Heresy and Schism as Social and National Movements," in *Schism, Heresy and Protest,* ed. Derek Baker (Cambridge: Cambridge Univ. Press, 1972), 37–49. For the tensions between the churches of Rome and Carthage, see Werner Marschall, *Karthago und Rom: Die Stellung der nordafrikanischen Kirche zum Apostolischen Stuhl in Rom* (Stuttgart: Hiersemann, 1971).

37. For Augustine's early views on the church, see David C. Alexander, *Augustine's Early Theology of the Church: Emergence and Implications, 386–391* (New York: Peter Lang, 2008).

38. For the background to this, see W. H. C. Frend, *Saints and Sinners in the Early Church: Differing and Conflicting Traditions in the First Six Centuries* (London: Darton, Longman & Todd, 1985), 94–117.

39. James S. Alexander, "A Note on the Interpretation of the Parable of the Threshing Floor at the Conference of Carthage of A.D. 411," *Journal of Theological Studies* 24 (1973): 512–19.

40. For a good account of the issues here, esp. in relation to the political response of Catholicism to Donatism, see John von Heyking, *Augustine and Politics as Longing in the World* (Columbia: Univ. of Missouri Press, 2001), 222–56.

41. For an excellent account of Augustine's conversion, see Colin Starnes, *Augustine's Conversion: A Guide to the Argument of Confessions I–IX* (Waterloo, Ontario: Wilfrid Laurier Univ. Press, 1990).

42. Augustine of Hippo *Confessiones* 10.29. "Da quod iubes, et iube quod vis." See further Peit F. Fransen, "Augustine, Pelagius and the Controversy on the Doctrine of Grace," *Louvain Studies* 12 (1987): 172–81.

43. Robert Evans, *Pelagius: Inquiries and Reappraisals* (New York: Seabury Press, 1968), 66.

44. Gerald Bonner, "Rufinus of Syria and African Pelagianism," *Augustinian Studies* 1 (1970): 31–47.

45. Eugene TeSelle, "Rufinius the Syrian, Caelestius, Pelagius: Explorations in the Prehistory of the Pelagian Controversy," *Augustinian Studies* 3 (1972): 61–95. For further details, see esp. Guido Honnay, "Caelestius, Discipulus Pelagi," *Augustiniana* 44 (1991): 271–302.

46. Jean-Michel Girard, *La mort chez Saint Augustin: Grandes lignes de l'évolution de sa pensée, telle qu'elle apparaît dans ses traités* (Fribourg: Éditions Universitaires, 1992), 133–38.

47. Two important studies of Pelagius should be noted in this respect: Peter Brown, "Pelagius and His Supporters: Aims and Environment," *Journal of Theological Studies* 19 (1968): 83–114; Peter Brown, "The Patrons of Pelagius: The Roman Aristocracy Between East and West," *Journal of Theological Studies* 21 (1970): 56–72.

48. For the Roman context of the Pelagian movement, see Charles Pietri, *Roma christiana: Recherches sur l'Église de Rome, son organisation, sa politique, son idéologie de Miltiade à Sixte III (311–440)* (Rome: École Française de Rome, 1976), 1222–44.

49. F. G. Nuvolone and G. Solignac, "Pélage et Pélagianisme," in *Dictionaire de spiritualité* (Paris: Beauchesne, 1986), 12:2889–2942.

50. For the issue of dating, see Yves-Marie Duval, "La date de 'De natura' de Pélage: Les premières étapes de la controverse sur la nature de la grâce," *Revue des études Augustiniennes* 36 (1990): 257–83.

51. See, e.g., Sebastian Thier, *Kirche bei Pelagius* (Berlin: de Gruyter, 1999).

52. The best exploration of this point is Gisbert Greshake, *Gnade als konkrete Freiheit: Eine Untersuchung zur Gnadenlehre des Pelagius* (Mainz: Matthias Grünewald Verlag, 1972).

53. Pelagius *Epistula ad Demetriadem* 16.

54. For the question of the attitude of the Roman bishops to Pelagius's teaching, see Otto Wermelinger, *Rom und Pelagius: Die theologische Position der römischen Bischöfe im pelagianischen Streit in den Jahren 411–432* (Stuttgart: Hiersemann, 1975).

55. See Josef Lössl, *Julian von Aeclanum: Studien zu seinem Leben, seinem Werk, seiner Lehre und ihrer Überlieferung* (Leiden: Brill, 2001), 250–330.

56. The writings of John Chrysostom were attracting attention at this time: see Duval, "'De natura' de Pélage," 280–81.

57. For an excellent account of Augustine's views, focusing on a later variant of the Pelagian controversy, see Donato Ogliari, *Gratia Et Certamen: The Relationship Between Grace and Free Will in the Discussion of Augustine with the So-Called Semipelagians* (Louvain: Peeters, 2003). For a detailed account of Augustine's doctrine of grace, see Agostino Trapè, *Sant'Agostino: Introduzione alla dottrina della grazia,* 2 vols. (Rome: Città Nuova, 1990).

58. Augustine of Hippo *De natura et gratia* 3.3.

59. See esp. Pelagius's treatise *De induratione cordis Pharaonis*.

60. For more detailed discussion, see Timothy Maschke, "St Augustine's Theology of Prayer," in *Augustine: Presbyter Factus Sum,* ed. Joseph T. Lienhard, Earl C. Muller, and Roland J. Teske (New York: Peter Lang, 1993), 431–46.

61. Stephen J. Duffy, *The Dynamics of Grace: Perspectives in Theological Anthropology* (Collegeville, MN: Liturgical Press, 1993), 89.

62. Augustine of Hippo *Tractatus in Johannem* 27.7.

63. This point is emphasized in Ronald W. Dworkin, *The Rise of the Imperial Self: America's Culture Wars in Augustinian Perspective* (Lanham, MD: Rowman & Littlefield, 1996). Note esp. his comments on Pelagianism (39–58).

64. Dworkin has spotted it: Dworkin, *Rise of the Imperial Self,* 59–73.

CHAPTER 8: CULTURAL AND INTELLECTUAL MOTIVATIONS FOR HERESY

1. For comment on Newman's views, see Rowan Williams, "Newman's *Arians* and the Question of Method in Doctrinal History," in *Newman After a Hundred Years,* ed. Ian Ker and Alan G. Hill (Oxford: Clarendon Press, 1990), 263–85; and Thomas Ferguson, "The Enthralling Power: History and Heresy in John Henry Newman," *Anglican Theological Review* 85 (2003): 641–62.

2. H. M. Gwatkin, *Studies in Arianism,* 2nd ed. (Cambridge: Deighton Bell & Co., 1900), 17–21, 274. For a landmark response to Gwatkin, which some regard as marking the origins of modern Arius scholarship, see Maurice F. Wiles, "In Defence of Arius," *Journal of Theological Studies* 13 (1962): 339–47.

3. For an important early statement of this approach, see Pascal Boyer, *The Naturalness of Religious Ideas: A Cognitive Theory of Religion* (Berkeley: Univ. of California Press, 1994). For a recent overview, see Justin L. Barrett, "Exploring the Natural Foundations of Religion," *Trends in Cognitive Sciences* 4 (2000): 29–34.

4. A good example of this is Daniel C. Dennett, *Breaking the Spell: Religion as a Natural Phenomenon* (New York: Viking Penguin, 2006). For a critique, see Justin L. Barrett, "Is the Spell Really Broken? Bio-Psychological Explanations of Religion and Theistic Belief," *Theology and Science* 5 (2007): 57–72.

5. I here draw on Robert N. McCauley, "The Naturalness of Religion and the Unnaturalness of Science," in *Explanation and Cognition,* ed. F. Keil and R. Wilson (Cambridge, MA: MIT Press, 2000), 61–85.

6. E.g., R. P. C. Hanson, *The Search for the Christian Doctrine of God: The Arian Controversy, 318–381* (Edinburgh: T. & T. Clark, 1988).

7. This latter idea is known as "monarchianism" and played an important role in second- and third-century Christian thought. For its relevance to this discussion, see D. H. Williams, "Monarchianism and Photinus of Sirmium as the Persistent Heretical Face of the Fourth Century," *Harvard Theological Review* 99 (2006): 187–206.

8. Mark J. Edwards, "Justin's *Logos* and the Word of God," *Journal of Early Christian Studies* 3 (1995): 261–80. This study corrects some influential older misunderstandings of Justin's approach.

9. Augustine of Hippo *De doctrina Christiana* 2.40.60–61.

10. Augustine of Hippo *De civitate Dei* 10.10.21. See the comments in Leonard Robert Palmer, *The Latin Language* (London: Faber & Faber, 1954), 191–94.

11. For the development of the Christian understanding of justification, see Alister E. McGrath, *Iustitia Dei: A History of the Christian Doctrine of Justification,* 3rd ed. (Cambridge: Cambridge Univ. Press, 2005).

12. Cicero *Rhetoricum libro duo* 2.53: "Iustitia virtus est, communi utilitate servata, suam cuique tribuens dignitatem." Cf. Justinian *Institutio* 1.1: "Iustitia est constans et perpetua voluntas suum unicuique tribuens." See further D. H. van Zyl, *Justice and Equity in Cicero* (Pretoria: Academica Press, 1991).

13. For his life and thought, see Josef Lössl, *Julian von Aeclanum: Studien zu seinem Leben, seinem Werk, seiner Lehre und ihrer Überlieferung* (Leiden: Brill, 2001). More specifically, see Andreas Urs Sommer, "Das Ende der antiken Anthropologie als Bewährungsfall kontextualistischer Philosophiegeschichtsschreibung: Julian von Eclanum und Augustin von Hippo," *Zeitschrift für Religions- und Geistesgeschichte* 57 (2005): 1–28.

14. Ps. 31:1 (my emphasis). For analysis of this important point, see McGrath, *Iustitia Dei,* 6–21.

15. For a full discussion, see Alister E. McGrath, "Divine Justice and Divine Equity in the Controversy Between Augustine and Julian of Eclanum," *Downside Review* 101 (1983): 312–19. There is also some useful material in F. J. Thonnard, "Justice de Dieu et justice humaine selon Saint Augustin," *Augustinus* 12 (1967): 387–402.

16. Austin Farrer, "The Christian Apologist," in *Light on C. S. Lewis,* ed. Jocelyn Gibb (London: Geoffrey Bles, 1965), 23–43; quote at 26.

17. See the examples in Caroline P. Bammel, "Pauline Exegesis, Manichaeism, and Philosophy in the early Augustine," in *Christian Faith and Greek Philosophy in Late Antiquity,* ed. Lionel R. Wickham and Caroline P. Bammel (Leiden: Brill, 1993), 1–25.

18. The best study is George H. Williams, *The Radical Reformation,* 3rd ed. (Kirksville, MO: Sixteenth Century Journal Publishers, 1992).

19. See, e.g., Mihály Balázs, *Early Transylvanian Antitrinitarianism (1566–1571): From Servet to Palaeologus* (Baden-Baden: Valentin Koerner, 1996).

20. Art de Groot, "L'antitrinitarisme socinien," *Études théologiques et religieuses* 61 (1986): 51–61.

21. William S. Babcock, "A Changing of the Christian God: The Doctrine of the Trinity in the Seventeenth Century," *Interpretation* 45 (1991): 133–46.

22. See the important collection of research assembled in John Hedley Brooke and Ian Maclean, eds., *Heterodoxy in Early Modern Science and Religion* (Oxford: Oxford Univ. Press, 2005). An earlier study is also of importance: Michael Hunter, "Science and Heterodoxy: An Early Modern Problem," in *Reappraisals of the Scientific Revolution,* ed. David C. Lindberg and Robert S. Westman (Cambridge: Cambridge Univ. Press, 1990), 437–60.

23. See Stephen D. Snobelen, "Newton, Heretic: The Strategies of a Nicodemite," *British Journal for the History of Science* 32 (1999): 381–419.

24. Maurice Wiles, *Archetypal Heresy: Arianism Through the Ages* (Oxford: Oxford Univ. Press, 1996), 62–134.

25. William P. Alston, *Perceiving God: The Epistemology of Religious Experience* (Ithaca, NY: Cornell Univ. Press, 1991), 289.

26. A point emphasized in Alister E. McGrath, *The Open Secret: A New Vision for Natural Theology* (Oxford: Blackwell, 2008).

27. Emily A. Greenfield and Nadine F. Marks, "Religious Social Identity as an Explanatory Factor for Associations Between More Frequent Formal Religious Participation and Psychological Well-Being," *International Journal for the Psychology of Religion* 17 (2007): 245–59.

28. A pattern noted and assessed in Wayne Meeks's excellent study of the social realities of Pauline communities in the New Testament: see Wayne A. Meeks, *The First Urban Christians: The Social World of the Apostle Paul* (New Haven, CT: Yale Univ. Press, 1983), 84–103.

29. See A. H. M. Jones, "Were Ancient Heresies National or Social Movements in Disguise?" *Journal of Theological Studies* 10 (1959): 280–86; and W. H. C. Frend, "Heresy and Schism as Social and National Movements," in *Schism, Heresy and Protest,* ed. Derek Baker (Cambridge: Cambridge Univ. Press, 1972), 37–49.

30. This view is found in its classic form in W. H. C. Frend, *The Donatist Church: A Movement of Protest in Roman North Africa* (Oxford: Clarendon Press, 2000).

31. Robert A. Markus, "Christianity and Dissent in Roman North Africa," *Studies in Church History* 9 (1972): 21–36.

32. See, e.g., Augustine of Hippo *Epistula* 66.1.

33. Maureen A. Tilley, *The Bible in Christian North Africa: The Donatist World* (Minneapolis: Fortress Press, 1997), esp. 19.

34. See the detailed analysis in Oliver O'Donovan, *The Desire of the Nations: Rediscovering the Roots of Political Theology* (Cambridge: Cambridge Univ. Press, 1996).

35. Gerald Bonner, "Pelagianism and Augustine," *Augustinian Studies* 23 (1992): 33–51.

36. See Christine Trevett, *Montanism: Gender, Authority, and the New Prophecy* (Cambridge: Cambridge Univ. Press, 1996).

37. See David G. Hunter, *Marriage, Celibacy, and Heresy in Ancient Christianity: The Jovinianist Controversy* (Oxford: Oxford Univ. Press, 2007). Hunter's analysis of the complex interaction of heresy and asceticism (87–170) merits close attention.

38. See the classic study of Robert E. Lerner, *The Heresy of the Free Spirit in the Later Middle Ages* (Berkeley, CA: Univ. of California Press, 1972), esp. 10–13.

39. Norman Cohn, *The Pursuit of the Millennium: Revolutionary Millenarians and Mystical Anarchists of the Middle Ages,* rev. and expanded ed. (New York: Oxford Univ. Press, 1970), 151.

40. H. E. W. Turner, *The Pattern of Christian Truth: A Study in the Relations Between Orthodoxy and Heresy in the Early Church* (London: Mowbray, 1954), 97–163.

CHAPTER 9: ORTHODOXY, HERESY, AND POWER

 1. Rowan Williams, "Defining Heresy," in *The Origins of Christendom in the West,* ed. Alan Kreider (Edinburgh: T. & T. Clark, 2001), 313–35.

 2. See John B. Henderson, *The Construction of Orthodoxy and Heresy: Neo-Confucian, Islamic, Jewish, and Early Christian Patterns* (Albany: State Univ. of New York Press, 1998).

 3. For accounts of critical realism, see Andrew Collier, *Critical Realism: An Introduction to Roy Bhaskar's Philosophy* (London: Verso, 1994); and Margaret Archer, Andrew Collier, and Douglas V. Porpora, eds., *Transcendence: Critical Realism and God* (London: Routledge, 2004).

 4. Karl Marx and Friedrich Engels, *The German Ideology* (New York: International Publishers, 1972), 64. For an assessment of this approach, see Hans Barth, *Wahrheit und Ideologie* (New York: Arno Press, 1975), 73–190.

 5. Engels's depiction of the Peasants' Revolt as fundamentally based on class warfare has subsequently had a significant impact on historical studies of the movement: see, e.g., Peter Blickle, "Communal Reformation and Peasant Piety: The Peasant Reformation in Its Late Medieval Origins," *Central European History* 20 (1987): 216–28.

 6. George V. Zito, "Toward a Sociology of Heresy," *Sociological Analysis* 44 (1983): 123–30; quote at 126.

 7. Max Weber, *The Sociology of Religion* (Boston: Beacon Press, 1993), 68.

 8. For a somewhat speculative exploration of this theme, see Meerten B. ter Borg, "Canon and Social Control," in *Canonization and Decanonization,* ed. A. van der Kooij and K. van der Toorn (Leiden: Brill, 1998), 411–23.

 9. For an exploration of this issue, see Virginia Burrus, *The Making of a Heretic: Gender, Authority, and the Priscillianist Controversy* (Berkeley: Univ. of California Press, 1995), 19–21.

10. Rowan Williams, "Origen: Between Orthodoxy and Heresy," in *Origeniana Septima: Origenes in den Auseinandersetzung des 4. Jahrhunderts,* ed. Wolfgang A. Bienert and Uwe Kühneweg (Louvain: Peeters, 1999), 3–14.

11. See Rowan Williams, "Does It Make Sense to Speak of Pre-Nicene Orthodoxy?" in *The Making of Orthodoxy,* ed. Rowan Williams (Cambridge: Cambridge Univ. Press, 1989), 1–23.

12. See the discussion in Timothy D. Barnes, *Constantine and Eusebius* (Cambridge, MA: Harvard Univ. Press, 2006).

13. For a standard introduction to the issues, see William P. Haugaard, *Elizabeth and the English Reformation: The Struggle for a Stable Settlement of Religion* (Cambridge: Cambridge Univ. Press, 1970).

14. For these historical developments and their subsequent outcomes, see Lewis Ayres, *Nicaea and Its Legacy: An Approach to Fourth-Century Trinitarian Theology* (Oxford: Oxford Univ. Press, 2004), 100–104. There are indications that Constantine himself was not entirely happy with the outcome of Nicaea, especially its treatment of Arius's supporters.

15. The Council of Constantinople was convened by Theodosius I, whose authority was restricted to the eastern region of the empire. For its significance, see Henry Chadwick, *East and West: The Making of a Rift in the Church from Apostolic Times Until the Council of Florence* (Oxford: Oxford Univ. Press, 2003), 20–26.

16. For an overview of this analysis, see Ayres, *Nicaea and Its Legacy,* 167–260.

17. See the account in Judith Herrin, *The Formation of Christendom* (Princeton, NJ: Princeton Univ. Press, 1987).

18. Kathleen Cushing, *Papacy and Law in the Gregorian Revolution* (Oxford: Oxford Univ. Press, 1998).

19. Jane Sayers, *Innocent III, Leader of Europe, 1198–1216* (New York: Longman, 1994).

20. Cyprian of Carthage *Epistula* 72: "[S]alus extra ecclesiam non est."

21. Jean-Maurice Rouquette, *Provence romane: La Provence rhodanienne,* 2nd ed. (La Pierre-qui-Vire: Zodiaque, 1980), 50.

22. Francis Sullivan, *Salvation Outside the Church? Tracing the History of the Catholic Response* (Mahwah, NJ: Paulist Press, 1992).

23. As pointed out in R. I. Moore, *The Origins of European Dissent* (London: Allen Lane, 1977).

24. See the discussions in Richard Landes, "The Birth of Heresy: A Millennial Phenomenon," *Journal of Religious History* 24 (2000): 26–43; and R. I. Moore, "The Birth of Popular Heresy: A Millennial Phenomenon?" *Journal of Religious History* 24 (2000): 8–25.

25. Heinrich Fichtenau, *Heretics and Scholars in the High Middle Ages, 1000–1200* (University Park: Pennsylvania State Univ. Press, 1998), 105–26.

26. The Cathars were also referred to as the Albigensians, from the town of Albi (Latin name: *Albiga*), northeast of Toulouse. For an accessible introduction, see Stephen O'Shea, *The Perfect Heresy: The Revolutionary Life and Death of the Medieval Cathars* (New York: Walker & Co., 2000). The term "Cathar" derives from the Greek term *katharos* ("pure"), referring to their emphasis on moral excellence.

27. Gabriel Audisio, *The Waldensian Dissent: Persecution and Survival, c. 1170–c. 1570* (Cambridge: Cambridge Univ. Press, 1999).

28. Kantik Ghosh, *The Wycliffite Heresy: Authority and the Interpretation of Texts* (Cambridge: Cambridge Univ. Press, 2002), 22.

29. Ghosh, *Wycliffite Heresy,* 67–85.

30. Richard Kieckhefer, "The Office of Inquisition and Medieval Heresy: The Transi-

tion from Personal to Institutional Jurisdiction," *Journal of Ecclesiastical History* 46 (1995): 36–61.

31. For an early statement of this case, see Herbert Grundmann, *Religiöse Bewegungen im Mittelalter: Untersuchungen über die geschichtlichen Zusammenhänge zwischen der Ketzerei, den Bettelorden und der religiösen Frauenbewegung um 12. und 13. Jahrhundert und über die geschichtlichen Grundlagen der deutschen Mystik* (Berlin: Emil Ebering, 1935).

32. See Martin Brecht, *Martin Luther,* 3 vols. (Minneapolis: Fortress Press, 1990–94).

33. Norman E. Nagel, "Luther and the Priesthood of All Believers," *Concordia Theological Quarterly* 61 (1997): 277–98.

34. See the discussion in Alister E. McGrath, *The Intellectual Origins of the European Reformation,* 2nd ed. (Oxford: Blackwell, 2003).

35. B. B. Warfield, *Calvin and Augustine* (Philadelphia: Presbyterian and Reformed Publishing Company, 1956), 322.

36. See the important collection of material assembled in Leif Grane, Alfred Schindler, and Markus Wriedt, eds., *Auctoritas patrum: Zur Rezeption der Kirchenväter im 15. und 16. Jahrhundert* (Mainz: Verlag Philipp von Zabern, 1993); and Leif Grane, Alfred Schindler, and Markus Wriedt, eds., *Auctoritas patrum II: Neue Beiträge zur Rezeption der Kirchenväter im 15. und 16. Jahrhundert* (Mainz: Verlag Philipp von Zabern, 1998).

37. For Melanchthon's important statement of this position, see the classic study of Peter Fraenkel, *Testimonia Patrum: The Function of the Patristic Argument in the Theology of Philip Melanchthon* (Geneva: Droz, 1961). This analysis has been extended in Irena Backus, *Historical Method and Confessional Identity in the Era of the Reformation (1378–1615)* (Leiden: Brill, 2003).

38. For details, see Massimo Firpo, "The Italian Reformation and Juan de Valdes," *Sixteenth Century Journal* 27 (1996): 353–64.

39. The historical details of this controversy are not directly relevant here, as our concern is to note the difficulties Protestants faced when confronted with new ideas that could not easily be reduced to older heresies. Those wishing to follow through the historical and theological issues should consult Nicholas Tyacke, *Anti-Calvinists: The Rise of English Arminianism, c. 1590–1640* (Oxford: Oxford Univ. Press, 1990); Martin Mulsow and Jan Rohls, eds., *Socinianism and Arminianism: Antitrinitarians, Calvinists, and Cultural Exchange in Seventeenth-Century Europe* (Leiden: Brill, 2005); and Benjamin Myers, *Milton's Theology of Freedom* (New York: Walter de Gruyter, 2006).

40. See Maurice Wiles, *Archetypal Heresy: Arianism Through the Centuries* (Oxford: Clarendon Press, 1996).

41. See esp. Benjamin Myers, "Following the Way Which Is Called Heresy: Milton and the Heretical Imperative," *Journal of the History of Ideas* 69 (2008): 375–93. On Milton's libertarianism in general, see Hugh Wilson, "Milton and the Struggle for Human Rights," in *Milton, Rights, and Liberties,* ed. Christophe Tournu and Neil Forsyth (New York: Peter Lang, 2007), 21–30.

42. *Complete Prose Works of John Milton,* ed. Don M. Wolfe et al., 8 vols. (New Haven, CT: Yale Univ. Press, 1953–82), 7:247–48.

43. I develop this point in Alister E. McGrath, *Christianity's Dangerous Idea: The Protestant Revolution* (San Francisco: HarperOne, 2007).

44. Michel Foucault, *Discipline and Punish: The Birth of the Prison,* 2nd ed. (New York: Vintage Books, 1995).

45. This point also applies to orthodoxy. For the concept of "dogma" as a belief that is formally accepted by the community of faith as a whole, see Alister E. McGrath, *The Genesis of Doctrine* (Oxford: Blackwell, 1990), 8–13.

46. Hilary Lawson, *Closure: A Story of Everything* (London: Routledge, 2001), 4.

47. Lawson, *Closure,* 327.

48. This is a theme explored in Karl Rahner, "Chalkedon—Ende oder Anfang?" in *Das Konzil von Chalkedon: Geschichte und Gegenwart,* ed. Alois Grillmeier and Heinrich Bacht, 3 vols. (Würzburg: Echter-Verlag, 1951–54), 1:3–49.

49. This is the view expressed in Rowan Williams, *Arius: Heresy and Tradition,* 2nd ed. (London: SCM Press, 2001). See further his essay "What Is Catholic Orthodoxy?" in *Essays Catholic and Radical,* ed. Kenneth Leech and Rowan Williams (London: SPCK, 1983), 11–25.

50. See further Alister E. McGrath, *The Genesis of Doctrine* (Oxford: Blackwell, 1990), 1–8.

CHAPTER 10: HERESY AND THE ISLAMIC VIEW OF CHRISTIANITY

1. Richard C. Martin and Mark R. Woodward, *Defenders of Reason in Islam: Mu'tazilism from Medieval School to Modern Symbol* (Oxford: Oneworld, 1997), 202–3.

2. See the points made in Alister E. McGrath, *Christianity's Dangerous Idea: The Protestant Revolution* (San Francisco: HarperOne, 2007), 474–76.

3. Wilfred Cantwell Smith, *Islam in Modern History* (Princeton, NJ: Princeton Univ. Press, 1957), 17–18.

4. Surah 4:167–70; 5:77. This could easily be interpreted, in quasi-pagan terms, as the divine Father, Son, and Mother.

5. For some examples, see David Thomas, "The Doctrine of the Trinity in the Early Abbasid Era," in *Islamic Interpretations of Christianity,* ed. Lloyd Ridgeon (Richmond: Curzon Press, 2001), 78–98.

6. The name of this sect derives from the Greek word *kollyris,* "loaf of bread"—a reference to its practice of offering bread to Mary as a goddess.

7. For a detailed study of the issues, see Vasiliki Limberis, *Divine Heiress: The Virgin Mary and the Creation of Christian Constantinople* (New York: Routledge, 1994), 114–21.

8. Schwager Raymund, "Christologie und Islam," in *Penser la foi: Recherches en théologie aujourd'hui: Mélanges offerts à Joseph Moingt,* ed. Joseph Doré and Christoph Theobald (Paris: Éditions du Cerf, 1993), 203–15; David Thomas, "Explanations of the Incarnation in Early Abbasid Islam," in *Redefining Christian Identity: Cultural*

Interaction in the Middle East Since the Rise of Islam, ed. J. J. van Ginkel, H. L. Murre-van den Berg, and Theo Maarten van Lint (Louvain: Peeters, 2005), 127–49.

9. For an excellent account of this point, see Peter Widdicombe, *The Fatherhood of God from Origen to Athanasius* (Oxford: Clarendon Press, 1994).

10. Gnosticism and Nestorianism are often noted as possible influences on the Qu'ran. E.g., the Qur'an appears to refer to a story of Jesus giving life to birds that are made of clay (Sura 3:49; 5:110), found in the Gnostic Infancy Gospel of Thomas (4:2). Syrian influences should also be noted. See further Gabriel Said Reynolds, ed., *The Qur'an in Its Historical Context* (New York: Routledge, 2007).

11. Second Treatise of the Great Seth 55:16–35. See further Paul Gavrilyuk, *The Suffering of the Impassible God: The Dialectics of Patristic Thought* (Oxford: Oxford Univ. Press, 2004), 79–90.

12. Surah 4:157–58.

13. For this and other examples, see David Pinault, "Images of Christ in Arabic Literature," *Die Welt des Islams* 27 (1987): 103–25.

14. Mahmoud Mustafa Ayoub, "Towards an Islamic Christology, II: The Death of Jesus, Reality or Delusion?" *Muslim World* 70 (1980): 91–121.

CONCLUSION

1. These concerns are noted sympathetically, though not endorsed, in Eleonore Stump, "Orthodoxy and Heresy," *Faith and Philosophy* 16 (1999): 147–63.

2. This concern was present even in the patristic age, as noted in Robert M. Grant, *Heresy and Criticism: The Search for Authenticity in Early Christian Literature* (Louisville, KY: Westminster/John Knox Press, 1993).

3. Robert A. Segal, ed., *The Allure of Gnosticism: The Gnostic Experience in Jungian Psychology and Contemporary Culture* (Chicago: Open Court, 1995).

4. Patrick Henry, "Why Is Contemporary Scholarship So Enamored of Ancient Heresies?" in *Proceedings of the 8th International Conference on Patristic Studies,* ed. E. A. Livingstone (Oxford: Pergamon Press, 1980), 123–26. Henry's concerns are not met by the kind of response found in Virginia Burrus, *The Making of a Heretic: Gender, Authority, and the Priscillianist Controversy* (Berkeley: Univ. of California Press, 1995), 1–2.

5. See Philip E. Tetlock, Orie V. Kristel, S. Beth Elson, Melanie C. Green, and Jennifer S. Lerner, "The Psychology of the Unthinkable: Taboo Trade-Offs, Forbidden Base Rates, and Heretical Counterfactuals," *Journal of Personality and Social Psychology* 78 (2000): 853–70.

6. For a critical account of this phenomenon, see the recent revisionist account of Timothy Larsen, *Crisis of Doubt: Honest Faith in Nineteenth-Century England* (Oxford: Oxford Univ. Press, 2006).

7. Arthur Michael Ramsey, *The Christian Priest Today* (London: SPCK, 1972), 21.

8. A representative case for the necessity of doctrinal statements, including a critique of the notion of an "undogmatic faith," can be found in Alister E. McGrath, *A Scientific Theology,* vol. 3, *Theory* (London: T&T Clark, 2003), 3–76.

9. G. K. Chesterton, *Orthodoxy* (New York: Doubleday, 1959), 129–47; quote at 129–47. It is important to note that Chesterton bases his case for faith not so much on the basis of Christianity's truth as on its capacity to answer our need for "an active and imaginative life, picturesque and full of poetical curiosity" (3).

10. I borrow this phrase from William Lynch, *Christ and Apollo: The Dimensions of the Literary Imagination* (Notre Dame, IN: Univ. of Notre Dame Press, 1960), 157.

Index

Abraham, 21, 61, 115, 131
Abu Hamid, al-Ghazali, 228
Al-Qiyadah Al-Islamiyah Islamic sect, 34–35
Alston, William, 186
Ambrose of Milan, 193
antiauthoritarian culture, 2, 3, 8–9
anti-Semitism, 131
anti-Trinitarianism, 185–86, 214
apocryphal writings, 47–49
apologists, 181, 183, 184, 186, 189
apostasy, 155
Appeal (Luther), 209
archaism, 66
Arianism
    Athanasius's critique of, 146–47
    Constantine's involvement in dispute, 149–50, 203–4
    Council of Nicaea's rejection of, 140, 148–49
    debate reopened by Constantius, 204–5
    as distinguished from Ebionitism, 108–9
    endorsement of divine *monarchia,* 149–50

fundamental themes of, 54, 93, 143–47, 150–52
identity of Jesus in, 144–47, 150–52
impact of, 28–29, 86–87, 186, 219
motives behind, 171
nineteenth-century views on, 175
revival in Anglicanism, 215
similarities to Islam, 87, 144, 150
and social norms, 96, 184
Thalia, 142, 203
use of biblical "proof-texting," 143–44, 171
Arius, 54, 86, 142–52, 171, 203, 204, 221
Arminian controversy, 214–15
Arminius, Jakob, 214–15
asceticism, 191, 193
assimilation, 84–86, 91, 101, 178, 180–83, 189
Athanasius of Alexandria, 48, 66–67, 86, 87, 146–48, 204, 213
atheism, 2, 233
Augustine of Hippo, 29, 156–60, 162–70, 179, 181–83, 188, 192, 212, 213
authenticity, 27–28, 101–2, 232
authoritarianism, 150, 193, 194, 216
authoritative resources, 46, 47–49
Ayoub, Mahmoud Mustafa, 228

Baigent, Michael, 3–4

Barth, Karl, 108, 185–86

Basilides, 120, 125

Bauer, Walter, 2–3, 56, 73–77, 81, 119, 125, 133, 197, 201, 203

belief, 22

belief system. *See* framework of beliefs

Benedict of Nursia, 191, 192

Berbers, 95, 153, 155, 187

Berger, Peter, 7–8

Bible
   in anti-Trinitarianism, 185, 214
   contemporary theories of the, 5
   Hebrew Bible, 61, 127, 201
   "heresy" in various translations, 37–38
   sacred boundaries in the, 6
   See also New Testament; Old Testament

biblical interpretation
   biblical "proof-texting," 143–44
   the church's power over, 207–8
   difficulties posed to Protestantism, 51–53, 216–17
   divergent interpretations of New Testament, 51–54
   and doctrinal formulations, 102
   Irenaeus on, 124
   Luther's challenge to papal authority, 209, 210–11
   Marcion's biblical canon, 129–30
   Milton on, 216–17
   problems of Protestant, 51–53
   Waldensian literalism, 207

Bossuet, Jacques-Bénigne, 67

Bourdieu, Pierre, 35

Brown, Dan, 3–6, 218

Caecilianus, Bishop, 139, 152–54

Caelestius, 161, 162, 192

Calvin, John, 212

Calvinism, 215

Carlyle, Thomas, 86–87

Cathars, 7, 188, 207

Catholic Church
   authority over biblical interpretation, 51, 211
   concern over "doctrinal development," 67
   First Vatican Council, 68–69
   Inquisition, 103–4, 208, 214
   as inventing ideas to secure power, 4–6
   reaction to Protestantism, 211–14
   Second Vatican Council, 213
   suppression of heresy, 3, 6, 7, 74, 104, 203
   See also imperial Christianity; medieval church

Cerinthus, 111–12

choice, 7–8

Christian faith
   consolidation of, 24–27
   as framework for life, 18–19
   heresy as threat to, 33–35
   as innovative and radical, 10–11
   intellectual core of, 17–18, 46, 49–50
   Jesus as center of, 17, 43, 90, 92–93
   naturalization of, 177–178
   the nature of faith, 20–23, 189
   preserving the mysteries of, 27–32
   quest for authenticity, 27–28, 101–2, 232
   sacraments of, 123, 153–55, 157–58
   saints and sinners in, 156–58, 167
   significance of heresy to contemporary, 231–34
   transmutation of the world, 19–20
   See also doctrine; early church; imperial Christianity; medieval church; orthodoxy; worship

church of Rome. *See* Catholic Church; imperial Christianity; medieval church

classic period. *See* imperial Christianity; Roman empire

clerical authority, 209, 210–11

clerical marriage, 210

closure, 219–20

cognitive science of religion, 176–80

Cohn, Norman, 193–94

Collyridian sect, 225–26

community identity, 32, 187–88

Confessions (Augustine), 159, 160

conspiracy theories, 6

Constantine, Emperor, 5, 46, 55, 138–40, 148–50, 153, 154, 202–4, 211

Constantius, Emperor, 204

contemporary views of heresy
  associated with choice, 7–8
  as challenge to authority, 8–11
  as fashionable, 1–2, 217–21, 232–33
  heresy/orthodoxy and power, 2–6, 200, 217–21
  as liberating, 7, 191

Council of Chalcedon, 67, 69, 219, 220–21, 226, 228

Council of Constantinople, 204

Council of Nicaea
  and the Arian controversy, 140, 148, 204
  creation of uniform imperial church, 55
  imperial political authority and, 148–50, 203
  Luther's reference to, 211
  on nature of Jesus, 4, 26, 29, 151

councils, church's hold over, 209, 211

creation/creator
  in Arianism, 144
  church doctrine of, 24–25
  in Gnosticism, 119, 120–21
  Marcion's view, 128–29
  Pelagius on, 163–64

creeds, 22–23, 28, 89–90, 124

critical realism, 198

crucifixion, 116, 227–28

cultural and intellectual motivations for heresy
  accommodations to secular reason, 180, 184–86
  assimilation to cultural norms, 85, 164–65, 180, 181–83

and the cognitive science of religion, 176–80

ethical discontent, 180, 190–94

as historically misunderstood, 175–76

naturalization of Christianity, 177–78

and the need for cultural engagement, 180, 194–95

overview of, 175–77, 180

religious contextualization, 180, 189–90

shaping of social identity, 180, 187–88

cultural influences on orthodoxy, 101–2, 179–80

culture, contemporary. *See* contemporary views of heresy

Cyprian of Carthage, 154–55, 206

Da Vinci Code, The (Brown), 3–6, 218, 236n12

Darwinism, 35, 69, 198

Dawkins, Richard, 131

"Death of God" debate, 233

Decian persecution, 55, 137

Decius, Emperor, 136–37

deism, 185, 186

Demetrias, 163, 164

Demiurge (*demiurgos;* workman), 121–22, 123

democratization of faith, 209–11

depositum fidei (deposit of faith), 46

Diocletian, Emperor, 137, 139, 152

Diocletian persecution, 137, 139

diversity, contemporary religious, 7, 8

diversity of early church
  allowing establishment of Marcionism/ Valentinism, 132
  crystallization of orthodoxy among, 55–58, 79–80
  five factors contributing to, 46
  and geographic spread, 43–45
  in interpretation of New Testament, 51–54
  in New Testament documents, 49–51

diversity of early church *(continued)*
    uncertainty over authoritative
        resources, 47–49
    unity within, 45–46, 77
    in worship, 46, 54–55
divine justice, 182–83
divine revelation, 28, 30, 141, 150, 223–24
Docetism
    early accepted presence of, 28
    identity of Jesus in, 94, 111–12, 129
    influence on Islam, 226, 228
    matter as fundamentally evil in, 132
    origins of, 112–16
    revelatory emphasis in, 141
doctrine
    of creation, 24–25
    creeds, 22–23, 28, 89–90, 124
    development of early, 3, 24–28, 56–57,
        66–71, 102
    as framework for Christian life, 18–19
    heresy and orthodoxy in development
        of, 65–66, 70–71, 87–91
    identity of Jesus, 146–48, 150, 151–52
    of Incarnation, 25–26, 142
    preserving and protecting the faith,
        30–31, 80, 124–25
    as quest for authenticity, 27–28, 101–2
    of revelation, 28, 30, 141
    secondary to faith and commitment, 22
    of the Trinity, 95, 123, 150, 184–86, 214,
        224–26
    Vincent's checklist of conformity, 53–54
    See also grace; salvation
Donatism
    challenged by Augustine, 156–59
    Constantine's involvement in dispute,
        202, 203–4
    heretical aspects of, 158–59
    Luther and, 212
    parallels to Pelagianism, 167, 170
    rigorist stand of, 139, 152–56
    as shaping orthodoxy, 171
    social identity factor in, 95, 187–88

Donatus the Great, 154
Dryden, John, 52
Dunn, James, 50

early church
    creeds of, 22–23, 89–90
    development of doctrines, 3, 24–28,
        56–57, 66–71, 102
    geographic spread of, 43–45, 101, 117
    heresy in the, 37–39, 73–74, 201–5, 219,
        222
    Luther's continuity with, 212–13
    overview on heresies of the, 101–4,
        132–33
    and political power, 201–5
    "received view" on the origins of
        heresy, 64–66
    relationship to Judaism, 43, 44, 61–62,
        87–88, 101
    Roman persecution of, 44, 55, 84,
        136–37, 152
    separation from the world, 88–89
    texts of the, 45, 47–49
    threats to, 84–87, 91
    See also diversity of early church
Ebionitism
    Christian assimilation to Judaism, 189
    early accepted presence of, 28
    historical context of, 108–10, 252n10
    location of Jesus Christ in, 94, 105–10,
        140, 145
    recent reemergence of, 110–11
Edict of Decius, 137
Edict of Milan, 55, 138
egalitarianism, 77–78, 233
eidolon (phantom), 114–15
Eleusinian mysteries, 117
"Elixir, The" (poem; Herbert), 20
Engels, Freidrich, 199
Epiphanius of Salamis, 61–63, 225–26
*Essay on the Development of Christian
    Doctrine* (Newman), 68
ethical concerns, 180, 190–94

Eutychianism, 93
evangelism, 51–52
Evans, Robert, 160–61
evil, 121, 123, 128, 132, 165–66, 182

faith
consolidation of, 24–27
nature of Christian, 20–23
preserving the mysteries of, 27–32
relational faith, 23
vs. belief, 22
Farrer, Austin, 184
First Vatican Council, 68–69
forgiveness, 158–59
Foucault, Michel, 218–19
Fox, Robin Lane, 76–77, 128–29
fragmentation, 86
framework of beliefs
choice and postmodern, 8
in Christianity, 17–20, 23
ideologies, 199
Judaism's influence on Christian, 140–41
orthodoxy and heresy in, 33, 35, 96
religious contextualization and, 189
See also doctrine
free will, 163, 165–68
future of heresy, 231–34

Gay, Peter, 1–2
Gemeinde (community), 210
Ghosh, Kantik, 207
Glaerius, Emperor, 137, 138
Gnostic Gospels, 47
Gnosticism
beliefs on the creator, 119, 120–21
Cathars resembling, 207
as challenge to early church, 28
and Christian religious
contextualization, 189–90
connection to Marcionism, 129
as conservative, 10–11, 218
contemporary response to, 9, 77–78,
117–18, 232, 233

difficulties in defining, 118–19
forcing clarification of faith, 89
influence on Docetism, 114, 116
influence on Islam, 226–27
Irenaeus's response to, 118
Sethian, 120, 121, 123, 226–27, 228
two main presuppositions of, 119
See also Valentinism
God
in Arianism, 144–45, 151
core beliefs on, 49–50
divine justice, 182–83
divine revelation, 28, 30, 141, 150,
223–24
in doctrinal development, 70
framework for the experience of, 18,
28, 31
in Gnosticism, 121–22, 123
human nature and grace, 167–69
mysteries of, 29, 30
nature of faith in, 20–23
rejection of Old Testament, 128–29,
131
suffering of, 25
God Delusion (Dawkins), 131
Goldstein, Ronnie, 114, 115
Gore, Charles, 26, 30, 69
Gospel of Judas, 9–10
Gospel of Thomas, 78
grace
in divine justice, 183
healing in, 166–67
medieval church's compromise of, 212
to restore free will, 165–66
salvation through, 181
as viewed by Pelagianism, 167–69
Greek thought/culture
Arianism's connection to, 145, 146
Christianity as irrational to, 142, 184
"doubles" of mythological heroes,
114–15
influence on early church, 26, 101
See also Platonism

Green, Garrett, 9
group identity, 32, 39, 82, 180, 187–88
Grundmann, Herbert, 103, 208, 213
Gwatkin, H. M., 175

hairesis/haeresis (act of choosing; heresy),
    7, 36–39
Hanson, N. R., 20
Harnack, Adolf von, 131
Hauerwas, Stanley, 18–19
healing, spiritual, 158–59
Hebrew Bible, 61, 127, 201
Helen of Troy, 114–15
Hellenistic culture/philosophy. *See* Greek
    thought/culture
Henley, William Ernest, 163
Herberg, Will, 2
Herbert, George, 20
heresies, early classic, 101–4, 132–33. *See
    also* Ebionitism; Docetism; Gnosticism;
    Marcionism; Valentinism
heresies, later classic, 135–36, 171–72. *See
    also* Arianism; Donatism; Pelagianism
heresies, medieval, 103–4, 205–8
heresiology, 58
heresy
    characteristic features of, 11–12, 31,
        33–34, 81–84, 198
    as constructed notion, 33, 82
    defiling church purity, 31–32
    as evaluative notion, 33, 62–63
    future of, 231–34
    as ideas lost to orthodoxy, 1–3, 12–13,
        31, 33, 81–82, 197
    incoherence in, 86, 93–96, 148, 198
    innovations as, 64, 65
    Islam's view of Christianity influenced
        by, 224–29
    linked to suppressed nationalism,
        155–56
    medieval notions of, 103–4, 208, 213, 219
    present in every worldview, 35–36
    Schleiermacher's model of, 92–96

    subscribing to apocryphal sources, 48
    threat to the faith, 33–35, 80, 83–84, 198
    as Trojan horse, 34, 96
    See also contemporary views of heresy;
        heretics; origins of heresy
"Heresy of the Free Spirit," 193
heresy-orthodoxy dichotomy
    appropriation of alternative/
        supplementary wisdoms, 179–80
    in the Bauer thesis, 73–77, 197, 203
    and doctrinal concepts, 79–80, 91, 102,
        171
    emergence of, 39, 79–80
    in every worldview, 35–36
    extremes of the theological spectrum,
        12–13
    importance to modern church life,
        231–34
    in the Middle Ages, 103–4, 208
    politicization of, 139–40, 222
    in quest for authenticity, 27–28, 101–2
    in "received view," 64–66
heresy-orthodoxy dichotomy and power
    contemporary views, 2–6, 200, 217–21
    heresy of Protestantism, 208–13
    and the Middle Ages, 205–8
    overview on, 197–98, 221–22
    in the patristic age, 201–5
    postmodernists views, 217–21
    problem of heresy to Protestantism,
        213–17
    sociological approaches, 198–200
Heretical Imperative (Berger), 7–8
heretics
    biblical interpretation by, 124
    contemporary views of, 2
    focus on moral character/motives of,
        63, 64, 175–76
    as insiders, 35, 58–59, 71–72, 76
Hippolytus of Rome, 85–86, 106, 113
holiness, 157
Holy Blood, Holy Grail (Baigent, Leigh,
    and Lincoln), 3–4

Hooker, Richard, 93
human nature
    as flawed, 165–66, 169
    and free will in Pelagianism, 163–67, 170
    God and grace, 167–69
    healing and redemption of, 157–58, 167
    New Testament view of, 170
    in Schleiermacher's model of heresy, 94
    as sinless, 166–67
Hurtado, Larry, 79
Hussites, 103, 188, 212

Ibn al-Juwayni, 228
identity of Jesus
    in Arianism, 144–47, 150–52
    contemporary views, 4–5
    Council of Chalcedon on, 220–21
    in Docetism, 94, 111–16, 129
    in Ebionitism, 94, 105–10, 145
    in Gnosticism, 122
    heresy as misunderstanding, 93–95
    and the heritage of Judaism, 125–27,
        140–41
    influence of Platonism, 141–42
    Islamic views of, 226–28
    Jesus's self-proclaimed divinity, 107
    in Marcionism, 128–29, 130
    in orthodoxy, 146–48, 150, 151–52, 166
    in Pelagianism, 163, 168
    See also Incarnation
ideologies, 199
Ignatius of Antioch, 112–13
imperial Christianity
    Constantine's impact on, 138–40,
        148–50, 202–4
    creating unity in, 55, 202–4
    early lax moral vision of, 191–92
    legalizing the faith, 137–38
    overview on heresies of, 135–36, 171–72
    persecution preceding, 136–37
Incarnation
    in anti-Trinitarianism, 185
    Arianism at odds with, 144–47, 150–52

    as denial of Gnosticism, 123
    Docetism on, 114
    emergence of doctrine, 25–26, 142
    as incoherent, 184
    suffering in, 25
    as transformative notion, 218
incoherence, 86, 93–96, 148
Innocent III, Pope, 205
Inquisition, 103–4, 208, 214
intellectual incoherence, 86, 93–96, 148
intellectual pressure. *See* cultural and
    intellectual motivations for heresy
interpretation of Bible. *See* biblical
    interpretation
"Invictus" (poem; Henley), 163
Irenaeus of Lyons, 16, 47, 51, 53, 58–59, 89,
    111, 113, 115, 118, 122–25, 128, 130
Islam
    Al-Qiyadah Al-Islamiyah Islamic sect
        debate, 34–35
    Arianism's similarity to, 87, 144, 150
    emergence of political structure, 56
    heresy shaping views of Christianity,
        224–29
    uneasy dynamic with Christianity, 223,
        229
    See also Qur'an

James, William, 17, 20
Jerome, 31–32, 48
Jesus of Nazareth
    center of Christian faith, 17, 43, 49, 90,
        92–93
    contemporary cultural views of, 4–5
    crucifixion accounts, 116, 227–28
    and doctrinal development, 31, 70
    early Christian beliefs in, 28–29
    in the Gospel of Judas, 9–10
    nature of faith in, 21–23
    New Testament core beliefs, 49–50
    sanctifying the church, 157–58
    as source of divine revelation, 223–24
    See also identity of Jesus

John, Gospel of, 22, 54, 111
Josephus, 37
Jovinian, 193
Judaism
    creation doctrine, 24
    early Christianity's relationship to, 43,
        44, 87–88, 101
    framework for identity of Jesus, 140–41
    Gnosticism's trajectory away from, 125
    Hebrew Christians, 110–11
    Jesus as fulfillment of, 125–27
    Jewish Christology of Ebionitism,
        105–6, 109–10, 145
    Jewish *haireses,* 37
    the Law in, 126–27
    Marcion's proposed break with, 61–62,
        87, 127, 129–31
    orthopraxy of, 87
    purity beliefs, 31–32
    Sethian Gnosticism derived from, 121
    threat of Christianity's assimilation
        into, 84–85, 91, 189
Julian of Eclanum, 161, 164, 181, 182, 183
justice, 182–83
Justin Martyr, 119, 125–28, 133, 141,
    178–79

kerygmata (proclamation), 50
King, Karen, 53, 119
King James Bible, 37–38
Koester, Helmut, 74–75
Kurtz, Lester, 35

Lambert, Malcolm, 96
language, 30, 36
lapsi (lapsed clergy), 139, 153–55
Law of Moses, 161, 168
Lawson, Hilary, 219–20
Leigh, Richard, 3–4
Lewis, C. S., 19, 184
libertarianism, 191, 193, 222
Lincoln, Henry, 3–4
Logos (word), 126, 141, 144, 178

Louth, Andrew, 29–30
Lucian of Samosata, 47
Luke, Gospel of, 129–30
Luther, Martin, 185, 199, 208–13

Marcion of Sinope, 61–63, 85, 105, 127–32,
    201
Marcionism
    as anti-Semitic, 78
    influenced by Stoics, 65, 85
    matter as evil in, 132
    proposed break with Judaism, 61–62,
        87–88, 110, 127–31, 189
    as voluntarily heretical, 131–32, 201
Marcus Tullius Cicero, 182, 183
Mark, Gospel of, 21
Mark, Karl, 198–99
Markus, R. A., 88
martyrdom, 152, 153
Marxism, 198–99
Mary, mother of Jesus, 225, 227
matter, as fundamentally evil, 121, 123,
    128, 132
McCue, James, 75–76
medieval church
    authority of Rome, 7, 103–4, 205–6
    clerical authority, 209, 210–11
    heresy and power, 205–8
    Luther's challenge to, 208–11
    notions of heresy, 103–4, 208, 213, 219
    overview on heresies of, 103–4, 205–8
    papal authority, 104, 209–11
Melanchthon, Philip, 65
Mensurius, Bishop of Carthage, 152, 153
millennial generation, 206
Milton, John, 216–17
missionary work, 51–52
Mithraic mysteries, 117
monarchia (total cosmological authority),
    149–50
monasticism, 192, 193
monotheism, 144, 145, 149
Montanism, 71–72, 78, 192–93, 218, 248n6

morality
  and church participation, 154–55,
    157–59, 167
  as focus of Pelagianism, 162, 167, 170,
    191–93
  grace to inform, 168
  moral discontent with orthodoxy, 190–91
motivations for heresy. *See* cultural and
  intellectual motivations for heresy
Muhammad, Prophet, 56, 224, 228, 229
mythology, 7–8, 114–15, 19

Nag Hammadi documents, 5, 73, 75, 116,
  120, 228
nationalism, 155–56
natural theology, 186
naturalization of Christian belief, 177–78,
  189
negative association, 36–39
Nestorianism, 93
New Testament
  Christ healing the paralytic, 169–70
  concern about false teachings, 89–90
  contemporary cultural views on, 5, 9
  creation in, 25
  critical of Jewish orthopraxy, 87
  disciples faith/trust in Jesus in, 21–22
  diversity in early church interpretation
    of, 46, 51–54
  and early church documents, 46, 47,
    49–51
  haeresis in, 37–39
  Islamic interpretation of crucifixion
    accounts, 228
  Jesus as central focus of, 49, 90
  message as radical, 11
  parables on saints and sinners, 156–57
  power and canonization of, 201
  salvation by grace/justification by faith,
    181
  translations of the, 37–38
  unity in, 50–51
  view of human nature, 170

Newman, John Henry, 68, 171, 175
Newton, Isaac, 186
Nicene Creed, 89
North Africa, 95, 139, 152–56, 158,
  187–88
Numidians, 153–54, 187–18

Old Testament
  God of the, 128–29, 131
  justice of God in, 182
  Marcion's rejection of, 87, 128–29, 130
  power and canonization of, 201
  Ten Commandments, 161, 163, 168
Origen, 202
original sin, 161, 165
origins of heresy
  case of Marcion of Sinope, 61–63
  from within the church, 34–35, 58–59,
    71–72, 76, 83
  and the cognitive science of religion,
    176–80
  in development of doctrine, 65–66,
    70–71
  development of the term, 36–39
  "essence" of heresy, 82
  Pagels's revisionist account, 77–79
  and the quest for authenticity, 101–2
  "received view" on the, 64–66
  shaped by threats to early Christianity,
    84–87
  See also cultural and intellectual
    motivations for heresy
orthodoxy
  authority over biblical interpretation,
    53, 54
  contemporary views of, 2, 3–6, 233
  crystallization of, 48, 55–58, 79–80, 171
  cultural influences on, 101–2, 179–80
  early Christian diversity and, 53, 55–58,
    133
  as emergent phenomenon, 79–80, 221
  heresy as ideas lost to, 1–3, 12–13, 31,
    33, 81–82, 197

orthodoxy *(continued)*
    on identity of Jesus, 146–48, 150, 151,
        166
    moral discontent with, 190–94
    Protestantism as, 212, 213
    proto-orthodoxy, 79, 201
    and Roman politics, 133–40, 136, 203
    and "the other," 82–83
    See also doctrine; heresy-orthodoxy
        dichotomy

paganism
    difficulty with Incarnation concept, 142
    as part of heresy, 65, 72, 86
    in Rome, 136, 137
    worship of Jesus as, 226
Pagels, Elaine, 53, 77–78, 233
papal authority, 104, 209–11
patristic period. *See* early Church
Paul of Tarsus, 44, 88, 90, 101, 119, 127,
    129, 130
Peasant War in Germany (Engels), 199
Pelagianism
    as amalgam of ideas, 161–62
    as disciplinarian, 78
    divine justice in, 182
    human nature and free will in, 163–67,
        170
    ideas advanced by Caelestius, 161
    interest in cultural assimilation, 181–83
    moral discontent in, 162, 167, 170,
        191–93
    as shaping orthodoxy, 171
    sin and grace in, 94, 166–70
    upheld by medieval church, 212
Pelagius, 160–64, 162, 167–70, 181, 191–92
Peterson, Erik, 149
"philosopher's stone," 19–20
philosophy, 85, 86, 179
Platonism
    Christianity's engagement with, 28, 65,
        71, 85
    Demiurge in, 121

Logos in, 126, 141, 178
naturalization of Christianity, 178–79,
    189
pleroma (fullness), 120
politics
    Christianity and imperial Rome,
        136–40, 148–50
    in the Donatist debate, 155–56, 158
    history of church-state relations, 205–6
    monotheism and political authority,
        149–50
    threat of heretical communities, 34
postmodernist views. *See* contemporary
    views of heresy
power. *See* heresy-orthodoxy dichotomy
    and power
predestination, 215
priesthood of all believers, 210–11
Protestantism
    approach to heresy, 213–17
    Catholic Church's recent attitudes
        toward, 213
    difficulties of biblical interpretation to,
        51–53, 216–17
    as heresy, 208–13
    Reformation, 65, 184–85, 208–13
    Reformed Protestantism, 212, 214, 215
proto-orthodoxy, 79, 201
purity, 31–32

quest for authenticity, 27–28, 101–2, 232
Qur'an
    codification of the, 56
    divinity of Jesus, 226–28
    doctrine of the Trinity, 225–26
    reflecting heretical Christianity, 224–29
    as source of divine revelation, 223–24
    view of crucifixion, 227–28

Rahner, Karl, 186, 220–21
rational norms, 180, 184–86
redemption. *See* salvation
Reformation, 65, 184–85

Reformed Protestantism, 212, 214, 215
"Religio Laici" (poem; Dryden), 52
religious accommodation, 180, 189–90
religious choice, 7–8
religious identity, 187–88
renewal, 158–59
revelation, 28, 30, 141, 150, 223–24
righteousness, 182–83
Roman empire
    Christianity's spread through, 43–45, 101
    consonance with Pelagianism, 164,
        181–82
    criticism of Christian writings, 47
    persecution of Christians, 44, 55, 84,
        136–37, 152
    politics following collapse of, 205
    righteousness and justice in, 182–83
    social-political forces in North Africa,
        95, 139, 152–56, 187–88
Rufinus of Syria, 161, 162, 192
ruling class ideology, 199

sacraments, 123, 153–55, 157–58
salvation
    Arianism's incoherence around, 146–
        47, 151–52
    dependent on Christ, 50, 94, 158–59
    "economy of salvation," 123
    in Gnosticism, 119
    institutionalization of, 205–6
    and the justice of God, 182–83
    through grace, 181
Sayers, Dorothy L., 152
schismatic bishops, 153–55
Schleiermacher, Friedrich Daniel Ernst,
    92–96
Second Treatise of the Great Seth, 116,
    226–27
Second Vatican Council, 213
secularization, 85–86
self-transformation, 164, 170, 232
Sethian Gnosticism, 120, 121, 123, 226–27,
    228

sin, 156, 161, 163, 165–67
sinners, 156–58, 167
Smith, Wilfred Cantwell, 224
social factors
    in Donatism, 95, 139, 152–56, 158,
        187–88
    heresy posing social threat, 34
    motivating heresy, 95, 96, 180–84,
        187–88
    sociological approaches to heresy,
        198–200
    suppression of heresy as social control,
        104
Socinianism, 52, 185
sophia (wisdom), 121
Sozzini, Fausto Paolo (Faustus Socinus),
    185
spiritual healing, 158–59
Stesichorus, 114, 115
Stoicism, 65, 85
Stroumsa, Guy, 114, 115
suffering, 25, 114

Ten Commandments, 161, 163, 168
Tertullian, 28, 63–65, 71, 85, 86, 89, 128,
    130, 175, 189, 193
Thalia (Arius), 142, 203
Theodotus, 122
Torah, 126, 127
traditore (surrenderer), 153–55
transmutation of the world, 19–20
Trinity, 95, 123, 150, 184–86, 214, 224–26
trust, 20–23, 49
Turner, H. E. W., 45–46, 57, 66, 194
Tyndale, William, 37–38
Tyndale Bible, 37–38

Umar, Caliph, 56
unbelief, 33
unity
    early Christian, 45–46, 57–58, 75
    in early Islam, 56
    of God, 144

unity *(continued)*
    in imperial Christianity, 139, 148, 202–4
    medieval Catholicism's enforcement
       of, 7
Unity of the Catholic Church (Cyprian),
    154–55
University of Paris, 211–12

Valdés, Juan de, 207, 214
Valentinism
    Christ as redeemer in, 122
    Demiurge in, 121–22, 123
    Docetist view of Christ, 113
    emerging within orthodoxy, 75–76
    influence of Gnosticism on, 190
    influence on Docetism, 113
    Irenaeus's response to, 122–25
    matter as evil in, 132
    Tertullian's response to, 65, 85, 130
    views of, 119–23
    as voluntarily heretical, 201
    See also Gnosticism

Valentinus, 64, 85, 105, 113, 116, 119, 120,
    122, 123, 132, 190, 201
Vincent of Lérins, 53–54, 124–25
Virgin Mary, 225, 227

Waldensians, 7, 103, 207
Warfield, B. B., 212
Weber, Max, 201
"Will to Believe, The" (essay; James), 17
Wisdom (*sophia*), 121
working hypothesis, 17–18, 20
worldview. *See* framework of beliefs
worship
    connection to belief, 74, 146, 147
    diversity of early church, 46, 54–55
    Jesus at center of early Christian, 90,
      91
    role of, 17
Wright, N. T., 10–11
Wycliffe, John, 207–8

Yaldabaoth, 121